EXOTIC

PETS

Arthur Rosenfeld

Illustrations by Glenn Wolff

A FIRESIDE BOOK

PUBLISHED BY SIMON & SCHUSTER, INC.   NEW YORK

A FIRESIDE BOOK
Published by Simon & Schuster, Inc.
Simon & Schuster Building
Rockefeller Center
1230 Avenue of the Americas
New York, New York 10020
FIRESIDE and colophon are registered trademarks of Simon & Schuster, Inc.
Designed by Eve Kirch
Manufactured in the United States of America

10 9 8 7 6 5 4 3 2 1
10 9 8 7 6 5 4 3 2 1 (pbk.)

Library of Congress Cataloging in Publication Data
Rosenfeld, Arthur.
    Exotic pets.
    "A Fireside book."
    Bibliography: p.
    1. Pets. 2. Wild animals as pets. I. Title.
SF413.R67 1986   636.08'87   86–13081
ISBN: 0-671-63690-1
        0-671-47654-8 (pbk.)

Acknowledgments

I would like to thank Joan Tayman for her typing assistance and Herbert Schaffner for his editorial and production efforts. I'd also like to thank Bob Stene and Gary Sipperley for their tireless efforts to provide quality photographs. Special thanks go to Bryan Brown, without whom this book would not have been possible.

To my parents, for their unimaginable forbearance.

Contents

PARROTS

AMPHIBIANS

List of Illustrations

CONTENTS

Photograph sections appear after pages 64 and 126.

Introduction

Deep in a frozen winter, not too long ago, Mother Nature played a sadistic joke on the hibernating public. It had not snowed yet, but the weather was bitter cold. Leaves on the ground were turning to frozen mulch, and ponds were almost skatable. I had just finished insulating my windows with tape and plastic when the thaw hit hard. It began on a Thursday, escalating and intensifying until by Saturday you could just as well forget about the expected consequences of this planet's movement around the sun. This was no winter—this was spring!

Of course I was not the only one who thought so. Flocks of birds that had begun the trek south seemed confused and wheeled about aimlessly in the sky. Squirrels and rabbits appeared on the roads, begging to be squashed, and all the amphibians and reptiles came out of their long sleep, unwound and went to search up some grub. I breathed deep in my shirt sleeves and felt great, but I eyed the sky with distrust.

The front hit during the night. The wind began howling at 3 A.M. The storm windows shook in their brackets and I ran about my home clad only in wrapper and slippers, checking and resealing every way into and out of the house. The temperature dropped nearly 40 degrees and the snow started, not stopping until it was nearly a foot deep. The next day, when I returned from grocery shopping, I stumbled and fell on the way from the garage to the house. I looked down to see what had caused my loss of footing, and there, frigid and immobile amid the scattered foodstuffs, was a baby snapping turtle.

15

I scooped him up and brought him into the warm house, forgetting all about the groceries. As I placed him in tepid water in the sink, my wife watched over my shoulder, shaking her head and pronouncing him dead. She did not recant until his tiny black head began to move slowly and rhythmically. Before long he was investigating the porcelain world with evident interest.

The last thing I needed to add to my zoo was a baby common snapping turtle. After all, on top of the forty parrots, several dozen finches, hundreds of aquarium fish, scores of frogs, salamanders, snakes, lizards, crocodiles and octopi, I already had seventy or eighty of the most interesting, rare and exotic turtles in the world. I was more than a little overburdened, and have to admit to being slightly annoyed at any new responsibility. I wanted to toss him back outside and be done with him, yet I admired the little guy's spunk, traipsing through the ice and braving all that snow to find the only sucker on the block. As I considered his vain and pathetic attempts to climb from my sink, I was more than a little ashamed. It was then that I started to consider the very nature of a pet.

A pet, I concluded, is any animal that depends upon you. Although I would only pull this little turtle through one winter, he was still my pet. It made no difference that come the real spring thaw, I would release him, fattened and fresh, in a pond nearby. It didn't even matter that I did not cuddle with him, take him for long walks or fill voluminous scrapbooks with unbearably cute snapshots of him. What did matter was my interest in his welfare. It strikes me that this is the general rule. The type of pet you keep is of no consequence. You can have a pet spider, a pet elephant or a pet sea sponge. What makes any or, in my case, all of them pets is involvement and commitment.

Until the age of twenty, I was plagued by allergies to animals with hair. As a result, I was drawn to a cascade of scaled, feathered and moist-skinned creatures that did not make me sneeze. I garnered and lost inexpensive small creatures as if they were so many Tonka toys. I could not walk them on a leash or teach them to sit, so my perceptions and appreciation took other routes. Through a combination of my own health problems and a fervent desire to understand these creatures better, I fell in love with the microcosm of exotic crawlers, fliers, runners and swimmers. While I do have a well-trained mastiff these days and am constantly wiping cat hairs off my pillow, it is my parrot that does a better job of barking at strangers and rolling over to play dead. Exotic pets need not take the place of domesticated animals in your life. Often they have less to offer in the way of companionship. A piranha, for instance, will not curl up at your feet like a poodle—at least, not without taking your toes clean off. Yet many of them do offer a bond, and in addition add a flavor to your home. An exotic creature provides the link with the mountains, deserts and bayous so often missing, especially from city life. For those of you less poetically minded, practicality may be the appealing feature. A fish tank can be left unattended for a week, and a cage bird does not need to be taken out and walked. Thus if you are a steward-ess or are confined to a wheelchair, an exotic pet may offer some-thing you thought you could not manage. It is difficult to enumerate the various ways in which the presence of an aquarium, aviary or vivarium enhances your living environment. When friends ask me why I have a twenty-foot chicken-eating Burmese python in my closet, I answer simply that I think she is beautiful and have enjoyed raising her from the size of a fat pencil. Attraction to living creatures is a personal thing. How indeed would you "explain" the pleasure you take in a beholding a beautiful sunset? This may take some self-exploration.

Explore gingerly, and use this book as a travel guide. Today we walk a very critical and delicate line when we keep a wild animal in our homes. That chord that is touched in us when we share our lives with a pet also demands our sensitivity to the state of the outdoors. When I was a boy, few people felt the threat to our wildlands, or worried about the snail darter. Now the great majority of wild beasts are best left in their own environment, which we must preserve and guarantee. You won't find elephant-training tips in this book, nor a discourse on how to build a sturdy rhino pen. Good conscience and responsibility also preclude my telling you how to build a flight cage for a pair of red-tailed hawks or how to convert your swimming pool into a dolphin tank. And concern for endangered species is just the half of it. You might not know, for instance, that the twenty-five-foot-long saltwater crocodile you covet covets you. Warnings all done with, I can tell you with great pleasure that there are still a myriad of exotic beasts that are not endangered in the wild and which may thrive in your home. If you approach these animals with warmth and interest, their care will challenge and reward you.

With our horizons thus broadened, the choices that confront us are a bit overwhelming. You have probably never heard of some of the animals in this book, and even if you have, you surely have never considered them as possible pets. Whether you are a seasoned hobbyist looking for a new approach or simply want a companion to brighten your days, this book will guide you through an abundance of creatures suitable for life in your home.

Whatever you do, do not let my enthusiasm get the better of your good judgment. Sometimes I get carried away. You must at all times remember that any pet, even a hermit crab, is a responsibility. It makes demands upon you and can even tie you down. Please forgo buying a pet just to "keep it for a while." Some of the creatures in this book have the habit of hanging around long enough to be passed down to your grandchildren. Despite my love for the topic, I am here to inform you, not persuade you.

I have tried to organize the book in such a way that it is easy for you to use. If you hate reptiles and are interested only in parrots, you will find that the parrot section—indeed, each and every section in the book—is a complete unit. Naturally, since I wrote the whole book, I would like you to read the whole book, but if you don't, at least read the introduction to each chapter. This will save you time in the long run by telling you right off whether you are headed in the right direction when planning a purchase.

Right off the bat you will notice that not all chapters are equal in length. This is because the book is about the *pet qualities* of animals, rather than all their biological characteristics. Lizards, for example, have more complex requirements than salamanders, so the section on lizard care is the lengthier.

Another thing you will see right away is all the Latin names floating around the text. They are there for a good reason. People in one place, it turns out, are apt to call one animal a "zod" whereas in the next county over the same creature is an "ibop." That is why we need scientific names. They are the names you can rely on, either at the time of a purchase or to impress someone at a cocktail party. Most of the time you can just ignore them, but it is good to know they are there. A Latin scientific name has two essential parts. The first word, which has a capital letter, indicates the genus. The second word, no capital, is the species name (sometimes abbreviated "sp.") and applies to a specific kind of animal within the group. Man, for instance, is often termed *Homo sapiens. Homo* means the group, or genus, of all men; *sapiens* tells you that we are thinking beings. Every once in a while you may see a third name tacked on there. This refers to the subspecies or race. Races are just geographical variations of the same animal. *Terrepene carolina,* for example, is the Eastern box turtle; *Terrepene carolina triunguis* is the "three-toed" Southeastern race of the box turtle.

Each section in the book includes a bit on the biology of a given group. This should give you a much better understanding of a beast's life in the wild. I have also included housing and feeding information for each type of animal. At the end of each chapter is what I call the "recommended" section. This is a list of some twenty animals in each category. A lot of thought and heart wrenching went into these lists. I have tried to represent a given group and at the same time to choose animals that are available and affordable. I have canvassed dealers nationwide to arrive at prices, but availability and cost may well have changed by the time you read this. Animals that are easily had in Oregon, moreover, may be a bit hard to come by in New Jersey, and vice versa.

Another aspect of exotic pets that is out of my hands is the law. Particularly where amphibians and reptiles are concerned, statutes tend to develop rapidly and without much notice. It is now on the books, for instance, that any creature that is illegal to catch or keep in its foreign homeland is illegal to own or sell in this nation as well. Some of the animals that I mention, though very few, are subject to such restrictions. In such a case, you are bound to acquire them from dealers or private individuals who may legally trade in such a species. The animal either was imported before the legislation went into effect or was bred domestically.

Speaking of breeding, you may notice that I have deliberately omitted any mention of specific breeding tactics. While breeding is a very desirable and important goal for any keeper of a rare and valuable animal, it requires rather more experience (as well as "green thumbness") than is generally to be found in the beginner. This is the kind of information it would be all but impossible for me to give you. There is a cookbook formula to help you keep a parrot alive for fifty years, but the recipe for making baby parrots remains in the heads of the birds themselves and some skilled and devoted folks. The same, incidentally, goes for animal medicine. The subject is just too complex. If your pet gets sick, the best course of action is to take it straight to a veterinarian.

Now that all the admonitions, explanations and excuses are out of the way, I hope you have an idea of what this book is all about. You read *this* introduction, so you may as well proceed to the next one!

Introduction to Reptiles

I got my leg up into the world of exotics from a turtle. I caught him on a fishing line while on a canoe trip. Nobody would have guessed that it was the turtle who hooked me, rather than the other way around. Maybe it was my capture at such a tender age that made reptiles my favorite. Though I love all exotic creatures, lizards, snakes, crocodiles and turtles are the ones that live closest to my heart.

Do you know what I like best about reptiles? They don't make any noise. I mean, they are absolutely silent. Sure, a snake will hiss once in a while and a giant tortoise will grunt at the peak of reproductive ecstasy, but all in all, reptiles are a tight-lipped bunch. Millions of years ago, reptiles and their dinosaur kin ruled the earth. Imagine what the woods must have sounded like then! It was before the time of birds, so nobody would have been cooing in the trees. Elephants were not in existence either, so the wild would be free of trumpeting. In short, when the crickets and locusts and bees were asleep and the reptiles were afield, the world must have been a deadly silent place. Yet even though they have taken a vow of silence, reptiles give off vibes. If I, who know them pretty well, could take a time machine back to those days, I bet I would know they were there.

As pets, reptiles have a variety of requirements and offer a range of rewards. Some reptiles are as responsive as the average house cat, while others disdain human contact and will scurry from view if not managed with circumspection. Unless you choose a giant python with an appetite for chickens and pigs, reptiles are also inexpensive to feed. Whatever may turn you on about a reptile pet, you are not alone. The reptile fancy is not a new one, and there are scores of clubs and organizations across the country devoted to the care and breeding of this fascinating group. These organizations, by the way, are one of the best sources of specific information on care and breeding, particularly if you end up with a collection.

Reptiles are grouped with amphibians in the academic field of zoology, though this is a matter more of historical convention than of good sense. Scientists and hobbyists alike have found the terms "reptiles" and "amphibians" a bit clumsy when said together over and over. They have thus coined the term "herps," from the Greek word for "crawling thing," to cover both.

Reptiles are a vanishing class of beasts. When I was a boy, there were loads of creatures that could be had for a couple of dollars and kept in a gallon jar under the bed. Now many of those same friends are living under threat of their lives in some shrinking jungle somewhere. Crocodilians, for example, which I raised in abundance in my younger days, are nearly all ecologically threatened. I therefore omit them from discussion. There are still many other reptiles, however, thriving in the wild. These are not protected by legislation and are thus available to us as responsible pet owners. It is to this myriad of fascinating forms that this portion of the book is devoted.

I have divided the reptile section into three chapters: snakes, turtles and lizards. The chapters should be read as a whole, however, since there is some information common to all three groups. Most of the "hard-core biology" that applies to reptiles appears in the snake chapter. I have paid particular attention to the advantages and disadvantages of each group and have supplied you with information on what it takes to feed, clothe and house your prospective pet. Each chapter closes with a list of some twenty animals in each group that I have found make exceptionally good housemates in the time they have spent at my place. This list is no mean feat, as it takes into account hardiness, charm, price and availability.

SNAKES

Everglades ratsnake

Y ou are a technical adviser for a major motion-picture studio. Your field of expertise is horror and science-fiction thrillers. You have been handed a screenplay for an exciting new movie that calls for a wild beast on the set. The creature may have neither hair nor feathers, yet cannot resemble a fish. It must be fairly advanced, with a decent-sized brain and built about a recognizable frame. It must be extraordinarily dangerous, yet have characteristics, such as a need for food, water and air, with which the viewers will identify. To fit into the plot without inconsistency, it must have all of man's senses plus some outrageous sixth sense that can be elaborated upon in the script. In short, it must possess capabilities that neither man nor machine can match.

Where do you start? At your local pet shop, by buying yourself a snake and taking it back to the studio.

Although the fascination with snakes goes back into time just about as far as snakes go, there is probably no animal on earth that has been more maligned and misunderstood. This timeless preoccupation, a sort of ongoing love/hate relationship, has not been so good for the snake. People have killed snakes on sight for millennia.

Personally, I have for many years now borne the brunt of being a snake lover. This has yielded not only sidelong glances, but also a shortage of dates, especially in high school. Yet whatever else people may have felt, there was always a horrified fascination. Nobody is indifferent to a snake. What is the root of this fascination? I'm not sure. Frankly, I doubt that the fear is instinctual. "Instinct" is usually a word employed when we mean "I don't know." More likely, this fear is learned, based upon the reputation of a small number of snakes that are in fact hazardous. The fact is that, of all the world's snakes, only a small percentage are potential threats. The rest are by and large not only harmless but useful, as they cut down on rodents—eaters of grain and spreaders of disease.

When I was a little boy, I was terrified of snakes. It was only because I liked turtles and fancied myself a budding herpetologist that I forced myself to overcome my fear. The psychology of snake-fright might well be likened to the "*Jaws* effect," though thank goodness no one has made a film about a killer snake terrorizing Long Island parking lots. The odds of being attacked by a shark while swimming are infinitesimal, yet many people, including me, now shun good fun in the waves. By the same token, although the notorious "dangerous to man" animal corps is minute and shrinking daily, few people heed statistics. The small but very human death toll exacted every year is the spine-tingling stuff of which headlines are made. This, regrettably, causes beautiful, interesting and harmless creatures to be spurned instead of appreciated as wild creatures or wonderful pets.

A pet snake is an exotic alternative to the usual domestic fare. Some people prize snakes' almost feline aloofness and self-sufficiency, while others simply find them beautiful and sensual. I like the feel of a snake against my skin. It is cool and smooth, and as far from slimy as can be. Most snakes can be tamed to the extent that they tolerate handling without vicious response, and some specimens seem to positively enjoy the warmth of the human touch. You never fail to create a stir when you keep a pet snake. Some of us even find the conquest of a strong fear motivation enough.

Even if you hate aloof animals, could not care less about a serpent's dry, smooth touch and are perfectly satisfied with having a phobia here and there, the snake has one last thing to offer as a pet. The snake is possibly the easiest of all exotic pets to keep happy and healthy! Snakes take less care than any other animal with a backbone. Warm, close quarters, an occasional meal and a dish of water are all that most snakes ever require.

SNAKE BIOLOGY

Okay, they are exotic, they are intriguing, they are different, but what makes a snake tick? The heart of it all, if you will pardon the pun, is a three-chambered affair a lot more primitive than our own. In humans the blood coming from the lungs, filled with oxygen and destined for the tissues, is kept separate from the blood going back to the lungs for freshening. We keep the "full" and "empty" blood separate by having a four-chambered heart that allows no mixing. The snake heart, by contrast, is three-chambered. In terms of his circulation, the snake is less efficient than we are. Lots of what scientists call "lower" vertebrates (this should mean they are closer to the ground when they walk, but probably doesn't) have three- and even two-chambered hearts. You have probably caught on by now that snakes are vertebrates, meaning simply that they have a spine.

Although they are backboned, snakes are considerably more flexible than even the most devout yogi. Each bone in the vertebral column has special articular surfaces (surfaces that meet and move against each other). In addition to having special shapes, these bones are incredibly numerous. Some snakes have as many as three hundred vertebrae. Talk about contortions! A snake can literally tie himself in knots.

Having a backbone entitles the snake to share in the usual gamut of vertebrate organs and structures, but these are elongated to fit the long, slender body. Like all the more advanced vertebrates, snakes use lungs to breathe air. They don't, however, always have a pair of lungs. In some species a lung is missing. When they do have two, the left one is smaller than the right. Snakes have a long gut to digest their prey, which they eat whole. The excretory system of the snake is simple when compared with our own and involves an organ called a cloaca. The cloaca is present in all herps and also in birds. The organ takes care of reproductive functions as well as providing the final link in the excretory chain. In snakes the cloaca is just ahead of the base of the tail. The organ communicates with the outside via a slit that runs across the body.

You want to get down and dirty about snakes? Fine. The male has paired reproductive organs, the hemipenes, housed in the cloaca.

These organs are quite varied in form, resembling anything from a sausage to a strip of corrugated tin. These shapes may sound arbitrary to you, but to a snake they are serious business. The shape of the gonads is so reliably constant within a given snake species that scientists use these structures to identify and classify serpents. The female has no such equipment. Her ovaries look a bit like Styrofoam in cross section, and the rest of her plumbing is elongated to fit her slender build.

Snakes copulate in a very dramatic way. They writhe and intertwine until the male organ (one side only, so his aim need not be too good) is inserted into the female's cloaca. Fertilization of the snake eggs takes place within the body of the mother, just as in people. While so far this is all birds-and-bees stuff, what happens next is not so straightforward. In some cases the egg develops inside, just like the egg of a bird. The female then lays her clutch (which can number anywhere from a few to as many as sixty eggs) and goes her merry way. In other snakes, however, the eggshell never develops and the young are born live. This is complicated enough, but to make matters worse, there is a third course that nature may follow. In some species a shell is formed around the embryo but is then fully or partially resorbed. The mother then gives birth to young plus some bits of shell. Just in order to stymie those of us who think we have her understood, the female snake may also decide to hold her eggs within her body and simply not lay them at all! You have to work hard to get a snake upset enough to do this. In any case, the mother takes no care of her young and may never even see them.

Although snakes are generally sexually mature within the first two years of life, it is not a good idea to breed females when they are too young; these animals need all their energy just to grow. Snakes have elaborate courtship rituals that help to ensure that the right snakes breed with one another. Without the characteristic twitchings and bobbings of head and body, different species might try to breed with each other.

Speaking of mating and eggs, the reptile egg has played a very important role in vertebrate evolution. It was the leathery shell of the reptilian egg that in eons past was instrumental in allowing backboned animals to colonize the land. You see, the first step from the water was made by creatures that were ancestral to our modern-day amphibians (frogs, salamanders and the like). These creatures had it all over fish, since they had legs and lungs, but they shared with the fish the jellylike, vulnerable egg. If you have ever eaten caviar or plucked a string of frog eggs out of a pond in your back yard, you know how goopy and without form amphibian eggs are. You also know that when removed from the water for any period of time they dry out and blow away with the wind. Not so with the reptile egg! By developing a tough, leathery shell for her eggs, the reptile unshackled herself from the lake and stream. Eggs could be laid in any relatively moist environment, even one far from the water. In this way, reptiles began the conquest of areas that amphibians could never lay eyes upon.

The reptile itself is as tough as its egg. The scales that cover snakes and their kin are strong plates that resist the wear and tear of life on land magnificently and also retain precious water. This type of covering further freed some of the first reptiles from the local watering hole.

While scales hold water well, they do a lousy job as insulators. Heat can travel across them and be lost to the snake quite easily. More than likely, on cold days the snake wishes he were a Teddy bear. This knife cuts both ways, though, as heat can as easily enter the snake from the sun or warm ground as it can leave. Incidentally, if you still find yourself wishing snakes looked like Teddy bears this far into the chapter, you probably will never own a pet snake!

So the snake's scales bear on its temperature relationship with the outside world. This introduces us to a key business. Let me state right now that there is absolutely nothing more important to the reptile than how warm or cold he is. All reptiles (there are a couple of exceptions, but let's forget them) lack the body machinery to produce their own heat. A snake that has just come in from an exhilarating run down the slopes will have to sit in front of the fire a lot longer than you or I will in order to warm up. To tell the truth, this is a poor joke because there is no way that a snake could avoid freezing to death, never mind finding skis that fit. Since he cannot make his own heat and is lousy at keeping it in anyway, the snake must find other ways of keeping warm. All the functions of a snake depend upon temperature-sensitive chemicals known as enzymes. Without the correct body temperature, these enzymes don't work and the snake cannot eat, sleep, crawl around or compose sonatas. Lest you think this unusual, bear in mind that our body works the same way; it's just that we aren't aware of a shutdown unless we freeze to death or boil over. Our body, you see, has means of making its own heat.

Since the snake cannot make heat, he must find it. Heat is often hiding on warm rocks, in the rays of the sun and even on a toasty desert road after sunset. In captivity, the snake lacks the opportunity to travel around in search of a warm spot, so you must provide it for him.

Reptiles respond in amusing ways to changes in temperature. To best understand these reactions, consider the beast's body to be an engine, which it really is. Heat is the throttle that controls how fast it goes. High temperatures speed the snake up; low temperatures slow it down. Sometimes a tame, docile snake can turn into a nasty son-of-a-gun if you warm it up too far. I once had an embarrassing interlude with such a reptilian Jekyll and Hyde. It was back in my college days and I was touring around in my spare time, giving lectures on reptiles at local high schools. I brought along to many lectures a pet Florida king snake whom I had kept for years. This was the consummate pet snake. You could breathe garlic all over him, sling him around the room and step on his head and he would not even dream of biting you. I had placed him around the necks of five-year-old children probably a hundred and fifty times and never regretted it.

One day I arrived at a school and unloaded my animals from a large satchel. I put the bags and cages out on the table for all to see and placed the satchel over by the radiator so that it would be nice and warm when I went to put all the animals back into it. Well into the lecture, having already dismissed the notion that snakes can be vicious with an imperious wave of the hand, I went for Elrond, my kingsnake. My old buddy was nowhere in the assemblage of bags before me, and it took me a few moments to realize that I had not taken him from the satchel that now sat, toasty warm, in the corner of the room. I whipped out beautiful black-and-yellow six-foot El-rond to a round of hoots and catcalls. I noticed that my old reliable friend was very, very warm to the touch. It would not be a lie to say that Elrond was sizzling. Upon being pulled from the bag, he hooked his tail securely through my belt and bit my ear. While I screamed, he chewed and nuzzled in true kingsnake fashion, trying to effect a reptilian needle job.

I got lucky after a while and Elrond let go. This is a good thing, since gaudy earrings are not my style.

High temperatures will speed up a snake, and may change his demeanor for the worse, while low temperatures will do precisely the opposite. A feisty, intractable snake will mellow with the cold and promptly also lose his appetite. If you keep a snake too cold for a long period, he will likely sicken and die. To tell the truth, some delicate exotics can expire quickly even if they just catch a chill.

You have probably guessed by now that keeping a snake warm will increase his appetite, the speed at which he digests his food and, ultimately, his growth. Snakes and other reptiles have to face a problem with growing that you and I never have to worry about. The skin of a snake is made up of layers of flesh that become progressively more distinct from each other as the animal grows. At a certain point the outermost layer (dead, like the surface of our own skin) can no longer accommodate the stretch, and it is shed, all in one piece.

Shedding the skin is one of the most peculiar events in the life of a snake. The way it is accomplished rivals for sheer uniqueness the way a snake swallows its prey. Shortly before the skin is to be shed, the snake becomes noticeably drab and lackluster in appearance and the eyes cloud over. These visible changes are not fully understood but are thought to be the result of minute changes in the structure of the skin. A snake in this condition is said to be "blue" or "opaque," in reference to the loss of vibrancy of color. After a variable length of time (usually three to ten days) the condition clears. At this point the snake is on the verge of shedding, but gives no sign.

Constriction of the blood vessels that normally allow fluid to exit the head causes the area to swell. This cracks the skin on the nose or chin. At this point the snake will snag the loose skin against a rough surface, anchoring it there while he proceeds forward and crawls out of it. The skin (assuming all goes well) is left in one piece and inside out. How frequently a snake performs this ritual and how long each stage lasts depends upon how rapidly the animal is growing. Just like children, young snakes grow more rapidly than their adult counterparts. Unlike people, however, snakes never completely stop growing. True, the *rate* of growth diminishes with time until an old reptile is enlarging at an infinitesimal pace, but no reptile ever really stays the same size. What a fix! Can you imagine how much you would spend on shoes, not to mention winter coats and underwear, if you grew like a snake?

Let me give you a more concrete idea of what to expect from a snake's growth rate. I have in my collection a rough-scaled sand boa from Kenya that I have had for many years. It is a couple of feet long

and lives under the sand in a ten-gallon aquarium equipped with a
screen cover. Every once in a long while, say every two or three
months, this snake comes out of the sand to feed. I know it is hungry
because I don't see it for ages and then all of a sudden there it is lying
in full view. Taking this as a cue, I toss food into the cage, and it is
gone in the morning. Food offered more frequently or at other times
is ignored. In the years that I have had this animal it has grown only
an inch and shed no more than nine times. I am also the proud owner
of a one-year-old Burmese python that was twenty-two inches at
hatching from the egg. This snake has shed as frequently as every ten
days for some time, but as it grows its shedding rate declines. At
present it is ten feet long.

If you have a snake that, like my Burmese python, is an eager
feeder, you can increase the growth rate by feeding the snake more
often. The animal, however, will accept only its natural prey. Snakes
are carnivores and in the wild eat just about anything they can catch,
subdue and swallow. Snakes kill their prey by constriction, by en-
venomation or simply by holding on and swallowing, depending
upon the type of snake. Constricting snakes, such as boas, pythons
and king snakes, have an elaborate body musculature that allows
them to exert a considerable squeeze. Each time the prey animal
breathes out, it shrinks a tiny bit and the snake tightens. Each subsequent breath that the ill-fated food animal takes is thus smaller than
the previous one until at last it cannot get enough air and it suffo-
cates. Constricting snakes do *not* exert bone-crushing force. Noncon-
strictors, however, may overpower their prey by squashing it against
something as they hold on with their jaws and proceed to swallow.
I will discuss venomous snakes below.

Some snakes eat rats, some mice, some lizards or frogs and some
snakes even specialize in eating other snakes. Whatever food item
you choose that is acceptable to the snake must be either alive or
freshly dead. One thing about snakes that I have never had any
trouble dealing with is feeding, although most people think that must
be the most difficult part. I have developed a philosophy about giving
living animals to my snakes for food. This way of looking at things
tells me that if I am to keep a snake, then I must provide it with food
to keep it alive. If I let it go someplace in the wild where it had a
reasonable shot at survival, then it would calmly and silently begin
the business of hunting and killing the same type of animal that I am
reluctant to offer it. In short, though I would leap at the chance to

spare a mouse, chick, rat, lizard or frog, there is no feasible food alternative for a captive serpent. I suppose that over the years I have come to accept that this is the normal way of things and that to interfere will only starve my pet.

Incidentally, if you are fascinated by and drawn to a pet snake yet feel that its feeding habits make it impossible to manage, there is an out. The African egg-eating snake, *Dasypeltis scaber,* is, as its name suggests, an ovovore. This amazing creature can actually swallow a bird's egg far bigger in diameter than its head. It manages this by "popping" the shell against a sharp bony protuberance in the throat. Once the shell is compromised, the contents are swallowed and the shell is expelled.

All snakes eat their prey whole. What is more, they eat prey so large that you would wager a fortune that it would never go down. Can you imagine eating a honeydew melon whole? Well, that is

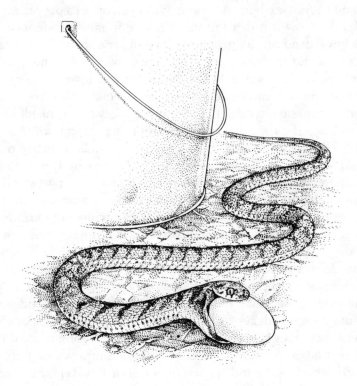

African eggeater

roughly equivalent to the feat of swallowing performed on a routine basis by a snake. An eleven-foot python about as thick as your leg has been seen polishing off a one-hundred-and-fifty-pound leopard. I have an interesting young Australian carpet python that ate an adolescent rat the size of my fist when the predator was no bigger around than two pencils side by side! This is neither a magical act nor an optical illusion. Snakes have a very special anatomy. When a snake opens his mouth, he actually unhinges his jaw. Imagine yourself in the dentist's chair being told to "say 'Ahh.' " You comply and take the entire dentist into your mouth, for your upper and lower jaws are not connected. The special hinge in the snake's jaw allows it to reconnect after the food has passed. This way the snake avoids standing around with its mouth open.

Just unhinging the jaw is not the whole story. Not only does the mouth unjoint, which permits expansion from top to bottom, it also has some lateral flexibility, allowing it to swell over its prey from side to side. But how is it that the snake is able to take a rodent or bird that is lying dead on the ground and get it far enough back into his mouth if he has no hands nor feet? The answer is that he *walks his prey into his mouth.* Not only are the upper and lower jaws capable of separate movement, but the lower jaws, which are in two halves, can move from side to side. This allows each row of tiny needle-sharp teeth to grasp the food and literally push it into his mouth. Another way of looking at it is to consider that the snake actually moves forward over the food item, never actually breaking it into smaller pieces. After a time the prey is in the mouth and then partway down the throat. All digestive organs must swell to accommodate the food as it goes through the system. A snake with a really big meal in him looks like a piece of radiator hose with a dinosaur stuck in the middle.

Why does a snake eat this way? What are the advantages and disadvantages of taking down such an enormous meal? Well, to a certain extent, the snake has no choice but to walk his food down, as he has no appendages to help out. Once it is down, especially if the meal was really big, the snake is incapacitated for a while during the time it takes to digest. The fact is that he simply cannot lug that lump in his middle around. That is obviously a disadvantage. The flip side of the coin is that he gets so much energy from the endeavor that he may not have to feed again for months! Imagine all the free

Bull snake

time you would have to fool around, get more work done or just play golf if you ate but once every two or three months! In captivity we wish to keep our pets healthy and growing, so we feed them once every week or two, especially if they are young. In the wild, which holds no guarantees, the snake can get away with prodigious fasts.

We have looked briefly at how a snake is put together and how his body machinery runs. We have seen how he grows and what he eats. Let's change gears a moment and talk about how he goes about finding his prey, a mate or even a warm spot in which to bask. In short, how does the snake see the world? What senses has he got?

When you look at the side of a snake's head, you will notice that he lacks ears. To put it more precisely, he has neither external ear openings nor eardrums. We, of course, have both. You can feel your eardrum if you stick your finger way into your ear. When you reach a stop and it feels as if you shouldn't be doing it, you are touching (with clean fingers, I hope) the drum. Sound moves this delicate membrane, and the motion is communicated to three tiny bones in the middle ear. These in turn impinge upon a fluid-filled sack in the inner ear. The snake's three bones are fused to one that connects to the jawbone. What all this tricky anatomy amounts to is that although they may be able to pick up vibration through the jaws and lungs, for all practical purposes snakes are deaf. While they don't rely much on hearing, snakes do have and use relatively good eyesight. The eyes, which are directed to the side, give a wide field of vision. They respond well to movement, which accounts for their use in pursuing prey even when the outline is dim or camouflaged (as in a brown mouse on dirt). A snake cannot see at any distance. Beyond a few feet, a general shape is all that he discerns. Interestingly, snakes differ from the average backboned animal in having a unique system to help them focus their eyes. To understand this, let's have a look at our own focusing system, just the way we did with our ear. When you hold a finger in front of your face and quickly focus back and forth between your finger and a painting at the other end of the room, the sensation you experience in your eye is the muscle system within the eye itself acting upon the lens and changing its shape. Snakes cannot manage this feat because they lack these particular muscles. Instead, a snake focuses by moving the lens forward and back, the same way you focus when you look through the lens of your snapshot camera.

Virtual deafness and limited vision are not the whole story. If they were, you might well envision that the snake is unaware and out of touch with his environment, moving mindlessly about until he lucks into a warm spot or a sleeping rat. This could not be further from the truth. The snake gets a sensitive and accurate picture of his surroundings from cues delivered courtesy of an extremely accurate and sensitive organ at the roof of his mouth. Somewhere between what we call taste and smell, the vomeronasal organ, sometimes called the "organ of Jacobson," allows the snake to follow a trail of scent. A very sensitive conglomeration of cells of the palate, this organ relies on the tongue to help it function. When stimulated, hungry or very warm, the snake flicks his protrusible forked tongue out into the air with considerable frequency. When the tongue is withdrawn, any particles that have adhered to the moist surface of the tongue are deposited on the special lining of the "sixth" sense organ and the snake gains information concerning the world around him.

The snake's sense of taste itself has been somewhat diminished by the presence of this additional organ, but it is still functional. If you have ever watched a snake approach a prospective meal, you know that the tongue is almost constantly active, assessing the air around the prey item as the snake slowly nears his dinner. The best way to think of what information the snake is gaining is to imagine being able to taste the air. Wouldn't it be great if you could judge a restaurant just by testing the air out on the sidewalk by the front entrance?

In addition to the unusual organ I have just described, some snakes are endowed with an even more astonishing feature. Richly inner-vated pits in the lips or in other special spots permit detection of minute changes in temperature, even at a distance. Rattlesnakes and other vipers, as well as boas and pythons, possess infrared receptors that make this extreme sensitivity possible. A rattlesnake is known to be able to detect a change of one-tenth of 1 degree Celsius at a distance of seven inches. Imagine being able to tell if the roast is beginning to burn just by measuring the oven temperature from the bedroom. A rattlesnake uses this capability to sense a passing mouse or a human foot.

The powers of the rattlesnake may be great, but his pet qualities are not. Venomous snakes are taboo for a number of reasons. Snakes are master escape artists, and sooner or later a snake is going to get out on you, no matter how closely you follow my advice in the following section. A lethal creature loose in your home may seem a picnic to you if you are the suicidal type, but it is completely irresponsible. Houses abut and apartments connect and nothing says that your escaped death adder will remain in your closet. I have learned that no matter how expert you become and no matter how careful you are, the moment will come when you slip up, and the snake will be waiting.

This happened to me in a rather inglorious episode involving a large, beautifully patterned tree snake from Thailand. The mangrove snake feeds at night, principally on birds. While the animal is poten-tially quite dangerous, its fangs are positioned so far back in its mouth that it has a hard time getting them around human flesh. Because I knew this, I didn't take the animal seriously enough. The incident occurred late in the afternoon one July several years ago. My five-footer had recently shed, and while cleaning its cage I no-ticed that it was suffering from a fairly common serpent malady best described as an incomplete shed. A snake in the best of health and condition will, if supplied with the right temperature and humidity, shed his skin in one piece, crawling out of it as described above after having rubbed it loose at the nose or lips. Sometimes, however, the skin comes off not intact but in shreds and pieces. The clear scale that covers the eyes is especially prone to difficulty. There are a number of ways to cope with this problem. A blunt probe, such as a bobby pin, can be inserted very gently and carefully under the edge of the eye cap and will sometimes lift the eye cap off. Alternatively, a piece of tape can be pressed onto the cap and will sometimes stick to the cap well enough to remove it. The last option is to moisten the eye, which often loosens a stubborn bit of skin and was the tack I had taken with my mangrove snake. I had a firm grip on the snake and was holding it over the bathroom sink, applying a warm wet compress. Removing an eye cap is no picnic, as the procedure puts your fingers perilously close to the fangs. In this case, I managed to retain control of the animal by utilizing the classic behind-the-neck grip. If grasped right behind the jaw, a snake cannot turn around and nail you. Even if he wraps up your arm and exercises other bodily functions upon your clean person, you are well out of harm's way.

Eventually I did get the eye cap off. Holding the snake in the neck grip, I opened his cage and dropped him in. As he fell he turned his head to the side and, with mouth wide open, caught my finger on his fang as he went down.

I stared at the prick marks on my finger and a deadly calm came over me. I headed for the phone and called my doctor. The secretary asked me if I could call back in the morning, as it was five o'clock and everyone was going home. I said no and insisted on speaking to the doctor, who let out a string of curses inappropriate for the written page. I moseyed over to his office, and the two of us sat by the sink scrubbing my finger with a surgical rub and a nailbrush, discussing what we might do about the whole thing.

I was lucky that day. It turned out that the snake had failed to get any venom into the wound. This experience was my cue to leave venomous snakes to the care of institutions equipped to deal with them safely. Resist the temptation, if you feel it, to prove something with a venomous animal. There are numerous fascinating and beautiful harmless snakes that make fine pets. If you read on, you will find out specifically what they are and how to care for them.

HOUSING THE SNAKE

I have said that snakes are the easiest of all vertebrates to have as pets. Whenever I make a statement like that I get this terrible feeling in my gut that somebody is going to prove me wrong. You can kill anything if you try hard enough, just as you can keep almost anything alive with sufficient knowledge and devotion. Your goal as a prospective keeper should be an understanding of the animal's natural history so that you may learn to think the way it does. Yet it is often hard to be in tune with a snake. In the ensuing discussion I will endeavor to point out obvious signs of distress and will go into fair detail concerning how you can meet their simple but occasionally elusive requirements.

The Cage

If you have ever collected snakes in the wild, you know that these masters of the art of concealment and surprise are rarely out in the open. They are so creative in finding old boards, rocks, ledges and holes to secret themselves in or under that even clever amphibians and rodents who share these habitats don't know where to expect them. Snakes, though carnivores themselves, are vulnerable to predation and feel most secure when tightly confined.

While they may relish a shoe-box existence, snakes are also persistent when it comes to the urge to sow some wild oats. They will try to get out of anything, and succeed much of the time. As a fancier, you want them out of your Cheerios, yogurt and cowboy boots and in their cages. Very active snakes will be the first ones out, putting their nose into even the slightest indentation or crack and pushing for all they are worth. If there is just the tiniest amount of give, any snake will be enthralled and keep pushing until he ultimately makes good his escape.

Although I have learned my lesson, over the past fifteen years numerous snakes have escaped from me. When I was in college I lost one of my prize animals, an Eastern indigo snake named Diane. I made the classic mistake of assuming that just because I had never seen her make any attempt to escape, I could leave the screen top loosely fastened over her aquarium. One day I came home to find her missing. This caused my roommates enormous concern. They had been as tolerant and forbearing as saints, but a six-foot, rodent-eating reptile crawling around loose in the room was just a bit much. Able to go without food and water for weeks, the indigo decided to stay lost. She was missing for so long that after holding a tremendous search in which I enlisted the aid of many friends, I simply gave up and forgot about the creature. It was not until I got dressed up one evening that I found her—or more precisely, my big toe found her—curled up at the bottom of a pair of boots! She ate and drank with gusto when I replaced her in her home, none the worse for wear.

Another dramatic escape occurred when I was in college. I had a one-hundred-and-twenty-pound, fourteen-foot-long Burmese python living on the floor of my one and only closet. One morning I opened the closet door, reached for a towel from the rack and forgot to close the door. I left the room for the dormitory bathroom down the hall and took a shower. On my return to my quarters, whom should I run into in the hallway but all fourteen feet of Ganymede, my python, stretched out against the cold floor, inching her way toward the stairs. As no one else ever saw her, I managed to finish my degree program without incident.

Because they grow to different sizes and display different habits, there is no "best" container for snakes, nor is there a rule of thumb to help determine cage sizes. Racers and rat snakes, for example, like to move around a lot, so a cage should be almost as long as the snake and perhaps half as wide and tall. Pythons and boas, conversely, are astoundingly lazy. What they want most is to sleep all day long, and this is just what they do. As a result, even a large example of one of these constrictors can do with limited cage space. No snake needs to be able to stretch out to full length. While our backs would doubtless become painfully and irreparably kinked in such a situation, a snake doesn't mind curling up for months.

It turns out that your own creativity provides the only boundary to what will make a good snake cage. I have successfully utilized everything from grapefruit-juice containers to six-foot-long aquaria. What I have found, however, is that the two best readily available snake containers are plastic shoe boxes for small animals (say up to two feet long) and aquaria with securely fastened screen tops for larger animals. Clear plastic shoe and sweater boxes come in a variety of styles. The ones best suited for our purpose are those that slide into and out of a cover, complete with a small handle. While there are a wide variety of other plastic containers available, none provide such a secure closing mechanism. Sliding boxes cost no more than a couple of dollars and are available at the five-and-ten. While they close securely enough to contain the snake, especially with the help of a strip of tape, they are not airtight and thus allow the snake to breathe. Often these boxes have grooves at the top and bottom that allow them to be stacked. If you end up with more than one small snake, this stacking makes an attractive display. The clear plastic furnishes a good view of your pet from all angles, and the boxes hold humidity well so that your animal does not dehydrate (more on this below).

Because snakes so love confinement, one of these boxes will also serve as a fine home for a juvenile that may ultimately reach a large size. You have little to lose by investing in this type of container, for if your snake outgrows it, you can use it to store anything from tools to knitting needles or even shoes! If you're purchasing a snake and the type of setup I will next discuss stretches your budget too far, you might want to go this route. Even if you have a giant python baby and the box lasts only a couple of months, you have still spread your expenses a bit.

Bigger snakes such as the larger kingsnakes, rat snakes, boas and pythons will not be content in a shoe box. A commercially manufactured fish aquarium is, as I have already suggested, the best choice. Aquaria are put together without metal rims these days, which makes them much easier to move around and a good deal less expensive to buy. The size you choose should be determined in accordance with the snake you plan to own. For all except the biggest snakes, a twenty-gallon aquarium is ample. A tank half that size will often suffice. Again, remember that highly active animals such as racers need a bit more room than lethargic species. You will find information about the habits of the animals I recommend below.

Since snakes use ground space in a tank, but for the most part not height, the *shape* of the aquarium you purchase is all-important. While fish may do fine in odd-shaped aquaria, snakes derive no benefit from such designs. The twenty-gallon aquarium I have suggested provides a good example. This size is available in a "tall" version, in a "long" version, and as a hexagon. Only the long version is advisable for snakes, since the ground space, for the size and price, is maximized.

Speaking of price, the rule of thumb for aquarium prices is to multiply the number of gallons the tank holds by one and one-half to arrive at a dollar cost. Thus a ten-gallon tank should set you back fifteen dollars, a twenty-gallon tank ought to cost thirty dollars and so on. A money-saving tip that I can offer is to buy a used and/or leaky tank. Since a snake cage need not be watertight, you can use a tank that would be all but useless for fish. Ask at your local pet shop for used or cracked aquaria and you can usually end up paying less than half the cost of a new unit. The classified ads in your local paper may provide some leads as well. You can always put in a want ad for a cage. Don't be afraid to take a larger aquarium if one comes your way. If you have the space for it, the larger size won't hurt anything.

I have made the aquarium sound like the simple, perfect serpentarium, which it can be. The major problem, however, is that aquaria don't come with snakeproof lids. The glass "hoods" that are used for fish work fine with mollies and cichlids, but are not worth anything when it comes to keeping in a determined python. What you need is a screen top. A number of pet-supply companies manufacture these. The difficulty comes, though, when you try to fit the screen to the tank. Although there are standard dimensions for most aquaria, the minute manufacturing differences between tanks from different factories make the fit of the screen tenuous. You may have

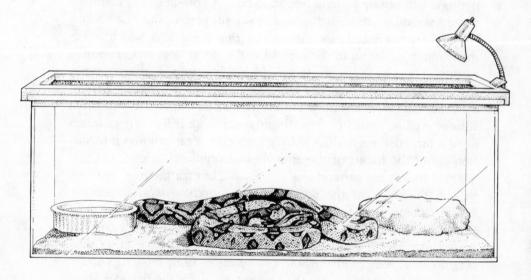

Boa constrictor

to experiment carefully to find a twenty-gallon screen top, say, that exactly fits *your* twenty-gallon tank. The screen tops that fasten with screws should fit well, but I don't like them. Tightening the screws to make the top really secure seems always to cause the plastic of the top to bow out, creating a small but "snakable" space. There is no beating the plain, all-metal top that was made in heaven for your particular aquarium.

Screen tops can be costly. They may cost half again as much as the tank. If you are good with light tools such as a staple gun and handsaw it may behoove you to put together a wooden frame that sinks well over the top of your aquarium and then cover this with hardware cloth.

While we are on the subject of making your own snake paraphernalia, I might suggest that, if you are in fact a do-it-yourselfer, you consider making your own cage. A well-put-together wooden box can be the best home a snake can have. Fitted with a tempered (for strength) glass or Plexiglas top, it provides visibility and freedom from drafts. Your own cage will probably fit the decor of your home better than a commercial aquarium and may cost less. Many snake boxes have been knocked together out of plywood, but I prefer a heavier, harder wood as it will last longer and is less likely to splinter and injure your snake. A sliding door is best, since it is "inesnakable," and you should fit one if you can. Otherwise a hinged door is fine. The inner surface, if not the outer, should be finished in polyurethane or varnish so that it may be easily cleaned. I have seen some great cages put together from old refrigerators, sinks and freezers rescued from the junkyard and furnished with clear doors for viewing. Beyond remembering to drill air holes, the cage design is up to you.

One last option is the specialty cage. A number of companies build snake tanks for zoos and other institutions. If you have money to burn you may want to go with one of these cages. Usually of metal, they are easy to clean, very professional-looking, tough to get out of and incredibly expensive. Glas 'Technic is one small outfit that claims to "serve the needs of the professional herpetologist." It manufactures a nice fiberglass tub for a more reasonable price than most. For a few extra dollars, the company will fit a sliding Plexiglas front to the unit, making it complete and snake-ready. Cages anywhere from the size of a ten-gallon fish tank all the way up to elaborate six-foot-long examples are available. The address is Glas 'Technic, Route 110 and Allen Street, Clinton, Massachusetts 01510; (617) 368–8831.

Whatever type of cage you settle on, remember that it must close tightly. Don't make the mistake of thinking that a pile of books or rocks on top of the lid will keep a snake in. Remember that he need not lift the whole lid to escape but only apply pressure to one corner. Especially if the fit is less than perfect, a good roll of tape is indispensable. The best is duct tape, a tough cloth material that can be yanked and reaffixed a number of times. You can find this gray tape in any hardware store.

The Cage Floor

While I have seen nearly every imaginable material in use at the bottom of a snake cage, most substances (gravel, for example) are either too abrasive or not absorbent enough. There are, however, three readily available choices that do the job well: newspaper, dried corn cob and pine-bark chips. Until I discovered the other two, I raised hundreds of snakes on newspaper. All you have to do is make a little pile of the papers as you finish with them each day and presto, free snake flooring! Aside from costing next to nothing, newspaper is highly absorbent and makes cleaning a cinch. Pluck out the paper when it becomes soiled and throw it away. The paper should fit the bottom of the tank precisely, with no spaces left uncovered around the edges. If the fit is less than perfect you will pay in the end, as snakes seem to know what the most annoying spot for them to mess is, and will choose it unfailingly. Instead of excreting liquid urine, snakes excrete primarily solid uric acid. There is rarely enough liquid to soak through more than one or two sheets of newspaper, so cleaning really is as easy as just throwing the paper away.

A timesaving tip that I can offer is to cut a number of sheets to size at the same time. Take a stack, mark off the size of the tank either with a pencil or by creasing the newspaper and then use a heavy scissors to cut, say, thirty sheets at once. If you do this, you can simply pluck a couple off the top of the pile each time the paper needs changing and fit them to the tank.

Although cheap and convenient, newspaper doesn't look so great and requires a complete change each time a mess is made. Dried corncob and pine-bark chips (*not* pine shavings, which can get caught in a snake's mouth and which contain a dust irritating to snake lungs) present neither of these problems and are also inexpensive. These materials both aggregate around waste materials and absorb well. Clumps can simply be picked out without the necessity of stripping the whole cage down. Pine-bark chips are available from any garden-supply house in various grades. The medium-sized chips (about the size of a nickel) are the most useful all around. Pine chips also have the added advantage of being slightly acidic, thus inhibiting the growth of some molds and bacteria. Dried corncob, sold under the names Bed O' Cob and Sanicel, tends to grow mold readily should you or your pet overturn a water dish onto it. Both pine-bark chips and dried corncob are attractive in color and tend to show off any snake to its best advantage.

A Place to Hide

A common complaint among new snake owners is that their snake will not feed. Often it not only refuses food but tirelessly looks for a way out of its new home instead of settling down quietly to enjoy the comfort and security captivity affords. When a snake is this unsettled, he can be nippy and his health can suffer. He may grow skinny enough for his ribs to show and his skin, when and if he sheds, comes off in dry patches instead of in one smooth throw. A potentially terrific pet can be reduced to a nasty, ugly animal.

Usually the circumstances just described indicate that the animal is feeling insecure and needs some simple change in his environment to make him feel right. If you remember what I told you about a snake's existence in the wild, you know that snakes are shy and don't like to be seen. Providing a snake with a place to hide will almost always eliminate these woeful symptoms.

A hiding spot, by the way, does not mean the space behind a water dish, near the wall of the tank. Nor does it mean a flap of newspaper under which you have seen the snake crawl every so often. A place to hide means a secure little cubbyhole, comfy by design. It should be warm and dark and have firm sides against which a snake can press for that good "tucked-in" feeling you may remember from your childhood. The hiding spot should be large enough for the entire snake to disappear into, yet small enough so that the snake is scrunched a bit fitting in. The entrance to the area should be no bigger around than the fattest portion of the snake's body.

Snakes vary in size, and you must match the hiding box to the snake. I have pressed a variety of items into service as hiding spaces over the years. Do you remember the indigo snake that escaped on me in college and ended up in my boot? Well, once I retrieved her, I made sure that she was secure and happy by sticking an old, tattered loafer into one end of her cage. After that the animal became the picture of contentment and never sought to leave again. When I fed her, I would dangle a mouse near the opening to the shoe. Out she would pop to grab it. Never another problem as long as she lived!

I was lucky that the snake never messed in the shoe. Normally a hiding box should be either washable or disposable. More conventional choices for hiding spaces include shoe boxes and flowerpots. Throw away the top of the box and cut a hole in one end of the bottom. Stick this in the corner of your snake's tank and you have a spot suitable for, say, a three- to five-foot kingsnake.

Flowerpots are great since they come in all sizes. Really small snakes such as brown, ringneck and DeKay's snakes can even use tiny flowerpots that are intended for seedlings. If you turn a pot on its side and wedge it into the corner of the tank, you may be able to use the drain hole already cut in the pot as an entrance. Otherwise you can just chip away a bit of one edge, plug the drain hole and stand the pot upside down.

While a hiding box generally will get a reticent snake to feed and a nervous one to calm down, not every snake requires one. Large pythons and boas, for instance, have few natural predators when they reach adult size. Thus they are less paranoid than more diminutive species (you'd have to be crazy to argue with one of these creatures, believe me) and are happy stretched out in full view, basking under a heat lamp or snuggling against a hot rock. There are few things more beautiful than one of the large constrictors lounging uncovered beneath good lighting. The iridescence of the scales, particularly immediately after shedding, is breathtaking.

Don't worry that if you give a snake a place to hide you will never see it again. You will always see it come out to drink and bask, and often to eat as well. Of course, you may also take it out to handle it (more on this later). The bottom line is that, to be happy, most serpents prefer seclusion, and as keepers with their best interests at heart, we must oblige!

Lending Warmth

As already emphasized, keeping a snake without a heat source is like driving a car without gas. Absolutely everything from the digestive system to the personality is affected. Regrettably, I have too often seen new hobbyists literally kill their pet with kindness. They have read somewhere that snakes are "cold-blooded" and they want to help. They either instantly cook their pet or slowly murder it by keeping it just a degree or two warmer than it requires for months on end without respite. One cannot simply put a snake on top of the water heater and go for life in the fast lane. Nor can you position your pet near a space heater and just blast the cage. No, the metabolic machinery of the snake is quite delicate. All snakes have preferred temperatures, a definite range within which they function best. Depending upon what is on the agenda for the day, the snake may wish to move his body temperature up and down by as much as ten degrees or more. Perhaps he will warm up to help digest a meal, then cool down if food is not forthcoming. It is difficult if not impossible for you as the hobbyist to know precisely what the snake's temperature requirements are at any given moment. Therefore you must provide a temperature gradient within the enclosure so that your pet can pick and choose where he wants to be. In other terms, keep one end of the tank warm and the other unheated and the snake will have the option of moving into and out of the heat as he desires.

What's a good rule of thumb? Well, it's a tough question. Desert species such as bull and gopher snakes like it hot, some of our temperate-zone woodland creatures such as ringnecks appreciate cooler temperatures, and rain-forest species may like it in between. The magic number, though, is 80 degrees F. If you stick with this figure you won't hurt anybody. From the 80-degree baseline, you can experiment, *very carefully,* by raising (not lowering) the temperature within a 5-degree limit, 1 degree at a time. Keep good notes concerning your snake's behavior, because this is your only clue. If the animal eats more than usual, write it down. If it refuses food when you think it ordinarily would have eaten it, write that down too. You may find, as I did with my friend Elrond, that a change in temperature brings about a change in disposition. If you play with the animal a lot (see the "Handling" section), it may be more important that he be tractable than that he eat and grow as fast as possible. Just remember, always give your pet an "out" by leaving one section of the tank cool.

If you have ever driven across the desert at night, you have no doubt seen the sad sight of many dead snakes on the asphalt. These animals crawl to the road and press themselves against its warmth, hoping to prolong the precious heat of the day, unaware of traffic. When the seasons begin to change in temperate zones, snakes will sometimes seek underground areas, often quite deep, that have remained warm and hibernate there until spring.

It should be no surprise that snakes also bask in the sun. One of the most beautiful sights that our Northeast has to offer is the Northern copperhead, *Agkistrodon contortrix,* curled up on a sunny and secluded pile of leaves, looking for all the world like a frond himself. If that image doesn't move you, how about a diamondback rattlesnake all curled up near the sagebrush?

The heat that a reptile needs must ultimately come from the sun. There are two ways that it can be delivered; basking and touching something warm. In captivity we can thus give snakes warmth in two ways, either with a warmed object or with a lamp.

Either method is acceptable. Snakes do not need much light, and the ultraviolet lighting that is so necessary (I discuss this in the lizard chapter) for other reptiles does nothing much for a snake other than darken his skin. If you do opt for a lamp, choose a small spotlight that focuses the beam, and the heat, into a narrow area. Screw it into a clamp-on socket or a gooseneck lamp and you can aim it exactly, allowing the snake to move into and out of the warmth as I have suggested. A 50- or 75-watt spotlight is more than adequate for all but the most gargantuan of reptiles. For fine control of heating, you can add a dimmer to the light, allowing you to compensate for fluctuating temperatures in your home. Don't forget to monitor the temperature in your snake's home with a thermometer!

Light offers not only heat, but energy. Ultraviolet light in particular is beneficial to nearly every animal in this book. While many creatures need this "high energy" light to help metabolize vitamin D and calcium, snakes have little use for it. In fact, ultraviolet light, in the form of so called "grow lights" or "full-wave" fluorescent bulbs is inadvisable for use with snakes because it causes an unattractive darkening of the skin. If you wish to use an ultraviolet light to achieve a desired cast in your snake tank, be sure to interpose a piece of glass. The ultraviolet portion of the light spectrum cannot pene-trate glass (the reason, incidentally, that you don't sunburn through a car window) and thus will not cause your snake's skin to darken. A better choice for making a tank "different looking" is to use a green or red spotlight. This has the added benefit of being a bit easier on your pet's eyes.

If you decide to warm your pet by providing a heat source against which he can coil up, be sure to *avoid* the "hot rocks" sold in pet shops for this purpose! These provide insufficient heat, and they are subject to rapid degradation by moisture if you or your pet spills a water dish on them. Instead, purchase a "Renacor wetproof heating cable for vivaria." This plastic heating cable is manufactured by Rena of France and is available nationwide in 15-, 25- and 50-watt ver-sions. A 50-watt unit will warm a fifty-gallon aquarium if coiled up inside one end of the tank. Of all the units I have tried over the years, this is the absolute best. If your pet shop does not carry it, have one ordered for you. You can achieve fine control of the unit by plugging it into a dimmer switch, but this should not be necessary as the heat is so localized with such a cable that your pet can move onto it or off of it at will.

Drinking, Soaking and Humidity

Flatly and sweepingly put, all snakes need water. Even desert serpents need to drink—something not true of all desert reptiles, some of which get their water from the food they eat. When a snake drinks, he puts just the snout, the lower part of the head or some-times the entire head into the water. If you watch the part of the head that would correspond to our temple, you will see a pulsating move-ment as the muscles move to help draw the water in. The average three-or-four-foot snake has to take a good long draught for you to be able to see the water level in a bowl fall noticeably. In captivity, snakes tend to drink most often after eating, but will take a nip at odd intervals too. Before I discuss the water bowl itself, I will dazzle you with some other important uses for water in the snake cage.

First off, snakes need humidity nearly as much as they need drink-ing water. In the preceding discussion I allowed that snakes from different environments had different temperature preferences. By the same token, some snakes crave the humid air of their native New Orleans or Houston, while others like the air lava-dry. Yet it rains even on a volcano, at least every once in a while, and a snake utterly deprived of humidity will meet his demise before long. I learned this lesson the hard way. At one point I was living in a bitter-cold part of the country with some eighty snakes. Heating eighty individual cages was, of course, a problem, and I had to resort to assigning them a room all their own, heated with an electric space heater to a toasty 80 degrees. My collection included a number of species from arid areas and also a variety of boids (serpents in the python and boa family) that hailed from the tropical rain forest. Soon after I moved into the area, all my boids went off their feed. No matter what trick I pulled out of my hat, these snakes showed no interest in food. They began to look somewhat unhealthy (more later on how to tell) and were obviously disgruntled. My desert animals thrived like bees in a hive. It took an embarrassingly long time before I figured out that the heater was drying the room too much. I increased the size of the water dishes in all the boid tanks, covered the tops of the tanks with tinfoil to keep the humidity in and set up a vaporizer in the room. Two days subsequent to these heroic measures, every single boid ate! The lesson to be learned here is that while in *most* cases humidity is not a problem, do keep it in the back of your mind, particularly if your house is heavily heated in the winter and you wake up in the morning with a dry throat. If you are parched, so is your pet.

The water dish serves not only as a humidifier, but as a tub. Sometimes you may find your snake curled up in his water bowl. Many snakes enjoy a good soak, and this is probably a natural urge having to do with moistening the skin prior to shedding. I have had numerous snakes that could not shed their skin easily and in one piece without a good soak at the right time. In fact, at present I have a pair of Ceylonese pink-headed pythons, *Python molurus pimbura,* which share a cage. The female spends upward of 70 percent of her life in her water dish, consistently shedding without difficulty. Her mate—living in the very same tank, remember—has never once entered the water. A battle of the sexes, perhaps?

Some experts, incidentally, feel that one should not allow snakes to soak indefinitely, as it can lead to water blisters. This is a rare condition, but if you literally never see your snake exit his bowl, you should check to be sure that the temperature is not too high.

I probably don't have to tell you by now that the bowl should be large enough for the snake to immerse himself completely and also be of a design that does not easily tip over. A wide bottom and some weight are the key ingredients of a good water dish. To help ease the burden of having to clean up spilled water or a fouled dish (you must of course keep drinking water free of urine and feces), I have one last suggestion. If you live in an area where humidity is not a problem, you might try giving your snake a full, clean water bowl only one day a week. This supplies adequate water for drinking, offers a chance to soak, precludes any possibility of blisters and makes life easier on you. I can get away with this strategy during the summer with some of my serpents. Naturally, when I see that a snake is about to shed (see the "snake biology" section if you have forgotten how to tell), I provide a water bowl full time.

One further caution in this respect: There are some snakes, hailing from Eurasian and American waters, that actually *live* in the water. Our own water snake, *Natrix sipedon,* is an example. Frankly, these are malodorous and foul-tempered beasts that have little to their credit in the pet department. I wouldn't bother with them. The completely aquatic Java wart snake, *Acrochordus javanicus,* is a bit more agreeable, but still there are far, far better pets.

FEEDING YOUR SNAKE

Fortunately for us, snakes require no special "health" foods. They don't fear preservatives, need not watch their salt or sugar intake, and have no cravings for junk food and ice cream to contend with. In fact, with the exception of adult pythons and boas, which are lazy and prone to obesity, snakes don't even have to watch their waistlines. No, all that most snakes need to keep happy and healthy is a mouse at the dinner table.

Before we delve too deeply and graphically into the feeding of our carnivorous friend the snake, let's take a look at our own diet. Ever been to a slaughterhouse? No? Why not? The answer probably is that you don't much fancy that sort of gore. You eat meat (unless you are a vegetarian) and probably enjoy it, but you rarely think of yourself as a being a carnivore or all that that entails.

If you elect to keep a snake, you are going to have to deal with a bit of meat eating. You certainly don't have to watch and relish it, but it is a fact of life to the snake keeper. I don't like giving my snakes rodents to eat. In fact, it took a long time before I could handle watching the process, and as a little boy just starting out with serpents

I had some pretty intense nightmares; giant rodents devouring me in my bed, that sort of thing.

Mice (and rats) are the most utilitarian and nutritious of serpent fare. From birth through adulthood, the various growth stages of the mouse provide us with food of the appropriate size for just about any but the largest snake. Newborn mice, known affectionately as "pinkies," are blind, hairless and tiny, and are appropriate food for baby king snakes, some boids and other small serpents. As the snake grows, so of course, must the size of its meal. To an extent, you have to gauge the size mouse your snake requires by trial and error. A good rule of thumb is to start with a rodent just about the size of the snake's head.

Mice are available from most pet shops, and most storekeepers will give you a break on the price if they know you are feeding the animal to a pet snake. Expect to pay about forty cents for a "pinkie," roughly fifty cents for a juvenile mouse and perhaps seventy-five cents for an adult mouse. These, like all prices in this book, are only guidelines. Choose mice that have no obvious lumps or skin lesions and that are alert and responsive. *You* wouldn't eat a sick mouse, so there is no sense feeding one to your pet. Check to see if the pet shop keeps (or has ever kept) the mouse you are about to purchase on cedar shavings. Cedar as a rodent flooring can be fatal to your snake. The mouse picks up a residue from the cedar in his fur and can transmit it, with dire consequences, to your pet. If you need pinkies regularly for one or more small snakes, you might consider ordering baby mice frozen. Snakes, as I will discuss in a moment, will eat thawed food, and it is often less expensive.

Speaking of cost, feeding rodents to more than a couple of snakes can be an expensive proposition if considered over a long term. Let's take a reasonable example: You read this book, become fascinated with snakes, get one, find out just how amazing they really are and end up after a period of time with half a dozen. They are young and growing animals, and they eat like crazy. Each one devours a mouse a week (more on this later). You frequent a pet shop that is more expensive than average and charges a dollar a mouse. Six mice a week is six dollars per week. Multiply this by fifty weeks for the year (you are bound to miss at least two feedings) and you arrive at a figure of three hundred dollars a year to feed a small collection; far from peanuts. Although you can often find private individuals who breed mice and are willing to supply you, and although you can often strike a deal with a pet shop if you are buying in quantity, you should realize that cost, especially if you get compulsive and end up with a bunch of snakes, can become a real factor. If you have more than, say, ten snakes, I would suggest that you look into breeding your own mice.

Next to the mouse, the most common snake food is the rat. Large king snakes, rat snakes, gopher snakes and most boas and pythons ultimately reach a size at which they should be fed rats. If you have purchased a snake that will ultimately grow big enough to eat rats, I have some great advice for you: think ahead! Snakes can be very stubborn about changing their diet. A snake that has eaten a mouse every week for a year or two is unlikely to wish to change over easily. You could become stuck with providing six to ten mice at each feeding, just to fill him up—a horrendously expensive proposition. Baby rats, or "rat pinks," are rarely much more expensive than mice. If you can interest a young snake in starting to feed on infant rats, you will have no trouble whatsoever graduating him to the larger models. My snakes tell me that, young and old, all rats taste the same.

While the price of an individual mouse is lower than that of an individual rat, the rat, in terms of body mass fed, is far cheaper. A large rat—food for, say, a six- or eight-foot boa constrictor—is at least the meal equivalent of six mice. Rats usually cost about two dollars, so your savings in feeding a giant snake can be substantial.

We have talked mice, rats and microeconomics, so now let's get on to how often to feed. As I begin this discussion, I hear far off in the distance a cry from my readers for a rule of thumb. Much as I hate rules of thumb, here goes. Try once every ten days. The average snake in good condition will eat this often, but if fed enough each time, not much more often. Now, while it is fresh in your mind, let me try to wriggle out of the rule of thumb. I have raised baby pythons that ate their limit of a couple of rat pinks once every four days. I have likewise had large, adult snakes that fasted for six months or more. The frequency of feeding is something to which you will have to become sensitive in your individual animal through trial and error. Start with my rule and your own thumbs will take over after a time.

Each time you feed, you should give the animal all he will eat. This is especially important, obviously, if the creature is young and growing rapidly. Conversely, if you have an aging (say, fifteen-year-old) boa or python, you should limit its food intake, as previously suggested, if it becomes obese. How will you know if it becomes obese? Believe me, you will know.

Although snakes will occasionally eat carrion, most snakes prefer live or freshly dead fare. Feeding your pet a live rodent is a bit risky, as both mice and rats, but particularly the latter, can injure or kill a snake. Some people just toss a live rodent into the cage and go out to a movie. If the snake is hungry, they reason, he will eat. If not they leave the mouse in there until he does, or return the rodent to the pet shop. This, by my lights, is not wise. If you must feed live food, stick around to be sure you can prevent injury to your pet.

A far better plan is to kill the food animal before offering it to the snake. Forgive me the vivid detail, but I want you to get this right so that the mouse or rat does not suffer: Using a pencil, press the animal firmly down right at the base of the neck, above the shoulders. This will provide a firm hold from which it cannot escape. While holding it there, give the tail a brisk yank. This is called "cervical dislocation"—a fond term for breaking the animal's neck. It sounds awful, but the nice part is that all the nerves are instantly parted from the brain, so the animal in fact feels absolutely nothing except the push of your pencil. If your snake does not eat, don't throw the food item away; freeze it instead in a plastic bag. Thawed thoroughly through and through and wiggled at the end of a forceps (pliers or barbecue tongs will serve) to make it look alive, it can be next week's meal. Don't use rodents that have been frozen for longer than six months, however, as they lose too much nutritional value, particularly vitamins.

All this stuff about biting, freezing, wiggling and dying doesn't sound like too much fun, and it isn't. Yet you must realize that if you weren't doing all this, the snake would be doing it himself somewhere in the wild. After a time it becomes very satisfying to watch your pet eat a good meal.

Well, the part we both dreaded most is over. Let me now sweeten the serpent pot a bit. I did promise earlier that snakes were really easy to keep. You might not think so after reading about killing rodents and all that. Ha! you are probably thinking—easy for *him*! Well how about this: It does not matter if you forget to feed your snake for a while. Having a hard time psyching yourself up for all this? Relax. You can let it go for a few weeks, as long as you are not trying to raise a hatchling. In fact, weekend trips and even month-long vacations are no problem, provided your snake is looked in on now and again to make sure it is warm enough and has water.

If you are dead set on having a snake, but feel you absolutely cannot give a snake a mouse to eat, there is a final option. A small number of available serpents can survive on frogs, fish, worms and crickets. They are not highly recommended as pets, but for the unswayable snake *and* rodent lover, they may be worth considering. Our native garter snake, *Thamnophis sirtalis,* and the venomous (but not dangerous to man) green vine snake, *Oxybelis fulgidus,* are two examples.

HANDLING AND TAMING YOUR PET

I bet you are dying to know! You are about to get the creature; you have gone ahead and learned all about how to care for it. You have set up its home and arranged to feed it. Now you want to know if you can play with it. The answer is (a qualified) yes! Below I will list the eight rules of snake handling.

1. *Never* handle a venomous snake of any variety, especially if you have been told it doesn't bite. (Remember Rosenfeld's Law; if it can kill you, it will.)
2. Don't handle hatchlings; they are too delicate.
3. Don't handle a snake for forty-eight hours after it has eaten or taken a long drink.
4. Don't handle a snake that is obviously agitated—for example, whipping around the cage.
5. Don't handle a snake for more than twenty minutes at a time.
6. Let the snake go where it wants to and adjust your grip accordingly.
7. Never pick up a snake by the head.
8. Support the snake in at least two places.

Snakes can be tamed, and there is no special technique beyond simply handling them a lot. Getting used to you is about all you can expect. Move slowly when you approach the animal to make sure he understands that you are not a mouse. I like to cover the snake's head with my open hand, pinning it gently, if the snake is strange to me or worries me at all. This procedure allows the animal to sense your odor, temperature and intention. Do this gently, lest he think your intention is to squash him.

Indian python

After five or six seconds he will relax and you can let his head loose. Go ahead and pick him up, following the eight laws. It is this simple procedure, repeated over a period of a couple of weeks, that will totally tame your pet. Just remember that he requires reminding now and then of who you are. If you go away on a two-week vacation, approach him warily when you get back, giving him a chance to recognize you. If your snake is very small—say, less than two feet long—you don't have to bother with all this mumbo jumbo. If he bites it will be no more than a pinprick and you probably won't notice it anyway.

If a larger snake should bite you, don't be alarmed. Generally the bite is a quick one-two affair drawing a tiny amount of blood, the snake letting go forthwith. If the snake hangs on or chews, persuade him to let go by prying his mouth open gently with the eraser end of a pencil or anything else that's soft and handy. If he still insists upon hanging on, immerse your hand (or whatever) in ice-cold water from the tap. (If your snake still won't let go, you need a new *snake.*) Once detached, wash the pinpricks and swab them with a disinfectant (snake mouths are generally dirty) and then forget the whole thing. If you have been bitten by something venomous, see a doctor immediately.

The majority of pet snakes don't bite. If yours does, see that he has more opportunity to get used to you; even wear gloves if you feel you must. If your snake is really aggressive, look to a fault in the environment, something that makes him insecure. Go over the preceding sections of the book to make sure you are giving him all he needs. Finally, lots of time can be saved by picking a docile individual in the first place. For advice on choosing a snake, see the next section.

ACQUIRING A SNAKE

If you have gotten this far, you clearly want to know what kind of snake to buy or catch. The species you end up with is important, since some snakes are, very simply, better pets than others. But first, you probably want to know whether the animal is young and healthy, how much you should expect to pay—and where, in fact, you even come up with a serpent these days.

Where to Buy

If you live in the Sun Belt, you may have the thought of at least trying to catch your own snake before you go rushing out to buy. Although people can and do make the attempt frequently, I wouldn't advise it. I am already having terrible dreams about all of you rushing out to grab the nearest rattlesnake by mistake. Until you really know what you are doing or can go out with someone who does, leave the field guide on the shelf and leave the hunting to the pros.

Pet shops, I have been told, exist to prevent snakebite. While I wouldn't go so far as to ascribe this to conscious effort on the part of pet dealers in this country, your local pet shop really is the best place to get your snake. A pet-shop purchase gives you the opportunity to be sure you really like the snake, to be sure it is in good health (see below) and to be sure it is nicely tempered. Most pet shops also guarantee their animals to some extent as well. If the creature sickens and dies quickly (a very unlikely proposition), you have someone to go and yell at. Also, if you get the animal home and your landlord evicts you (just kidding) you can most likely return the snake for credit.

Alas, pet-shop prices are usually a bit high and selection a bit low. What is more—and I hate to say it, since so many fine exceptions spring to mind—the *average* pet-shop keeper doesn't know his way around snakes well enough to answer all your questions and advise you properly. (For this reason you must keep one copy of this book by your bed, another on your desk and a pristine, unthumbed copy on your coffee table.) If you live away from a large urban center, you may not be able to find any snake for sale or the one you desire. If that is the case, you may have to explore some alternatives, the simplest of which is to consult a mail-order pet supplier.

Many large mail-order pet businesses operate on both a wholesale and a retail level. Some even specialize in reptiles and amphibians. You can find the names and addresses of some by phoning the zoo nearest you. Zoos receive flyers from big importers unsolicited and should even be able to tell you—unofficially, of course—who sells the best snakes for the lowest price.

Mail-order animal businesses depend upon repeat orders. While you certainly should not expect the very *best* examples of a given species, you will probably end up with a reasonable pet. If the places shipped one-eyed, scaleless, wheezing and decrepit beasts, they couldn't stay in business long. Speaking of shipping, you must realize that getting the snake from the supplier to you is the hidden cost in the mail-order game. The shipping charge can often be twenty-five to forty dollars. Many houses, moreover, will not ship and guarantee live delivery to the cold states in winter months or hot states in summer. Nobody wants to absorb the cost of a shipment that was left sitting on the runway in August in Arizona! One way to beat the shipping cost if you do decide to purchase by mail is to get a bunch of friends in on the order. This way you can all split the freight and have a heavier club to wave if something goes amiss.

The price list that most mail-order houses send out describes the animals by both common and scientific names. This is great, since it is the only way you can be absolutely sure that the species you are getting is the one you want. Most pet shops don't do this, but of course, you can see the animal yourself.

The last remaining marketplace option is in some respects the best. The private breeder who either has a couple of snakes and breeds them on occasion or runs an outfit that would put some zoos to shame is, some feel, the ultimate source for the serpent pet. I have mentioned this source last because although the quality is of the highest order, *it is very difficult to find such people.* There are only a few individuals around the country who really devote themselves to breeding reptiles full time. This is, understand, a poorly understood and financially risky venture. You wouldn't be likely to make your first million at it! Although a number of individuals do mail out price lists, the only way to find these people is through zoos or by word of mouth. Many private breeders have waiting lists for some of their most beautiful and exotic offspring. These are always sold as hatchlings and are frequently delicate and not appropriate for the novice. If you do buy a newborn of some exotic variety, listen carefully to the breeder's advice regarding getting it to eat and have him feed the animal in front of you. Very young snakes of this kind can be tricky!

To sum up, you have four options:

1. Catch the animal yourself: I don't recommend this unless you are very experienced and can positively tell the difference between venomous and nonvenomous varieties.

2. Buy or order a snake through your local pet shop: This is the best route, because even if the animal you want is not in stock, the dealer can mail-order it for you, thus taking the risk out of the mail-order ordeal and passing only a small price increase on to you. If the animal is in the store, you can get a sense of it before you commit yourself.

3. Order a snake by mail: Somewhat riskier than buying from a pet shop, since you don't get to *see* the animal, this route can also make rare species available to you and can save you money. Try to get some friends to join you in placing the order to cut shipping costs to each of you. Make sure the mail-order house has a good reputation by asking zoos, reptile clubs and other fanciers.

4. Buy from a private breeder: A good way to go if you can *find* a private breeder, but remember that these people get top dollar for their captive offspring and frequently have waiting lists.

How Old and Which Sex?

Unlike the giant turtles and tortoises that may, in rare cases, near the two-century mark, snakes are not especially long-lived reptiles. Nonetheless, a properly cared-for snake, under optimal conditions and with a healthy dose of luck, can live twenty years in captivity. In my experience there is a correlation between the size of the species and the longevity. That is to say that a secretive little foot-long insectivore (bug eater) such as a ring-necked or brown snake will not live to the ripe old age that a giant python will.

Twenty years, though, is a satisfactory lifespan for a pet, and any reasonably young snake that is healthy can be expected to live for a while. The ideal age at which to acquire a new snake is one year. By this time the animal either has gotten over any maladjustment or would have perished. Likewise, if there is any hidden congenital anomaly (such as a digestive problem, spinal malformation or other defect), it has either manifested itself or killed the animal.

Yet one year old is still quite young. Snakes do their most serious growing in the first two years, so you have plenty of time to "raise the baby" if that idea excites you.

There are exceptions to the rule, of course. If you end up with a giant boa or python (see more about this proposition below), then get him at just a month old or so, provided you have evidence that he is feeding well. I suggest this only because raising one of these giants is among the great thrills of snake keeping.

I have raised a number of creatures to the fifteen-foot mark and can attest to the fun of it. Also, as has no doubt occurred to you, it is great to know the animal when he is only the size of an elongated crayon. Imagine yourself hefting a monolithic, awe-inspiring serpent into your arms in front of your friends. This is the kind of beast that could pick his teeth with a woolly mammoth and have you and your buddies for dessert. Your friends gasp in awe, but you are secure, relaxed and comfortable (this sounds like an ad for a mattress and box spring), reveling in the knowledge that you knew the little tyke when he was hardly bigger than a pencil.

Recognizing a hatchling is easy. It is tiny, and there is probably more than one available. Recognizing a yearling is difficult because so many factors affect the size a snake has reached in a given period of time. To know for sure, you must ask the seller. If he or she does not know, you are left with finding out the animal's adult size and just guessing. Don't worry *too* much about this, though. As long as you don't get a really old snake, you should be okay. A really old snake looks like a really old anything else. It moves less, is less alert and just gives you the overall feeling that it has seen better days.

Sex—I mean the sex of the snake you wish to purchase—is a long and difficult topic. I have just four words of advice concerning the gender of your snake: *Don't worry about it.* It's true. There simply isn't much difference. This question should be of some concern to you only if you plan to breed the animal. I am, however, presuming that you are just looking for a first snake pet, and breeding is a bit beyond the novice's ken. Just relax and take whatever you get!

Healthy or Sickly?

Once you have seen a few snakes, you reach the point at which a quick glance will tell you almost as much as a thorough exam. For your first time out, though, consult the checklist below:

1. Does the snake have both eyes? Don't laugh—it's been missed before, and it will be missed again. Try convincing your pet shop that you "got him that way"!

2. Are all the scales in good shape? They should not show nicks or scratches, and there should be no scars. Areas where the skin is uncovered by scales means a snake was injured or burned.

3. Is the mouth clear of blood, mucus and any chalky substance? Any of these spells trouble. Pry open the mouth gently with a blunt instrument (such as a pencil eraser) while holding the head and supporting the body, and check.

4. Do the nose or lips look rubbed away? A hyperactive or maladjusted snake will rub his head against the cage looking for a way out. You don't want him.

5. Is the snake free of parasites? You can't look inside to see if he has tapeworms or flukes, but you can check to see that there are no mites (tiny little spiderlike creatures) crawling over him. These can be black or reddish and suck his blood. They can suck him dry. These creatures can be controlled, but it takes some doing and is beyond the scope of this book. If you feel that you must have that particular snake, then ask the shopkeeper to cure the animal and give you a call after the parasites are gone. Remember, incidentally, that these bugs

are *very* contagious. If one snake in the shop has them, chances are the rest do too.

6. Is the animal alert? Remember that there is a difference between alert and nervous. Your prospective pet should not be scooting all over the tank at your approach. Nonetheless, his eyes or his head should move to signal that he sees you coming. An overly lethargic snake may just be very well fed, but he could be dying too.

7. Does the animal feel heavy for his size? A serpent in good form has a hefty feel to him.

These are the critical points. If the snake you are evaluating meets these criteria, chances are he is in good shape.

SNAKES I RECOMMEND

In your heart of hearts, you probably still think a snake is a snake. Sure, there are big ones and small ones, but the bottom line is that they are just reptiles with no legs. Wrong! The variety of habits, shapes, modes of locomotion, methods of subduing prey, musculature, appearance, demeanor, color and scales would dazzle you completely!

Out of the multitude of the world's nonvenomous snakes that can adapt to captivity, there are a number that, as pets, stand head and shoulder(?) above the rest. Still, this is a tough job, since I have had to leave out some of my favorites. Yet in the selection I offer below, I believe there is something for everybody.

Kingsnakes

Kingsnakes are constrictors. Not *boa* constrictors, just plain constrictors. They wrap around their prey to kill it, exerting sufficient force to suffocate but not crush their victim. Found from Canada to South America, they derive their name from their ability to kill almost any other snake. They even have a high tolerance to venom and will dine with dispassion on rattlesnakes and field mice alike. In fact, they can even dine on each other, so remember to house them *alone.* I guess that does make them king of the snakes in this country, but I would hate to see one at war with a large python or a spitting cobra!

Chain kingsnake

1. Chain kingsnake *(Lampropeltis getulus getulus)*

The Eastern or chain kingsnake is the largest and most common of our domestic species. It feeds readily on just about anything you offer it (but forget chicken à la king). Being distributed all through the East, it is also easy to find in pet shops. This is a dark brown or black snake banded with yellow. (In snake lingo, by the way, a band goes around the body, while a stripe runs head to tail.) Chain kings are among the easiest snakes in the world to keep. They feed readily and adapt comfortably to captivity. The Florida race has speckling instead of banding and is also commonly available. Less frequently available, but worth seeking out, is the Midwestern variety, known as Holbrook's or the "salt and pepper" kingsnake. This understated and elegant kingsnake is a bit smaller than the average chain king but makes an equally elegant captive. Remember that kingsnakes must be kept alone, as they are cannibals.

FOOD: mice
SIZE: 3–6 feet
TEMPERATURE: 75–80 degrees F.
PRICE: $40–$70

2. Albino California kingsnake *(Lampropeltis getulus californiae)*

Kingsnakes are the most popular pets among our native serpents. They are hardy, showy reptiles which exhibit a myriad of patterns and colors just guaranteed to please. Technically you may have noticed that the California kingsnake has the same Latin name as the chain kingsnake, although it lives on the opposite coast. These are genetically one and the same animal, but they are quite different in appearance. California kingsnakes may come into the world with either stripes or hands, and both "morphs" or forms may even come from the same mother! To the untrained eye, the banded and the striped varieties look like completely different animals.

Enthusiastic breeders have been working with these animals for some years, and have at last come up with an albino form that is rapidly becoming a sought after reptile. The base color is white, covered with either bands or stripes of vibrant yellow. The eyes are red. At this time only a handful of pet shops sell these albinos, but they are commonly available from private sources.

> FOOD: mice of appropriate size
> SIZE: to 4 feet
> TEMPERATURE: 80 degrees F.
> PRICE: $75–$150 (Banded individuals at the time of this writing command a slightly higher price than do individuals with stripes.)

3. Mountain kingsnake *(Lampropeltis pyromelana* and other species)*

The mountain kingsnakes are a group of small, secretive, tricolored animals that are in some instances protected by law. Captive-bred individuals, however, are available. These little jewels are resplendent in different hues of gray, black, red, white, yellow and sometimes brown. The usual ground color is white. In your home these creatures *must* have a secure hiding place if they are to survive. They happen to look great curled up inside a piece of cork bark. I have included them here because of their stunning beauty, but mountain kingsnakes are not the easy captives that some of their relatives prove to be. Some insist on eating only small snakes and lizards and can only with difficulty be coaxed onto a more reasonable rodent diet. This you can

Corn snake (4 color phases)

Ringneck snake

Boa constrictor

Ball python

Chuckwalla

Madagascar Day gecko

Jackson's chameleon

Golden Tegu

GARY SIPPERLEY

Red-eared slider

GARY SIPPERLEY

Red-footed tortoise

Eastern box turtle

Lilac-crowned Amazon parrot

ARTHUR ROSENFELD

African Grey Parrot

GARY SIPPERLEY

African burrowing bullfrog

Bell's Horned frog

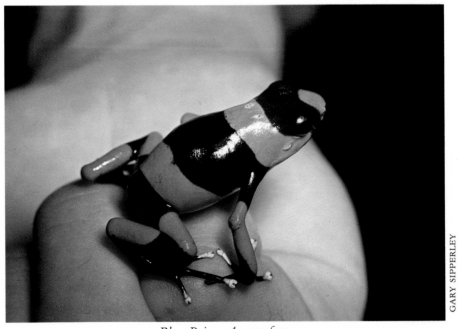

Blue Poison-Arrow frog

achieve by rubbing a mouse against a common pet-shop anole (lizard) in order to get the mouse smelling the way the snake wants it to. You should attempt one of these animals only if you can accept the fact that it might prove to be a bit stubborn and insist for a while on fasting. Your patience will be rewarded by success in keeping one of the most beautiful of all reptiles.

FOOD: lizards and mice
SIZE: 1.5–3 feet
TEMPERATURE: 80 degrees F.
PRICE: $175–$250

4. Milk snake (*Lampropeltis triangulum* sp.)

The milk snake is actually a kingsnake. It receives its name from any number of awful stories about its sucking milk from a cow. This is about as unlikely as an octopus' breeding with an elephant. The beautifully patterned, slender milk snake is a prodigious mouser, though, and does like to hunt around barns. The prudent farmer leaves him be. The milk snake's ground color is black or gray, and he is covered with rust or reddish blotches. There is often light gray or white between the blotches, but milk snake coloring is highly variable. Of our native varieties, the race from the Great Plains has the most color. Milk snakes from Mexico and Central America are occasionally available too, and bear especially attractive markings.

Like the mountain kingsnakes, these animals definitely need a hiding box, as they tend to be a bit nervous. If you are handling an unfamiliar milk snake, you should beware of one annoying habit they possess. Milk snakes bite sideways! You can be holding a seemingly well-adjusted animal in your hands when, as if planning an affectionate rub, the creature will move his jaw over the flesh of your of your finger and take it in sideways. This is more comical than anything else, as milk snakes are not big enough to inflict a worrisome bite.

Once a milk snake settles into captivity, it is a hardy and steady feeder that spends most of its time in hiding, awaiting your pleasure or its next meal.

FOOD: mice
SIZE: 2–2.5 feet
TEMPERATURE: 75–80 degrees F.
PRICE: $30–$200

Rat Snakes

While kingsnakes are relatively peaceful and quiet captives, the rat snakes, *Elaphe* sp., are not. These are large, powerful and active constricting snakes, less fond of handling than kingsnakes and more likely to try to escape from your grasp and their quarters. They are showy serpents that generally feed like clockwork and are not fussy. I don't know why they are called "rat snakes," as many of the species are arboreal (tree-dwelling) and eat birds. In captivity, however, they do best on rodents. Being active climbers, all rat snakes should have a branch or dowel for climbing added to their otherwise spartan dwelling.

5. Corn snake *(Elaphe guttata)*

The red rat snake or corn snake makes an outstanding pet. It is a beautiful, boldly colored red, orange and brown creature that enjoys a great reputation in the pet trade. Somewhat variable in color, depending upon its state of origin, this Eastern species is available regularly in many pet shops. As rat snakes go, this is a medium-sized animal. Very well adjusted, corn snakes can sometimes get away without a hiding box, being secure in the open. Many people breed these pretty snakes and have even isolated and selected for the albino strain. Albinos still cost twice as much as a normally colored individual, but are becoming more available all the time. They have lighter-than-normal coloration and red eyes. Totally white individuals are also to be had now and then. Don't forget to give your corn snake a branch on which to climb. This snake looks terrific curled on a branch with dried corncob as a background flooring.

> FOOD: mice
> SIZE: to 5 feet
> TEMPERATURE: 75–80 degrees F.
> PRICE: $40 (up to $200 for all-white albinos)

6. Everglades rat snake *(Elaphe obsoleta rossalleni)*

My favorite rat snake is the Everglades rat snake from Florida, a striking subspecies of the Southern yellow rat snake. This animal is one of the largest of our native serpents. It is clad in neon orange scales with occasional hues of pink. It can achieve the girth of a woman's arm and if purchased young is active and good-tempered.

Like all rat snakes, this one kills by constriction, and it may grow large enough to eat small rats. Being as robust as it is, it has little fear of lying out in the open and can often be kept without a hiding box. This is worth trying, as there are few more impressive sights than one of these enormous creatures stretched out in an exhibit cage. Since this animal looks so terrific stretched out, I would recommend a larger-than-normal cage so that the big yellow fellow can unkink.

FOOD: mice, rats for large adults (see pages 50–51)
SIZE: to 7 feet
TEMPERATURE: 80–85 degrees F.
PRICE: $75–$90

7. Trans Pecos rat snake *(Elaphe subocularis)*

The next rat snake is perhaps the most famous of all. The Trans Pecos rat snake is a peculiar little creature with exceedingly large, bulging eyes. There are scales between the eye and the lip that distinguish this animal from its rattish relatives and lend it the Latin *"subocularis."* This medium-sized rat snake from the Trans Pecos desert of Texas and New Mexico is tan striped with chocolate. This snake tends to be a bit more finicky as a feeder than other rat snakes, although I have never had one that failed to eat after an adjustment period of a month or so. Don't forget the hide box! This animal is not common and thus commands a bit more than some other rat snakes.

FOOD: mice
SIZE: 3–5.5 feet
TEMPERATURE: 80 degrees F.
PRICE: $120

8. Asian rat snake *(Elaphe taeniurus)*

The last rat snake we will look at is not native to this country. The Asian rat snake, is a very large serpent that uses its long teeth to catch birds in the forests of its homeland. When young it looks a bit like the preceding species except that its eyes don't bulge out and it is so much larger. When it grows it achieves a milky pearlescence that makes it look like something out of a fantasy film. I tend to think of adults as the "unicorns" of the serpent world.

FOOD: mice for young, rats for adults (see pages 50–51)
SIZE: to 8 feet
TEMPERATURE: 80–85 degrees F.
PRICE: $90

Pine, Bull and Gopher Snakes

Three domestic serpents that are actually regional variations of the
same snake, these are serious, full-bodied constrictors with a cast-iron
disposition and a ravenous appetite. The types of *Pituophis melanoleu-
cus* differ somewhat in size and coloration, but they are all great
captives. You can have some fun with them too, as they all have a
little flap of skin in the throat that amplifies the expelling of air into

Trans Pecos ratsnake

a thunderous noise for so small a creature. When annoyed, they hunker down and blow air, hissing as if they were entering a heavy-weight bout. All bark and no bite, they are usually well behaved and have no special dentition.

9. Pine snake *(Pituophis melanolencus)*

The pine snake is the Eastern form of the trio, being found from New Jersey to Florida. Pine snakes are black-and-white blotched and speckled creatures, although in Florida there are some completely black populations. At one time a common snake, the pine snake is now the most difficult of the three to come by. The head is conical, and the eyes are set a bit forward in the head.

Some years ago I raised a baby pine snake and found it to be a voracious and beautiful captive. When only the thickness of a pencil and not much longer, the animal was like a little jewel, perfectly scaled and tightly muscled. This particular baby loved to wrap very tightly about my fingers in a presumed demonstration of what it could do to me if I were a baby mouse!

FOOD: mice
SIZE: to 7 feet (rarely)
TEMPERATURE: 75–80 degrees F.
PRICE: $100 ($150 for the black variety)

10. Bull and gopher snakes *(Pituophis melanolencus)*

The bull and gopher snakes resemble each other more closely than they do their Eastern relative. From the Midwest and Far West, these creatures are tan, chocolate and yellow rather than black and white like the pine snake. Bull snakes may in rare instances reach eight feet long—notable, as this is just about as big as any serpent gets in this country. While a bit full of himself when first acquired, the average gopher or bull snake will soon stop hissing with his little throat flap and settle into a fine captive who will give you years of pleasure.

FOOD: mice
SIZE: to 8 feet (rarely)
TEMPERATURE: 85 degrees F.
PRICE: $50

11. Indigo snake *(Drymarchon corais)*

The queen and matriarch of North American serpents, the indigo is the obscure object of desire for many budding herpetologists. It is special in two ways; first as it is the last sizable domestic serpent to be considered here, and second as it does not constrict its prey but rather kills simply by using its head and jaws. This is absolutely the largest nonvenomous snake in the land. There are two varieties of the indigo. The larger and more desirable one occurs in Florida, the smaller and less attractive race in Texas. Indigos are muscular, blue-black animals with a marvelous disposition and a voracious appetite. While some Floridians who have grown up with indigos may dispute this, these animals have never been plentiful in the pet trade, especially in relation to other native species.

In the proper light, and especially just after a shed, the indigo glints with a rainbow iridescence. When I was a small boy I saw my first indigo in a small pet shop way up on the shelf in a metal-framed aquarium. The vision is so burned upon my mind that I can conjure it up now in an instant. There is a regal aspect to this snake that to me is perhaps utterly unmatched.

Unfortunately, the combination of its great desirability as a pet and the destruction of its habitat has resulted in the Florida indigo's becoming a threatened species. The animal is now protected by law. In order to obtain one you must first locate a breeder who is authorized to sell one (ask your pet shop to find you one from a mail-order house that does some breeding, or find a private individual). Next you must acquire a permit from the Department of the Interior. Anyone who legally sells you an indigo snake can provide you with an application for permission to own the animal. All this rigamarole is designed to preserve the species, and the species, as you will find out, is worth preserving.

Indigos, incidentally, should not be kept with other snakes, as they are irascible when it comes to dealing with their fellow serpents.

FOOD: fish, small snakes, frogs, mice, small rats (see pages 50–51)
SIZE: to 8 feet
TEMPERATURE: 80 degrees F.
PRICE: $150

12. Ringneck snake *(Diadophis punctatus)*

Before I leave our native fauna and go on to the snakes of South America and the Old World, I would like to mention a domestic snake that is about as far from being an indigo as a snake can be, and yet has much to recommend it. The ringneck snakes are minuscule animals that to me are the best example of how a snake can resemble a precious stone.

These are trickier captives than anything that I have mentioned so far and represent a departure from the norm in that they will fail if not left to their own devices. If you seek a pet snake that you can handle, forget a ringneck. If you instead want a gorgeous and terrifically executed miracle of nature in your home, he is a marvelous choice. These are dark-colored snakes, rarely exceeding two and a half feet. Most often they are a lot smaller and usually possess the girth of the good-sized earthworm that will provide them a meal. They eat a variety of soft-bodied insects, and I have even fed them crickets. When bothered, they coil and display their bright red or orange underbelly. Viewed from the top, their most noticeable feature is the bright yellow or red ring around the neck.

Normally I don't call the enclosure in which one keeps a snake a vivarium. This is a name that I reserve for a planted, organized micro-environment suitable for some lizards, frogs, insects and spiders, but not for snakes. Snakes root around in such confines, ruining painstaking decor and whacking all that is ordered into chaos.

Ringnecks, however, are exceptionally tiny, delicately built animals with a velvet touch. They do beautifully in a small vivarium. To prepare one, see the instructions in the lizard chapter under the heading "the forest vivarium."

There are several types of ringnecks, from our North, South, East and West. To me the Western subspecies or races are the nicest. Get the largest, healthiest-looking ringneck you can find, as the tiny ones can be difficult to find food for.

FOOD: soft-bodied insects
SIZE: 1–2.5 feet
TEMPERATURE: 78 degrees F.
PRICE: $5–$10

13. African eggeater *(Dasypeltis scabra)*

Let's leave this country and have a look at another unusual snake that is also small (though lots bigger than a ringneck) and has an offbeat diet as well. The African eggeater is a light brown or olive snake from the south of that continent. It is usually less than two and a half feet long and quite slender. It has few teeth, its mouth and throat instead being specialized to eat eggs many times the girth of its head. If you absolutely cannot tolerate the feeding of live animals to your snake, this snake presents an interesting option. You will have to have a supply of small bird eggs, though, since only a really large eggeater can down a chicken egg. Smaller eggs are available through poultry suppliers, restaurant wholesalers, mail-order biological-supply houses and some pet shops.

The eggeater has an amazing way of dealing with the size and shape of its favorite food. After getting its jaws closed around the egg, the snake punctures it with a sharp projection from the spine, present at the back of the throat. The contents are then swallowed and the eggshell expelled. It is a treat to watch one of these serpents feed. In most snakes the progress of the whole prey down the throat is visible, especially if the food item is large. When you watch the eggeater swallow, though, the bulge suddenly disappears and then out pops the shell.

Give the eggeater a branch. Since he subsists on bird eggs, he is used to climbing for his meal!

> FOOD: small bird's eggs
> SIZE: to 2.5 feet
> TEMPERATURE: 80–85 degrees F.
> PRICE: $100–$125

Boas and Pythons

Boas and pythons together make up a group called "boids." One can think of boas and pythons as New (the Americas) and Old (Europe, Africa, Madagascar and Australasia) World versions of the same thing. This is the special family that in addition to a large number of moderate-sized snakes, includes all of the so-called big six giant constrictors that may be more than ten times the length of a ringneck and thousands of times as weighty. All of these constrictors are related and occur in the tropical areas of the New and Old Worlds. They are the Burmese, reticulated, amethystine and African rock pythons, the boa constrictor and the anaconda. Believe it or not, two of these giants make terrific pets. The rest are unsuitable for one reason or another. The amethystine python, for instance, is neither exported from its native Australia nor bred here. The thirty-foot-long, deer-eating anaconda, in its turn, achieves hundreds of pounds in weight and must have an enormous pool in which to luxuriate while it digests.

How about an anaconda for the "guest bathroom" in your studio apartment??

Although this section may read like a science-fiction thriller or a horror novel, these giants are very much a part of the lives of people living in the tropics. In fact, none of these creatures are rare or even terribly costly. We are not talking about the Loch Ness Monster here, though some scientists believe that "Nessie" may indeed be some sort of giant reptile.

The two giants that make fine captives are the boa constrictor and the various races of the Burmese python.

14. Boa constrictor (Boa constrictor)

The boa only narrowly makes it into the Giant Club, whose members may reach thirty feet. The typical large wild boa is about ten feet long, though eighteen feet has been recorded. Even a ten-foot individual is a bruiser, though, since boas are heavy-bodied and muscular. There are numerous different subspecies or races of the common boa sprinkled all over Central and South America. These vary considerably in appearance. Boas from Mexico and Argentina, for example, tend to be either black and white or almost all black. Some boas from Peru and southern Brazil are very light tan with an orange cast to the head and fire engine–red tails. Boas have long been popular captives, easily available and easy to keep and even to breed. In the past there have been quite a few around. This embarrassment of serpent riches has resulted in a premium's being placed on certain color phases. There are aficionados to whom the various races differ in value and appeal as much as onions and diamonds. Frankly, this is a lot of nonsense. The best pets are the ones that appeal to you visually. All the various races can be beautiful and impressive animals with reliable dispositions. They are great if you want to handle your pet. Unlike the diminutive ringneck, these gentle giants will tolerate your most lavish affections.

Nearly all the young boas available these days have been bred domestically, as they are protected by law in most of their countries of origin.

> FOOD: mice for youngsters, rats for adults
> SIZE: to 18 feet (typically closer to 7)
> TEMPERATURE: 85–88 degrees F.
> PRICE: $85–$175

15. Burmese python *(Python molurus bivittatus)*

The Burmese python is even larger than the boa constrictor and is but one of three races. The common variety is olive green with brown markings. Upon hatching from the mother's egg, he is about twenty-one inches long and is ready to feed immediately upon mice or rats. Very young individuals can be a bit snappy, but they mellow with age. While I have raised more than fifty of these creatures and have never had a problem getting one to eat like a pig, it should be noted that making the commitment to a pet like this has a negative side to it. While young Burmese pythons are exciting and fun to grow and feed, an adult can be a real threat. A full-grown example makes meals of tougher customers than you! This is not a good first snake, and certainly not one to have if your space or commitment is limited. As your pet grows, you should garner advice from a nearby zoo as to how best to handle it. Do not procure one with the design of donating it to a worthy cause when it gets too large. Zoos and serpentariums have Burmese pythons coming out of their ears.

> FOOD: mice or rats of appropriate size. (See pages 50–51.)
> Large individuals—say, over 10 feet—can manage live chickens or rabbits without difficulty.
> SIZE: 20 feet or more is an exceptional adult
> TEMPERATURE: 85 degrees F.
> PRICE: $55–$100

16. Indian python *(Python molurus molurus)*

Closely related to the Burmese is the Indian python. While still an enormous reptile, this fine constrictor does not reach the same gigantic proportions as its cousin and is more attractively colored, being a café-au-lait brown. The temperament is unrivaled. Indian pythons are unfortunately a bit harder to find, being a threatened and protected subspecies. Try mail-order houses or private breeders for best results. If you do come across one, be sure and ask to see a permit stating that the animal was come by legally. There is perhaps no finer boid pet.

FOOD: rats of appropriate size
SIZE: to 11 feet
TEMPERATURE: 85 degrees F.
PRICE: $150–$200

17. Ball python *(Python regius)*

The regal or ball python of West Africa is a commonly available creature that marks our departure from the truly large into the realm of the markedly reasonable. This snake rarely reaches five feet in length and is considered somewhat of a dwarf in relation to its boid kin. Inasmuch as most of the world's snakes don't exceed three or four feet, it is not, in the larger scheme of things, small.

My first snake was a ball python, and the meaty little boids hold a special spot in my heart. Ball pythons are brown with black striping and blotching. They get their name from a tendency to coil up into a ball when disturbed. In this posture they can even be rolled along the floor! Tame captives lose this defense mechanism after a while. These stubborn fellows are capable of fasting for quite a long time, but have plenty of meat on their bones to keep them going.

FOOD: mice or small rats (See pages 50–51.)
SIZE: to 5 feet
TEMPERATURE: 85 degrees F.
PRICE: $75

18. Rosy Boa *(Lichanura trivirgata spp.)*

While scientists group this lovely little animal with the rest of the tropical boas, our native rosy boa is actually quite unique. Instead of hailing from steamy tropical ports, many rosys come from the desert areas of California and Mexico. These diminutive boas have adapted to life in a harsh and dry enviornment where temperatures vary considerably more than they do in equatorial countries. For this reason, the demure rosy is rarely a delicate or fussy captive and seldom resents handling. If you like the body form and constricting habits of a boa but are unimpressed by size, this little boa is for you. There are several varieties of this attractively striped serpent, ranging from chocolate and tan to pink and light gray. Rosy boas are commonly bred in captivity, and there are few finer pets than one of these born in captivity.

> FOOD: mice of appropriate size
> SIZE: to 3.5 feet
> TEMPERATURE: 80 degrees F.
> PRICE: $75–$150

19. Rainbow boa *(Epicrates cenchris)*

If you consider the ball python a miniature Burmese, then this next snake could be called a lightweight boa constrictor. The rainbow boa comes from South America and is well adapted for stalking and capturing nesting birds. This tree dweller does better on a captive diet of rodents and likes a branch to climb on. As a youngster the rainbow boa is a light orange brown with darker rings on its back and a beautiful boa sheen to its scales. As the animal grows it loses the pattern, but retains the iridescence. Unlike most other species I recommend, the rainbow boa, while hardy, needs to be handled regularly if he is to remain tame and takes a bit longer than most to grow accustomed to familiarity.

> FOOD: mice
> SIZE: 4 feet
> TEMPERATURE: 85 degrees F.
> PRICE: $75

Carpet python

20. Carpet python *(Morelia spilotes)*

The last serpent on my list is a great one. It is an Australian species (Australian reptiles, remember, are desirable but forbidden fruit, as all are protected) that is bred lavishly in this country. It has thus become easily available and affordable. The carpet python has a gentle disposition, the pattern of a brown Turkish rug, and the smooth, supple feel that makes the greatest snakes such a thrill to hold.

The availability of the carpet python is a testimonial to what determined breeders and hobbyists can do to make a fabulous animal available to the rest of us. It is, in my estimation, beginning to fill the void left by the boa constrictor, which was far more recently protected and which is not being bred and marketed with quite the same determination and enthusiasm.

FOOD: appropriately sized rats, or for the first year, mice (See pages 50–51.)
SIZE: to 9 or 10 feet
TEMPERATURE: 85 degrees F.
PRICE: $75

The tale of the carpet python is a fitting end to this section. Serious and devoted hobbyists who probably started out with a curiosity and interest like your own have ended up making a worthwhile contribution to the pet trade, to pet owners and to the wild populations. When an animal is as well understood, as well loved and as well attended to as this beautiful serpent has been, everyone benefits. Even the troubled boa makes out, by having the spotlight removed from it for a while, giving it a chance to make a comeback in the wild. You see? You can have a great time, learn a lot, enjoy an animal and do some good all at the same time if you take the right approach to an exotic pet.

LIZARDS

Green iguana

It used to be that reptiles took no guff from anybody. Millions of years ago they lorded over the earth. There was no room for pushy birds or upstart mammals. Everywhere you looked there were reptiles. You could find them in the ocean, in the mud underfoot, in the branches of trees and in the craters of moribund volcanoes.

Then something happened and the ruling dynasty fell. Nobody knows if it was a deadly reptile plague, a comet that poisoned the atmosphere, drastic changes in climate or simply the survival of "fitter" mammals. Whatever the cause, it left us considerably bereft of the "cold-blooded" elite. Modern reptiles are but relics of past glory, artifacts of a kingdom past. Now there are only four major groups of reptiles: the turtles, snakes, crocodilians and lizards. Lizards are in most ways the closest to the roaring roamers we see in the movies, comic books and museums.

Roaring roamers, however, don't generally make good pets. Nearly every animal group contains potential pets and potential problems, and the lizard group has its share of both. In fact, if the lizards as a group have a theme, it is diversity. There are three-foot-long black lizards that dive in the crashing surf and eat algae that they scrape from underwater rocks while holding their breath. There are others that look like walking thornbushes and strut through the outback utterly immune to approach. There are tiny ones with warty skin that can run up and down a pane of glass or leap from treetops only to glide to safety hundreds of feet below. There are twelve-foot giants that feast upon buffalo and deer, bringing down their ill-fated prey with a savage ripping open of guts, and there are tough-skinned and sluggish flower eaters that gourmandize the day away amid pastures of cactus.

The tiniest of the lizards are the tree geckos of the West Indies. If you have been to the tropics you may have seen one hanging upside down from the ceiling, watching a tiny insect run by a lamp in the corner. Suddenly he takes a step forward and thousands of tiny hooks on his feet grab the rough surface of the plaster, giving him a grip like superglue. He wipes the clear covering over his eyes with his long, agile tongue, just to make sure that what he sees is what he gets, then with a great silent rush forward is upon his prey, seizing it, all waving and crunchy, in his powerful little jaws.

Geckos of different sorts make great pets, with one notable exception: the dreaded *Tokay*. Some years ago I was trying to share a bit of lizard biology with some high school students. By way of illustration I was holding in my hand a foot-long tokay gecko. The tokay is the largest of the gecko family, a lizard group noted for its agility and coloring, with external ear openings that are quite obvious and an eardrum that is transparent and easy to see. I was eager to prove this to my students and went to great lengths to hold the lizard up to the light so that all could view the inner ear and daylight on the other side. One student asked me to point out the area in question. It never occurred to me that he was anything but sincere. Gingerly I raised my finger to the side of the lizard's head and indicated the orifice. This bit of manipulating caused me to lose control of the animal entirely, whereupon the aggressive little monster squirmed, turned around and sank his multitudes of tiny, needle-sharp teeth into the soft fleshy area between my thumb and forefinger. Shivers of pain coursing through my arm, I determinedly carried on as if nothing had happened, successfully squelching the attack cry forming at the base of my throat, as my students snickered and smirked. Redder of face and far redder of finger, I tried to instill some sense of propriety into the beast. Finally, all stoicism being for naught, I interrupted the lecture, strode casually to the sink (trying not to wince and gasp) and dunked my hand into some ice-cold water. The lizard let go—and I had learned a lesson in gecko grasping and student trusting. The general consensus on these lizards is best stated by a sign I saw recently on an aquarium full of tokays in a local pet shop. The sign read:

TOKAY GECKOS
YOU CATCH 'EM—$10. WE CATCH 'EM—$20

You will not find the tokay gecko in the "recommended" section!

The twelve-foot giant I mentioned above is named the Komodo dragon for the islands from which it hails. Some researchers think this gargantuan reptile is the source of the dragon legends that pervade the Orient. This animal, of course, makes a better reptilian assassin than pet, but other members of the "monitor" group make perhaps the most highly prized lizard pets of all. Monitors are large, carnivorous, predatory loners, so nicknamed for their wary habits. For years I had a *small* monitor living in my closet. He was one of my all-time favorite pets, and you will read about him below.

The vast majority of lizards are harmless. The only ones in all the world with venom are the bright orange-and-black Gila monster of our own Southwest and its relative the Mexican beaded lizard from south of the border. Lacking venom, lizards also require no special handling skills, apart from caution with a large, unfamiliar animal and keeping your large lizard's nails trim (best done by a veterinarian). In fact, life with a friendly lizard does not take much adjustment, as lizards are undemanding. Feeding and watering are accomplished with a minimum of fuss. A large lizard such as an iguana will live in a bare cage much like a snake house and require similar care to that given his legless cousin. Smaller lizards may need a more elaborate duplication of nature in the form of a vivarium. If you elect to set up the latter and populate it with more than one of these colorful specimens, you will be rewarded with a living showcase. Properly executed, this arrangement will all but run itself, just like a miniature forest or desert. Many lizards are quite long-lived (up to twenty years in captivity) and will provide you with years of pleasure.

If you are bedridden, elderly or confined for any other reason, a vivarium full of lizards makes a terrific choice. If you have an acute eye and a dose of curiosity about the natural world, you will soon be forsaking your television set in favor of your vivarium. If you are a budding student of animal behavior you will learn invaluable lessons from the little world in your sitting room. In the microcosm of the vivarium all the nasty rules of staying alive in the big bad world apply.

In sum, your lizard pet can be either a large, responsive creature with whom you may have a genuine one-to-one relationship, or a member of a small clan that re-creates desert, forest or jungle life for you right there on your coffee table. The choice is yours.

LIZARD BIOLOGY

This is a tricky and exciting topic on two counts. First, there is a lot more to lizard biology it than just the rudiments of meals and mates. We cannot cover everything here, so I will hit on some highlights instead. Second, I have just emphasized how diverse lizards are, and now I have to consider them all in one lump! Scientists have made our work a bit easier by dividing living lizards into two major groups: the ascalabotans and the autarchoglossans. (These are real names, not fictitious tongue twisters chosen to represent warring planetary factions on an old episode of *Star Trek*.)

As a quick guide, let's consider ascalabotans to be social lizards of all different shapes and sizes that use their eyes more than any other sense in evaluating their surroundings and in finding fun and food. Autarchoglossans, on the other hand, rely mainly on their chemosensory abilities—mainly their sense of taste—to provide clues to their surroundings. (See the snake section for an explanation of chemosensation and other very important aspects of biology that lizards and snakes share.) Believe it or not, tongues come into play here in understanding these groups. Ascalabotans have agile little tongues and can manipulate food in their mouths the way people do. Thus they tend to shred things and eat them a bit more delicately. The tongue of the autarchoglossan, however, is a key part of his sensory apparatus, yet has relatively little to do with moving food around in the mouth. As a result, autarchoglossans tend whenever possible to swallow food whole. Most lizards, by the way, are omnivores (they eat both plant and animal material), and a minority are herbivorous (plant eaters).

Lizards that spend a great deal of time on their own, hunting warm-blooded prey such as rodents and birds, are blessed with the type of intelligence that makes them responsive pets. These types tend to offer more when it comes to interacting with you. Desert iguanids (members of the iguana family that live in dry areas) and the chuckwalla (another desert lizard) from our Southwest are among the most active and responsive of lizards, but monitors have always seemed to me to outshine their kin in sheer presence and IQ.

Many years ago, I acquired an African savanna monitor lizard *(Varanus exanthematicus)* that had been raised from an egg in a local pet shop. Absolutely compulsive care had been given this animal, including ultraviolet lighting, intensive vitamins and plentiful live food. He was a tractable and friendly creature, and I paid many times the going rate for the species just to have this particular animal. I was not disappointed. For years this loyal and devoted fellow, whom I mentioned above, lived in my closet and came out to say hello when I came home. He was more responsive than a cat, pressing himself against my feet for warmth whenever I sat down. His name was Xan, taken from the Latin for his species. Xan loved chicken, especially when I prepared the bird Chinese style for wok frying. He would smell dinner cooking and appear at my legs, all yard and a half of him, eyes focused on me, tongue flicking in and out, claws on my trousers. As I prepared the boneless chicken breast I would cut a piece for me and a piece for him, a piece for me, a piece for him. I would toss each piece for him into the air and he would catch it on the way down, just like the best-trained of Frisbee hounds.

Smaller, insect-eating lizards are equally fascinating as objects of study and appreciation, but have a bit less interest in the give-and-take of the owner–pet relationship. Little guys such as geckos and fence lizards *(Sceloporus)* are pretty much unable to learn by trial and error. These are the vivarium types, who thrive in a natural setup where they don't have to make much of an adjustment to captivity and where you let them pretty well alone. If, for example, you give

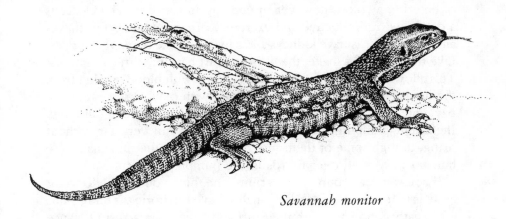

Savannah monitor

them too large a food bowl, they won't be able to figure out how to climb into it. The moral of the story is, small lizard, small bowl! And yet it is not the quantity of intelligence that is missing in the little guys so much as the quality. If you take the posture that intelligence and survival are strongly linked, then lizards (some of which have been around for hundreds of millions of years) are a lot brighter than people, who may not be around too much longer! You can broaden your definition of "brains" a bit by trying to understand how your pet goes about the business of his life. Viewed this way, any lizard has an admirable mentality.

Providing input to the lizard's gray matter are by and large the same senses we have. Many lizards can see color, and their visual acuity is quite good. Those lizards that must catch fast-moving bugs and the like and spend their time perched on tiny branches way up in trees have to be able to see clearly what is going on up front. The eyes of these animals are typically set farther forward in the head or in machine-gun-style turrets that move the eyes about like crazy. Talk about peripheral vision! If you are behind them and even *think* about moving, they know it.

Lizards cannot hear as wide a range of sounds as we can. Those tones they can detect, though, they hear better than we do. Some lizard ears are as sensitive as those of rodents.

All this talk of tongues and eyes and ears should give you the sense that in some important ways, lizards are recognizable. What I mean to say is that, like us, lizards are backboned animals with a familiar anatomy. When a lizard swallows its food, it goes down an esophagus just like our own and thence into a stomach and intestine. Instead of entering a colon, however, it ends up in a cloaca. The cloaca is a combined reproductive and excretory organ found also in snakes and birds. Lizards have kidneys and a liver just like other vertebrates. Like the heart of a snake, the lizard's heart has only three chambers. This allows blood going to the lungs to mix with blood coming from the lungs (mammals like us keep blood with oxygen separate from oxygenless blood) and makes for relatively inefficient pumping. Inefficient pumping means that lizards can't run very far without tiring, though some of them sure can scoot over the short haul. We humans have it all over lizards in the pumping department.

If you watch a group in a vivarium, one thing you will notice right away is that lizards, particularly males, have territories. Young studs are greatly concerned with their turf and have a characteristic stance and sequence of events that they perform in order to protect home and mates. Heads are butted, tails lashed, and sometimes you even see push-ups and throat ballooning (inflation of a loose flap of brightly colored skin under the chin). This is a heck of a lot nicer than cockfighting and quite fascinating to watch. Lizard combat, like most territorial conflict in the animal kingdom, is ritualized so as to avoid injury to the combatants.

Once the fighting for harems and territories is over, lizards settle down to a nice session of internal fertilization. Males have the same type of copulatory organs that snakes do: namely, hemipenes. A male lizard will lie alongside a female and insert the hemipenis of the appropriate side into her cloaca. (Remember that the cloaca is both an excretory and reproductive organ.) Like snake genitals, the reproductive organs of the male lizard may be equipped with lobes, hooks or spines, making an interruption of coitus difficult if not impossible. The actual act may last for anywhere from a few minutes to a full day. And they say *blondes* have more fun!

Once Lady Lizard has received the male's sperm (only lizards of the same species will get this far; different species do not interbreed), what does she do with it? There are two basic tacks she can take. The first is the formation of eggs and the subsequent laying and leaving, a process dubbed "oviparity" by scientists. Reptiles, with very rare exceptions, do not care for their young at all. The mommy leaves the clutch (which may number from one to sixty eggs, depending upon the type of lizard and how macho the father) in a drainage ditch, buries it and walks away. Young lizards are born with all the equipment they need to fend for themselves. A lizard may lay as many as five clutches of eggs per season. The number of eggs a lizard lays varies with her size. Big lizards lay big clutches; small lizards, small clutches.

The second tack is to give birth to live young. From the scientific standpoint the important difference is that Momma and the kids share a bloodstream. The baby lizards develop in the mother's "womb" just as we do. Scientists call live birth "viviparity."

One of the best experiences that I have had breeding lizards involved a viviparous ascalabotan. Hoehnel's chameleon *(Chameleo hoehnellii)* is a wonderful-looking creature with horns and a prehensile (grasping) tail. All of the Old World, or "true," chameleons are terrific terrarium animals (though they require special care), and these particular lizards were no exception. I had a trio of them in a tall, hexagonal aquarium of about thirty gallons capacity. Replete with branches, plants and dripping water, the setup was a true-to-life replica of a montane African forest. I had ultraviolet lighting and a quiet room for them, and the little devils really flourished, ultimately producing a litter of young.

The tiny pink babies were born one at a time, dropping from the branch to which the mother clung, straining. The young appeared pink because they were enmeshed in the membranes of the mother. As soon as they began to move, they rubbed off the mother's mucosa and began to clamber around the cage. I cannot think of a more rewarding moment in all the time I have spent keeping reptiles alive.

Lizard reproduction is complex and fascinating. Your contribution, as a fancier and hobbyist, to the breeding of species that are less than common can make a difference. Making some of these forms available takes the pressure off the native populations. Watching the animals court, mate and produce young is one of the great thrills of keeping any type of animal. Although some varieties seem bent on making babies no matter how you may botch their care, to breed most lizards takes a green thumb and a deep understanding of the species' needs. Don't expect that you will succeed, particularly at first.

I have wound up this section with a direct challenge deliberately! I hope you will succeed in keeping your lizard pet alive and happy and perhaps even encourage it to reproduce. I can't help you *too* much with the latter, as breeding reptiles is a vast topic, worthy of a book in itself. What I can do, however, is provide a thorough, though general, guide to housing and feeding. Read the next section, as it will help further in deciding if a lizard is the pet for you and will help you keep yours in good shape if you decide to go for it.

YOUR LIZARD'S HOME

There are, unfortunately for us, as many different ways to house lizards as there are lizards. I have to lump a bit, obviously, lest this section become a tedious description of three thousand cages. I have thus divided lizard houses into three types, and hope that you will experiment and expand a bit on each theme as your experience grows. The first type of lizard cage is for lizards too large and too destructive to occupy a tank that mimics the natural environment. Let's call this the "simple cage." Secondly we have the "desert vivarium" for species that like things hot and dry and are of medium size (less than sixteen inches). Lastly we have the "forest vivarium." This is an attempt, within realistic limits, to approximate the natural environment of the temperate or tropical forest.

The best way to use this information is to pick the animal that interests you from the "recommended" section and then refer here to learn how to house it. If you pursue this sequence, you will avoid the hassles and regrets that come with biting off more than you can chew or losing a pet for avoidable reasons.

The Simple Cage

The idea here is pretty much the same as for a snake cage. The cardinal rules are simplicity and security. Big lizards can be very active and destructive. There is no use in building a pretty setup for such an animal to simply demolish. You must do your best to keep your lizard clean and parasite-free. Think of these big guys as active snakes with legs. They resent confinement and will uproot plants, tip over water bowls and make a general mess of things. Their active nature makes them constantly search for a way out. Tops must be secured with bolts or latches, not simply weighted down.

All right, let's get specific. You have chosen a large, energetic lizard pet and need to set up a functional cage. Your first concern should be the size of the cage that you select or build for your pet. A good rule of thumb for a lizard cage is that it be *at least* as long as your pet measures from snout to tip of tail. Half the length of your pet will be an adequate width and height.

The handiest beginning is the home aquarium. Specimens of the big lizards, especially as juveniles, do just fine in a twenty- to sixty-gallon tank, though this will hardly serve for a full-grown five-foot-long monitor lizard. Most aquaria these days are made with fish in mind. They are constructed only of glass, with silicon sealing the sides and bottom and plastic protecting the edges. While these are adequate, it is better to try to hunt up a vintage, metal-framed tank, though this type is no longer manufactured. Metal tanks are undesirable for fish as they are unnecessarily heavy and the sealing material has a limited life. As lizard tanks, however, metal-framed tanks excel, thanks to their robust construction. If a monitor lizard, for instance, turns around and swats the side of an all-glass tank with his tail, there may be a storm of shards in the house. If his tail contacts a metal-reinforced pane, however, it may meet its match.

Finding a metal-framed tank may require a bit of sleuthing. Watch newpaper ads or even advertise that you are looking for one. Many non–lizard fanciers have old twenty-gallon tanks sitting in their attics and would be overjoyed to sell them for a few dollars. Ask your pet shop, too. There might just be an old "leaker" sitting in the back room. Your lizard won't care if the cage holds water!

Really big lizards such as large monitors or iguanas fit well in a steamer trunk that you modify yourself. Remove the hinged lid of the trunk and have some glass cut and drilled to fit as a cover. Don't forget to drill ventilation holes at each end of the tank and to cut out a hole for a light and reflector to focus the light into the tank for maximum heat. Try to avoid using Plexiglas instead of plate glass. While less expensive and easier to work with, Plexi has the annoying property of scratching if you so much as look at it the wrong way. A few days at the mercy of lizard claws and you won't be able to see in! (If finances demand Plexi, then place a layer of screen, with a half-inch of space, on the inside of the lid. This will keep the lizard off the stuff. It isn't beautiful, but it works.) Check a local army–navy store for a good selection of trunks.

Another possibility is a used tub or discarded refrigerator or freezer. As I have discussed in the snake section, any of these can be reasonably and successfully modified to fit the requirements of a reptile cage. The best source that I have come up with for one of these items is the junkyard.

A fourth option is to construct an enclosure out of wood. Plywood is not great, because spilled water and the heat from the warming lamps (more on this below) are likely to cause the cage to warp. Use a hard wood such as oak or maple and build a box that will stand both the test of time and your lizard's occasional exuberance. A simple box with a hinged, framed glass top is more than adequate. The top should fit flush. Any electric cords you may wish to put through can be threaded through holes drilled in the wood. You may need to thread a heat lamp cord into the cage, as lizards, like all reptiles, need supplemental heating. (Because large lizards and snakes have similar requirements, you will want to read the more amplified explanation of the simple cage in "Snakes.") It will suffice to say here that you are shooting for a tank temperature of between 80 and 85 degrees

F. (room temperature should be maintained at one end so your lizard can get out of the frying pan when he feels the need), and this is best accomplished with incandescent spotlights or Renacor heating cable.

Requirements differ, however, when it comes to lighting. While full-wave bulbs may cause a snake's skin to darken unattractively and offer no concrete benefit, lizards thrive on such lighting. General Electric ("Chromalux" is the brand name) and Luxor (here it's Vita-Lite) are two companies that produce fluorescent bulbs that do a decent job of mimicking the sun. These bulbs should be mounted inside the tank. Remember that the beneficial ultraviolet rays *do not pass through glass*! (The reason, incidentally, that you don't sunburn through a car window.) Such lamps stimulate growth in lizards by allowing them to metabolize their food properly. A good rule of thumb for deciding how much fluorescent, ultraviolet-giving light to offer your lizard pet (an incandescent lamp used for heating is separate; you may have two lamps on the animal) is to provide 1 watt of light for each gallon of tank capacity. A twenty-gallon tank thus requires 20 watts of full-wave light.

When providing water for your large lizard, follow the rules in the snake section. Use only plastic or metal bowls—no glass. The latter can be broken easily with one whip of the tail. Standing water breeds bacteria, so keep your pet's water bowl scrubbed clean and filled with fresh water.

Flooring, as for snakes, should be either newspaper or dried corn bits.

How about an idea of the kinds of lizards that go into a setup this substantial? Well, tegus (*Tupinambis* sp.), monitor lizards (*Varanus* sp.), iguanas (*Iguana* sp.) and blue-tongued skinks (*Teliqua* sp.) all fill the bill. Monitors have been mentioned already. Tegus are South American carnivores that resemble monitors in looks and habits. Iguanas come in all sizes and shapes, but in this context I have in mind the common green iguana *(Iguana iguana),* which is upward of six feet long when adult and predominantly vegetarian. Blue-tongued skinks are nicely tempered lizards that like to burrow and nudge.

I have had several blue-tongued skinks over the years, but the one who sticks in my mind was part of a teaching collection. I housed her in a twenty-gallon "long"-style aquarium and floored the tank with newspaper. The skink spent her entire life underneath the paper (one of the hazards of working with newspaper). I tried everything from tucking in the edges to weighting the paper down with rocks, all to no avail. She had to be visible so that my students could see her, but she spent all her time hiding! Finally I switched floorings. I gave the animal a few pieces of cork bark and put her on the same dried corncob I recommend for snakes. I started to pay her more attention because I saw her more often.

A few weeks after the changeover, I noticed that the lizard was going into a severe decline. She went off her nutritious diet of berries and bananas with an occasional dash of dog food. She moped around the cage without showing her usual spunk and grew thinner and thinner. As time went on she became gaunt and emaciated, even refusing water. I have said elsewhere that reptiles take a long time to die. This is especially true of turtles and snakes. Lizards as a rule are more active and alert and show decline more readily. Within three weeks my skink was near death. I tried everything. I offered kiwi berries and raspberries; I tried blender veggies and prime meats —all to no avail. The animal simply "wished" to die.

In an act of desperation I returned everything to the way it had been before she began to fade. I took out the bark, removed the pair of potted plants, yanked out the branch and, after pouring out the corncob, replaced the newspaper. The old hag shuffled under the paper, gave a little sneeze and was silent. I checked to see if she was still alive and then let her alone for a couple of days. On the third morning, she was out and active when I came to work in the morning, eyes clear and bright where they had been dull and filmy.

She liked life Zen-bare and simple and was not interested in having things any other way. The moral of the story is that some animals care for a natural setting and others don't. Be wise enough to know that we see the world differently from our reptile friends. For some species the Plain Jane cage is not only the best but the only option.

The Desert Vivarium

When we move from a simple cage to a vivarium, we take a qualitative leap. The word "vivarium" implies a place for the lizard to really live, not just exist. Lizards are social animals, and in the vivarium they may interact with each other as well as the environment. A community should be the aim, and we must forsake our usual definition of a pet. In a sense, a properly executed vivarium is itself the pet. This is not to say that the animals in it are just cogs in a machine, but rather that the setup works as a whole. You help the animals thrive by offering such a construction and they entertain and educate you with courtship rituals, pursuits of prey and warring over corner territories and under-rock hiding places.

Two lizards are enough for a start, but you may want more once you have the hang of things. I recommend small lizards such as utas (*Uta* sp.), fence or spiny lizards (*Sceloporus* sp.) and collared lizards (*Crotaphytus* sp.) (The chuckwalla, *Sauromalus obesus,* while large, also thrives in such a setup.) Smaller lizards are less destructive than their massive cousins whom we have discussed in reference to the simple cage, but can still wreak havoc on a setup unless you do things right. When mixing and matching desert lizards, keep in mind that nearly all are carnivores and may hassle each other a bit. Try to avoid disparate sizes. For a guide to selecting species, see the "recommended" section below.

To achieve a true balance, you must have space. A ten-gallon tank will work for two lizards, a twenty for four. Use this five-gallons-per-lizard rule as a minimum and you won't go wrong. An old motto among vivarium enthusiasts I know goes like this: "If you can't lose your animals in the vivarium, it is too small."

There are two readily available containers for your vivarium. One is the aquarium, the other a child's wading pool. If you use an aquarium, get a long, low model, as desert species need the room to scoot about, but not to climb. The only cover you need is a screen, as this will keep the humidity down and let in the critical ultraviolet lighting to be discussed below. Again, get as big a tank as you can afford *now.* If you don't, you may end up overcrowding your tank when you add a new animal here and there.

Wading pools are the second choice for an enclosure. These lightweight plastic items are made for kids to splash around in. If you have a family room, basement, attic or storage room, this is a good, inexpensive way to go. Wading pools offer a lot of space for few bucks. Remember not to just plop your little friends into the pool and imagine that they will stay there. As soon as you turn around, the little guys will make a break for it, scratching at the sides of the pool for a foothold. To avoid escapes, take a wide roll of window screening and either affix it to the sides of the pool or make up a wood frame. This should keep the beasties in and the humidity out.

Everything that you do in creating the desert vivarium is aimed at re-creating the true desert environment. You must think hot and dry!

Moisture, drafts and fluctuations in temperature are the hallmarks of disaster. Thus we use no water dish at all. In the simple cage, standing water, as for snakes, was recommended, but desert lizard physiology is aimed at economizing on the use of water and maximizing every last drop. Some desert lizards don't drink, while others may utilize an occasional ditch or pond that develops during heavy rains. Provide necessary water for your desert dwellers with a plant mister once or twice a day. More than enough water accumulates on the leaves of the plants you have provided to allow the lizards to lap up their fill. The hot, dry vivarium will soon cause the water to evaporate, so give the area a thorough soaking. Cover everything in a fine mist. I prefer to mist first thing in the morning, before the lights come on and dry everything up.

Speaking of lighting, the situation in the desert vivarium is much the same as it is with the simple cage, it's just that greater intensity is required. In the snake section I recommend using red or green spotlights for a big cage. Here you may use white, as desert lizard eyes are well protected against the brightness of a full sun. As many heat-producing spot lamps should be used as are required to keep the temperature up around 90 degrees. How many you need, of course, depends upon the size of your setup. You can overdo it and cook your lizards, so be careful to check out the temperatures in various parts of the vivarium with a thermometer before introducing any creatures. Just as in the snake cage, there should be a gradient, with one end of the tank at about 75 degrees to provide relief and the other a blazing 95. This tactic is much like applying a pressure-release valve to a water heater. When things just get too hot, there is an out. Remember that the temperature of the room in which your vivarium is situated will probably not remain constant, and it will almost surely (I hope!) be cooler than the setup. Thus heat is lost from the setup to your room. If the temperature goes up because of an unexpected warm spell, or just from the natural tide of the seasons, less heat will leave the tank and you will *fry* your lizards. Leaving one end of the tank cool can save lives.

Because desert lizards are exposed to so much direct sunlight in nature, their physiological need for ultraviolet is quite high. Double the 1-watt-per-gallon-of-tank rule for the desert setup. A forty-gallon aquarium thus requires 80 watts of General Electric (Chromalux) or Luxor (Vita-Lite) fluorescent lighting. Your plants will love it too.

As you know if you have ever spent any time in the desert, things may be blazing hot during the day, but they often cool down considerably at night. To duplicate this cycle, you should turn off all the lights at night. Fourteen hours on and ten off is a good schedule. I urge that you invest in a lamp timer that can do this work for you, lighting the vivarium at, say, seven in the morning and bringing "sundown" at nine at night. A timer can even reverse the day/night rhythm for you, if you work the night shift and can't see your pets while they are up in the heat of the day. What's more, with a timer in use you don't have to worry about weekends away. The lizards can even miss a couple of days of rain showers from your plant mister! (Incidentally, be sure not to exceed the recommended wattage of your timer. Plugging too many big spotlights into one timer can burn the thing out and even start a fire. Any hardware store carries these convenient, programmable devices.)

The next consideration in creating a desert vivarium is the flooring. Executed properly, the desert vivarium is a bit too elaborate to disassemble every time a change in corn bits or newspaper is called for. Thus we must take a different tack than we took with the simple cage. You must provide drainage good enough to keep the enclosure clean and odor-free for at least some months at a throw.

Start with a layer of "activated" charcoal. You can find this in the potting section of your supermarket or at the pet shop, being sold for aquarium filters. A one-inch-high layer at the bottom of your tank is sufficient. Charcoal serves to absorb wastes and purify whatever soaks through the layers above. On top of this add two inches of aquarium pebble gravel (buy it or find some in a driveway and and wash it). Finish off the flooring with several inches of fine sand. This top layer may be sculpted to taste, but most likely your scaled friends will shift through it, reducing dunes to ridges. Don't use less than three inches of sand, as burrowing lizards will bring the pebbles to the surface if you do, thereby spoiling the "clean" look.

Plants, at least from the standpoint of making your vivarium look like something, are indispensable. Leave them in their pots, though, rather than trying to plant them directly in the flooring. This protects the roots from burrowing lizards and facilitates easy removal for cleaning or rearranging. Cacti and other succulents naturally do well in this type of setup and look great. Stay away from varieties with large spines, however. In a confined space even desert lizards who know better can make a fatal dash and end up skewered.

Most desert saurians are secretive and like to hide. Rocks and driftwood present fine hide spots and look natural too. The "interior decoration" of your tank is up to you and can be a showcase of your taste. Keep in mind, though, that what you put in you also have to keep clean. Even in a vivarium the byword is simplicity!

The Forest Vivarium

What we have here, simply put, is a wetter desert vivarium overgrown and running wild. To understand it completely, you must read the preceding section. The principles and execution of forest and desert vivaria are nearly the same; only the details differ.

The majority of the world's lizard species can live comfortably in an appropriately sized forest vivarium. I have seen some beautiful

House geckos

setups that were handcrafted using the corner of a room. A wooden frame was built against the walls and glass was fitted, creating a closet-sized micro-environment. Although such a construction is beyond the scope of this book, I mention it to let you know that the only limits to what you can do for your lizards are your resources and your ingenuity. To construct a more moderate yet still lovely vivarium, begin with a *tall-style* aquarium as sizable as possible. A wading pool won't work here because height for climbing and plants is important.

Forests are humid compared with deserts, and we want to keep the humidity in. Therefore the cover of the tank should be glass rather than screen. This you can easily achieve by using a commercial "hood" designed for the tank. Be sure that there are no holes or openings in the hood—otherwise your forest dwellers will soon become apartment dwellers.

Since the tank is sealed and we know ultraviolet will not penetrate glass, the full-wave lighting that we used in the other setups (and which is important here) must be placed directly in the tank. This should pose no problem, for even if your lizards clamber on the glass, these bulbs do not get hot enough to burn.

A sealed, humid tank with fluorescent lights on it will build up heat quickly. Instead of employing the blazing spotlights recommended for the simple cage and desert vivarium, try a more moderate incandescent bulb. A flat aquarium fixture that sits atop the glass hood may be enough. One or more 40-watt tubular bulbs will do the trick. Even shining through the glass they will warm the vivarium, and it is fine to simply place a reflector over the tank, so long as you already have a fluorescent bulb shining unobstructed *inside* the cage. If you are using a *very large* aquarium—say, forty to eighty gallons—then you may have to rig a spotlight inside the cage. Try a clamp-on fixture attached to a branch with the beam safely away from flammable vegetation. Run the wire through a tiny hole punched in the hood and you are all set. A good temperature for the forest vivarium is 80 degrees, but as always a gradient from one end of the tank (or in this case even from top to bottom) is what you want. Try keeping one part of the tank at 70, another at 80 and maybe even a very warm spot at 85. This sounds tricky, but by moving lights around and experimenting with different wattages, you will be able to achieve it.

The flooring is a variation of the desert vivarium's. The purpose

is good drainage so you won't have to go ripping your work apart
to get everything clean all the time. A well-floored vivarium can go
many months or even a year without being changed. I have seen
some beautiful effects created by sloping the substrate. Sand may
shift, but soil is a bit steadier, and I encourage you to sculpt a bit in
the dirt. Start with a layer of pebbles about two inches deep. Next
place charcoal or activated filter carbon to another two inches in
depth. Following this, spread a one-inch layer of vermiculite (an
absorbent potting material available in the potting section of your
general store) and then three inches of good-quality potting soil.
Sphagnum or peat moss can be added for a velvet touch.

Like desert lizards, forest dwellers are secretive, so provide plenty
of hiding places. Cork bark, moss, rocks and driftwood are all effective nests. After a time, you will find that each and every inhabitant
of your vivarium has a favorite spot where he can invariably be
found. It is great fun to engineer new spots for your pets to hide in.
I find that cork bark is the most convenient provider of caves and
crannies. It is hollow and invites snuggling, yet can be lifted from
the tank without further ado should you require a tête-à-tête with
your pet.

Plants, of course, are what add warmth and color to a vivarium,
and the forest motif gives you a myriad of choices. Spider plants
(*Chlorophytum elatum*) and the philodendron group are sturdy species
that take readily to a wide variety of situations. Some experts recommend ferns and ivy, but I find that these types are too delicate and
end up looking a bit lizard-trampled. My all-time favorite forest plant
is the bromeliad, or urn plant (*Vriesia* sp.). This hardy little devil
grows low to the ground and provides natural cover for most animals. The only notes of caution in selecting plants are to avoid
weak-stemmed varieties that will succumb to being walked on and
to stay away from toxic plants such as the coleus varieties. These will
prove fatal to some herbivorous lizards. Leave plants in their pots,
incidentally, and sink the pots into the substrate. This will protect the
roots from prying lizard feet.

Bromeliads bring to mind an important point about the forest
vivarium: humidity. I have already said that this vivarium must be
humid, but the question is a bit more complex than it might at first
seem. The problem, you see, is that not all forests are the same, and
not all lizards come from one forest. The dripping jungles of Peru

are one type of forest, the pine barrens of New Jersey another. We have to adjust humidity, to an extent, to match the requirements of the animals who live in the tank. Bromeliads aid in keeping humidity high, as their cup shape holds water. They are thus useful in the re-creation of a rain forest. In such an environment, you must mist daily, and keep standing water in a dish (say, soup-bowl size for a twenty-gallon aquarium) at the bottom of the tank. With the help of an aquarium air pump, you can even fashion a crude vaporizer that will keep things *really* wet. Put a pan of standing water in the tank. Then affix some aquarium tubing to the pan with tape and hook the other end to a small pump. When you plug in the pump, the air will bubble through the water and create a tiny fountain. Wrap the pump in a magazine or some old clothes so that it won't buzz. Keep the water no more than an inch or two deep, so if a lizard happens into it, he won't drown. Most species can swim well, but a small rock in the middle of the pan for panicky saurians won't hurt.

In nature, lizards don't have forests to themselves. Lots of animals share the bark, leaves, branches and dirt. Tree frogs, for instance, make wonderful vivarium dwellers and won't soon become lizard fodder. That little tidbit should spark some creativity!

By now you should have the sense that a vivarium is not so much a cage as a living thing. Maybe my comment about a setup working as a whole makes sense now.

FEEDING YOUR LIZARD

Thank goodness this is a simple topic! The lizards of the world can be conveniently divided into three groups: the rodent and dog-food eaters, the vegetarians and the bug crunchers. Let's have a look at them one by one: The first one is easy.

1. Large carnivores like monitors, tegus and plated lizards feast on whole live animals in the wild. From the whole animal they gain much. There are the liver, heart, brain, bone and hair of the prey animal, not to mention the stomach and contents thereof. Eating another animal whole, the way snakes and some lizards do, virtually guarantees health and vigor. To duplicate this in the captive setting, you must offer rodents. If you really want what is best for your pet,

you will do this once or twice a week as opposed to feeding dog or
cat food, a mediocre substitute. (For information on feeding rodent
fare, see the snake section.)

If you are unable to deal with offering one animal to another as
food, you can get away with dog or cat food over the short haul.
Prolonged use without proper supplementation may result in nutritional problems for your pet. Choose a brand that has no sugar added
and as little fat as possible. Mighty Dog by Carnation is a fine choice.
Reptiles are lousy when it comes to breaking down fat. Use a food
dish, and leave some in the cage all the time. To stimulate the
appetite, a raw or cooked egg will sometimes be of benefit.

2. The next group are strict veggie eaters. There are not that many
of these creatures, but among the few are some of the best reptile
pets. Examples are the chuckwalla and the green iguana. All types
of fruits and vegetables are fair food. Particularly nutritious are kale,
cabbage, spinach, squash, tomatoes, carrots, melons, berries, apples
and bananas. The only real no-no is a diet of lettuce. Time and time
again I see animals wasting away from malnutrition and diarrhea
because they have been fed only lettuce. Lettuce is good for one
thing only, and that is stimulating the appetite. In and of itself, it has
no nutritional value, but mixed to flavor other foods, it can work
wonders. If a lizard is reluctant to feed I like to mix in some lettuce
for taste. After the animal is feeding steadily, I gradually cut out the
lettuce until he is eating exactly what I want him to. Use a blender
if you have one, and you can create a puree that is easily taken in.
Add a powdered dog vitamin in small amounts for extra nutrition
(this is largely precautionary, as the exact vitamin requirements of
most lizards are not known). Even if you don't need lettuce as a trick,
you can blend other fruits and vegetables together into such a mix
and store it in the refrigerator. (This tactic really cuts down on the
length of time you have to spend preparing food for your pet.) It is
fine to stop short of a puree; your lizard can deal with the chopped
format just fine. He should eat it just like a dog, sticking his head
in and chowing down. Use a food bowl in the cage and just keep it
full and fresh.

3. The last group is the largest. Most of the lizard pets that you
are likely to choose are insectivores. This is nice for you, as the
advantages of feeding insects to your pet are manifold. First off, I can
best describe the feeding process by simply saying that you dump a

bunch of bugs into the vivarium and watch the fun (how many you must figure out by trial and error; there shouldn't be too many left over when your pets have had their fill). It really is fascinating to watch the lizards stalk and capture the bugs. As a teenager I used to horrify my family with an imitation of the sounds issuing forth from a vivarium full of voracious cricket eaters at feeding time. It went something like this: *"Breeep breeep breeep auuuuuugghh!"*

Crickets are a convenient and inexpensive food. You might say they are the staple of hobbyists with insectivorous pets. Crickets can be bred, too, but it is a bit tricky. If you want to give it a go, try this. Place a clean empty tank, well sealed, in a warm dry spot. Put in empty egg cartons or rolled and shredded newspaper, along with a couple of well-soaked sponges for water. A pie pan filled with moss and covered with fine screen will stimulate the female crickets (the ones with the long spikes sticking out the back) to lay eggs. These long spikes are called "ovipositors" and are actually little pipes through which the eggs pass on their way to the moss. If crickets run rampant in your house by accident, a spray insecticide will end their jollies; just don't get the spray near your pets or feed insects so terminated to anything. If you don't wish to bother with breeding, crickets can be had inexpensively from most pet shops.

When you toss crickets into your vivarium, they will hide immediately. If your pets are alert, the crickets won't get the chance. Crickets will struggle and fight for their lives, so make sure you are not feeding big crickets to little lizards. Crickets are available as young or as adults.

Whiteworms, *Enchytraeus* sp., and mealworms, *Tenebrio,* also make fine food. The former are soft-bodied insects that are cheap to buy at a local bait shop or pet store and can be raised in a few inches of dirt and mulch. Feed them bread, cereal or dog snacks and keep their enclosure damp by covering it with plastic or glass. It is worth setting up a little "holding tank" for them so you always have them on hand.

Mealworms make good food as well. They are the larvae of a small black beetle. If you keep them in a container in order to breed a colony, be sure it is well sealed. The adult beetle is a fast-moving escape artist. Feed them fruit bits and some cereal, but keep them drier than whiteworms. Wood shavings make a good medium in which to raise mealworms. I have a caution, incidentally, about feeding too many of these fellows. Mealworms, you see, wear their skeleton on the outside of their body rather than the inside. This makes for a digestive problem. If fed to excess and over a long period of time, the skeletal material accumulates in the gut of the lizard, causing indigestion. It can even cause a fatal blockage. Use them, but don't rely on them as a staple in your pet's diet.

A familiar practice among lizard people is to provide vitamins and minerals to their insect-eating captives by "dusting" the food items. To do this, just add some vitamin powder to the bag of bugs and shake. This will coat the bugs with healthful additives. Whether or not this is really helpful can be debated, but it certainly doesn't hurt. A dog vitamin high in calcium and phosphorus would work well.

That's about all there is to feeding your pets. The tougher part is choosing which of the multitude of gorgeous lizards you wish to have grace your home. For some help in this difficult task, see the next section.

ACQUIRING A LIZARD

We have a lot to talk about! When it actually comes down to buying a lizard, there are scores of little points to consider, thrust upon us, as always, by the sheer diversity of the creatures in question. Snakes and lizards are grouped together by scientists because they are closely related. The signposts of lizard health greatly resemble those for snakes. Similarly, advice and guidelines for where and how to buy a lizard do not differ significantly from the same recommendations for snakes. As a result, most of this information is available in the snake section. Let's just run through a little checklist to make sure you have remembered some critical points.

1. Lizards can be found in pet shops or on mail-order price lists or collected yourself. Mail order is risky; collecting is fine if you happen to live in the right area for the animal you want. Exotic lizards, of course, cannot be collected locally.

2. A healthy lizard should appear extremely alert. Even the tamest and gentlest lizard will watch your approach like a hawk. The animal's scales should be even and show no blisters or breaks. The skin should also show no bagginess or looseness except when the animal

coils. The covering of the body should, in other words, fit like the work of a London tailor. The mouth, nose and eyes should be free of discharge. The gums should be pink and free of cankerous material. (If the lizard is really tiny, be very careful not to break teeth and hurt gums when examining the mouth.) Some lizards regenerate their tails, so fear not if the tail looks as if it didn't quite fit! Nails and toes should be intact.

3. Unless you plan to breed your lizard (a difficult proposition at best), don't worry too much about its gender. There is no across-the-board method for determining the sex of a lizard anyway. In some cases color will be the cue; in other cases it is the presence or absence of pores in the skin of the thigh. Sometimes it is the size and shape of the tail and other times the outline of the head. A guide to reliably "sexing" your lizard is well beyond the scope of this book.

4. Age is another parameter that is difficult to assess. Sometimes lizards have been in a dealer's care for a long period and have been inadequately fed. When they aren't fed, they don't grow and they give you the illusion that they are younger than they are because they are so small. If a dealer tells you an animal is a baby, ask him how he knows. If the species is supposed to grow to four feet long and the animal in his hand is all of four inches, believe him. Otherwise, be skeptical and assume you are dealing with an adult. An adult lizard, provided it is not decrepit, makes as good a pet as a juvenile if not better, as it is less delicate and has proved free of any congenital disease that might have killed it in the first few weeks of life.

5. If you elect to get the type of lizard that lives in a vivarium, you will most likely end up with several animals. Lizards tend to disappear in a vivarium, particularly if you have set it up correctly, and small vivarium-type animals are social and like company. If you are a real student of nature, you will wish to have a number of animals of the same species, thus more readily approximating the interactions that take place in the wild and encouraging the start of a family. Alternatively, you might wish to "specialize" in a *type* of lizard, filling your vivarium, for instance, with geckos. If you are more eclectic in your tastes, you may want to have a startling variety of fascinating creatures, each with something special to offer. Whichever option *you* choose, your lizards do not get to choose each other, and problems may conceivably result. There is no magic recipe for what species make the ingredients of a successful vivarium. A great

deal depends upon personality and pot luck. You should be prepared for the possibility that your pets may not get along.

If you stick to animals that are roughly the same size, the most likely cause of a problem will be one lizard's encroaching on another's turf. Some amount of "testing each other's mettle" is allowable so that the group can stabilize, but this should not include dire scrapping. If really serious fighting does occur, there is a good antidote for it and that is to turn the tank topsy-turvy and eliminate all hiding spots whenever you add a new member to the group. By rearranging the tank you take away the established order of things. Freddie Fence Lizard's hole under the round rock in the corner is no longer his to protect because there is no rock in the corner anymore, and so on. Even when you do exercise this precaution, be sure to keep a close eye on your pets, particularly at feeding time, for the first few days after introducing one or more new animals. At the time of purchasing a new pet for addition to the group vivarium, make sure of your option to return the animal to the seller should he not get along with the other members of your company. Remember to give a new recruit a few days to find his "niche."

6. Before I plunge into my list of the twenty "best" lizard pets, allow me to issue a little warning: *Set up the lizard's home before you buy!* I know, I know, it *is* obvious. Yet human nature being what it is, some of you are bound to rush into things a bit, once you have read about the goodies in store for you below. If you are unwaveringly bent on a particular animal that you have seen in a pet shop, a few dollars should hold it until you can get a home set up. Doing things this way ensures that you can handle everything financially and also spares the lizard at least a day of sitting in a paper bag or box while you make up his room.

Since I have your solemn promise, here goes.

LIZARDS I RECOMMEND

These are the twenty that I have selected from more than three thousand lizard species worldwide. I have tried for a wide range of choices, a representative sampling of the varieties available. At the same time I have borne in mind that some species, while fascinating, are just too difficult to keep alive. What you see, then, is a list that is varied, hardy and affordable. There are bare-cage dwellers, desert species and of course forest types. All of these can be kept by first-timers, though some are more challenging than others. The animals range in price from $1 to more than $300.

1. Green iguana *(Iguana iguana)*

This is the first of seven recommended lizards that belong to the "iguanid" family. When you see "ids" after a name, that just means "and kin." The best-known of the iguanids is the common green iguana from Mexico and Central and South America. This large vegetarian is a tree-dwelling giant. It isn't as bulky as some other lizards, though, because the tail is quite long. Iguanas need very roomy cages, and climbing branches are a must. This animal will use all the space you can provide. Iguanas swim well and have been seen leaping from overhanging trees into a stream from a height of two stories. When they become larger, iguanas can be treated as members of the family. They respond well to handling and grow extremely tame. Watch out for the claws, though, as without meaning to, your big green friend can give you a nasty scratch. It helps to keep the claws trimmed. For this service be sure and see your veterinarian. You are most likely to see a hatchling or juvenile at the pet shop.

> FOOD: fruits and vegetables of all kinds. Lean canned dog food should be given too. Some individuals show an interest in crickets. Insects and meat provide needed protein. As this is a large and fast-growing lizard, a vitamin/mineral supplement is useful.
> SIZE: to 6 feet
> TEMPERATURE: 85–90 degrees F.
> CAGE: simple, with branches for climbing
> PRICE: $25 for a hatchling, rising with size to more than $100 for a tame adult in good condition

2. Rhinoceros iguana *(Cyclura cornuta)*

Like the green iguana, the rhinoceros iguana grows to considerable size and weight and requires lots of space. Unlike his common, arboreal cousin, however, this rare and impressive animal dwells mostly in the scrub brush of Haiti and is not an avid climber. While a wild-caught adult is a formidable and potentially foul-tempered beast, a captive-born baby is a little jewel, who if treated kindly and handled often will develop into a marvelously responsive exotic pet. The name stems from the three horny protuberances on the top of the male's snout.

> FOOD: varied vegetables, mice of an appropriate size and lean cat food
> SIZE: to 3 feet
> TEMPERATURE: 85–90 degrees F.
> CAGE: large and simple
> PRICE: $300 for captive-born baby (adults not recommended) or juvenile at the pet shop

3. Collared lizard *(Crotaphytus collaris)*

A smaller iguanid that doesn't need so much space is the collared lizard from our own Southwest. This desert lizard can run on its hind legs to get away from danger or catch prey. A buff gray/brown with regular spotting, the male of this species is more colorful than the female, showing some blue under the throat and sometimes on the belly. Otherwise plain, the female develops reddish spots on her flanks before she lays her eggs. Once they are laid (between two and twenty-four of them), the spots go away. If you get lucky, a colony of several of these lizards might breed in a well-designed, spacious vivarium. Don't forget to provide a good rock to hide under!

> FOOD: insects
> SIZE: to 8 inches
> TEMPERATURE: 90 degrees F., but loves to bask in a 110 degrees spot under a light
> CAGE: desert vivarium
> PRICE: $10–$15

4. Haitian curly-tailed lizard *(Leiocephalus carinatus)*

Quite similar to the collared lizard, the curly-tailed lizard from Haiti and the West Indies is used to open scrub plain and brush. The curly-tail derives its name from the male, who carries his tail curled over his back. Curly-tailed lizards are responsive and hardy, learning to take food from your hand if you are patient. They are skittish and very quick, so be sure your tank is escapeproof. Trying to catch an escapee is no fun at all—take it from someone who knows! These lizards like a place to hide and seem to live in a series of mad dashes for security. They will shoot from one spot in the tank to another, hoping you are not watching, for the first few weeks you have them. After that, they settle down some.

This is a brown lizard with a speckled throat. When you touch his scales, you will notice that they feel rough. Examine each scale individually and you will perceive a ridge running down the middle of each one. Such scales are called "keeled" scales, and many reptiles have them. Curly-tails are great socializers and live well in groups.

FOOD: insects
SIZE: 7–10 inches
TEMPERATURE: 85 degrees F.
CAGE: desert vivarium
PRICE: less than $10

5. Fence lizard *(Sceloporus occidentalis)*

Another inhabitant of rough country is the Western fence lizard, named for its habit of basking atop rocks and fence rails. Fence lizards are also iguanids and are sometimes called spiny lizards or "swifts." Boy, can they take off when frightened! These common lizards are olive, brown or black with yellow under the legs. There is blue on the sides of the body, and the male has blue on his throat as well. These creatures come from our own Western states and become very tame, even taking insect prey from your loving fingers. In the wild there are vast populations, which provide food for small snakes and even young rattlers. These lizards are very hardy if provided with ultraviolet lighting.

FOOD: insects
SIZE: 5–9 inches
TEMPERATURE: 85 degrees F.
CAGE: desert vivarium
PRICE: $8–$12 or easily caught in areas where it occurs

6. Chuckwalla *(Sauromalus obesus)*

"Chucks," like fence lizards, are found in our own Southwest.
They are dull brown or black lizards with skin as rough as sandpaper.
These funny little guys live in rocks and crevices. If something
or someone threatens them, they blow up like a balloon, inflating
their lungs and torso to the point that they are thoroughly wedged

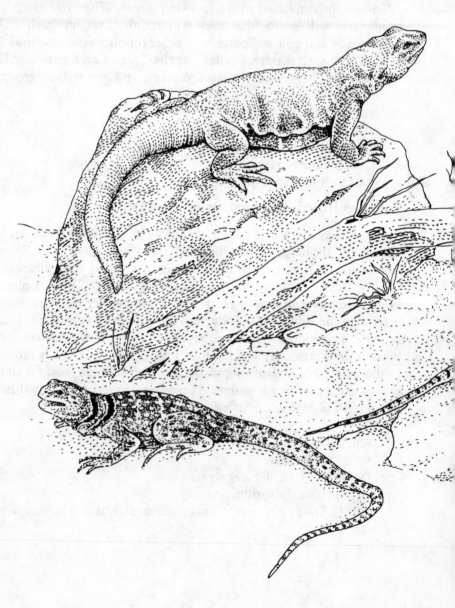

in and impossible to yank out. Bear this in mind when setting up a home and provide only hiding places that are easily dismantled if your chuck gets stubborn. These animals spend all their non-hiding time in the sun, and thus require loads of ultraviolet. Deprived of it, their metabolism falters and they succumb. *Give lots of UV light!* I mean, cram the top of the tank with bulbs. Hang bulbs from the ceiling, attach them to wires and hook them to

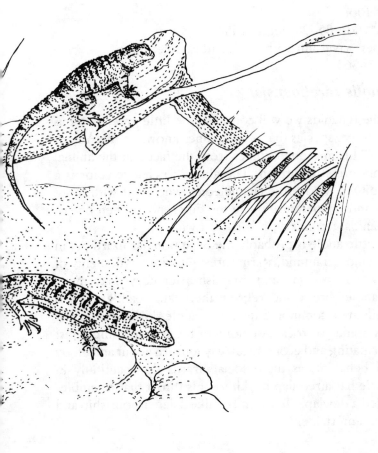

Lizards: chuckwalla, western fence lizard, alligator lizard, collared lizard

furniture—do whatever you must, but flood these babies with artificial sun!

Chuckwallas are my favorite domestic lizard because they are so superbly responsive and seemingly wise. They will grow to know you and whatever tankmates you choose for them. As a rule, young ones, though a bit harder to come by than adults, do better in captivity. They may be funny-looking, but these denizens of the desert are perhaps the best lizard pets of all.

> FOOD: all kinds of fruits and vegetables, especially berries, bananas and flowers
> SIZE: to 1 foot
> TEMPERATURE: 85–95 degrees F.
> CAGE: desert vivarium with lots of ultraviolet light
> PRICE: $45–$65

7. Anole *(Anolis carolinensis)*

The last of the iguanids we will consider, the little green anole is a slender, diminutive species that is sometimes known as the American chameleon. This misnomer comes from the fact that the animal can change from green to brown. The ability to change color is a hallmark of the Old World *true* chameleons, who do it with more finesse. Moods and temperature make the difference. When one of these little iguanids gets angry, it turns brown.

The elegant little anole is probably the most popular lizard pet in this country. It enjoys a humid, warm forest vivarium with plenty of tall plants on which to climb and establish a territory. Like many other lizards, anoles break and regrow their tails readily. This is lucky, as lost tails are a common outcome of anole skirmishes, minor disputes over a branch or rock. A colony of these lizards might just be the most fascinating and economical way to learn about and enjoy reptilian social behavior, as these social lizards do beautifully in groups. The male has a red flap of skin on his throat that resembles a fan and is called a dewlap. He extends it like a flag in courtship and battle—ever the entertainer.

> FOOD: insects
> SIZE: 4 inches

TEMPERATURE: 80 degrees F.
CAGE: forest vivarium
PRICE: $1–$2

8. House gecko *(Hemidactylus frenatus)*

This is the first of three lizards I will recommend from an enormous family of lizards found in the tropics of the world. Geckos are typically compressed from top to bottom and have vertically elliptical pupils. All of them are carnivorous, feasting on bugs, infant rodents and occasionally fingers. One of the most common geckos in the Mediterranean region is the world-traveling house gecko. This gecko is well known for hitching rides on boats and planes and making a go of it in a foreign land. Only a few inches long, this insectivore is a dull brown or gray in color and emits a characteristic faint click. House geckos breed easily, laying their eggs in corners of your warm, humid forest vivarium. The best way to ensure that these creatures breed is to buy several.

FOOD: small crickets, mealworms and other small insects
SIZE: 3–4 inches
TEMPERATURE: 80 degrees F.
CAGE: forest vivarium
PRICE: $2–$3

9. Leopard gecko *(Eublepharus macularius)*

The leopard gecko from Pakistan and India is a striking white lizard with purple, blue and yellow banding and splotching. Leopard geckos don't fit either forest or desert life too well. The best move is to put them in a desert vivarium that you mist lightly every day and provide them with a large water bowl. This is one of the rare species that will reliably breed for you without any special intervention on your part. You need only supply a male with a harem of five or six females (or service five or six females with a male, depending upon how you choose to look at it) to get things going. Add a slab of stone with some peat moss (available wherever you buy potting soil and easily stored in a plastic bag) under it to the hybrid vivarium and you may get as many as six clutches per year. Take the hatchlings out at once when they appear lest they be mistaken for crickets by their parents! If you so remove the babies, the parents will continue to breed.

Active at night, these lizards cruise the busy streets of Pakistani cities and are quite gregarious. They generally don't resent familiarity as many geckos do (remember the tokay?) and make spectacular pets, with the advantage of reproducing readily.

FOOD: Insects and, for adults, pink mice
SIZE: to 8 inches
TEMPERATURE: 85 degrees F.
CAGE: desert vivarium with a water bowl, regular misting and ultraviolet lighting
PRICE: $50–$70

10. Madagascar day gecko *(Phelsuma madagascarensis)*

This seven-to-ten-inch lizard is green with red streaks. No words can describe the electric quality of its beauty. The Madagascar day gecko appears to be composed of a score of little neon lights strung together and crammed into the body of a gecko. He is surely one of the most gorgeous of the world's reptiles.

Like most geckos', the day gecko's eyes are covered by a hard, clear integument. This animal lacks eyelids and keeps his "spectacle" clean by wiping it with an impressively long tongue used in a sweeping motion like a windshield wiper. *Unlike* most geckos, this species is active during the day rather than at night, thus its name. When a day gecko is sick or scared he fades in color—a reliable health indicator that most pets just don't offer.

Madagascar is closed to the export of its native reptiles, meaning that any day geckos you may come across must be captive-bred. In as much as these little jewels don't breed as readily as their leopard cousins, they are quite expensive.

FOOD: insects
SIZE: 7–10 inches
TEMPERATURE: 80–85 degrees F.
CAGE: rain-forest vivarium with some ultraviolet
PRICE: $125

11. Western skink *(Eumeces skiltonianus)*

Leaving the flattened little geckos, we move on to the skinks, a
group of cylindrical lizards with small though strong limbs and a way
of moving over the ground that is reminiscent of snakes. The Western skink has a brown-and-black body and a bright blue tail. The blue
is more vivid in the young. This somewhat skittish lizard lives in

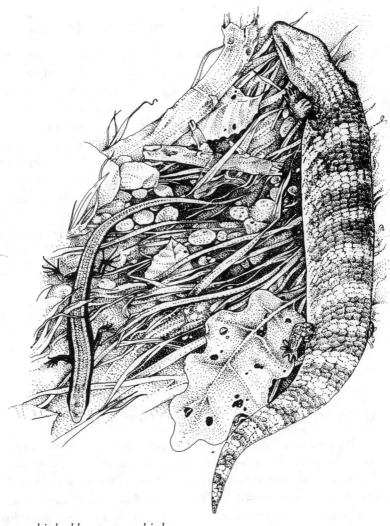

Western skink; blue tongue skink

various types of coastal brush and needs a hiding place to feel secure. Use low-growing plants rather than tall thin ones for cover in your skink's home.

> FOOD: small insects
> SIZE: 5 inches
> TEMPERATURE: 80 degrees F.
> CAGE: forest vivarium
> PRICE: $10

12. Blue-tongued skink *(Teligua scincoides gigas)*

Many times larger than the Western skink is the blue-tongued, which gets its name, as you might expect, from its tongue. You will notice that the Latin name of this animal has three parts. The third name, as you may recall, refers to the race. This particular race of the blue-tongue comes generally from New Guinea, while other races come only from the Australian mainland. While the Australian races can be had only with great difficulty, the New Guinea race is far more commonly bred and available. This is a large, heavy-bodied lizard with gold cross bands on a dark chocolate background. Because of its large size and active, friendly disposition it requires a simple cage, with a good hiding spot such as a shoe box or roll of cork bark. Blue-tongues tame very easily and may live fifteen years to become a real family pet.

> FOOD: lean canned dog food and various fruits including bananas and berries
> SIZE: to 2 feet
> TEMPERATURE: 80 degrees F.
> CAGE: simple with a hiding spot
> PRICE: $150–$175

13. Spiny-tailed agama *(Uromastyx acanthinurus)*

You may recall that the iguana-type lizards, or iguanids, live in the Americas and are known scientifically as the the "New World type." The iguanids' counterparts in Africa, Asia, Europe and Australia (the Old World) are known as "agamids." Agamids behave in a similar way, come from related forebears and look a lot like iguanids. The African spiny-tailed agama is a light brown or olive creature with a heavy body and clublike tail. He lives in very hot desert areas and stays cool by burrowing deep in the cool earth. While he won't drink from a dish, when you mist the vivarium this agama will actually absorb moisture through his skin! Spiny-tails become quite tame and responsive, but are not so common these days as they once were. You may have to hunt a bit to find one (figuratively speaking, of course), but it is well worth the effort. You could think of this vegetarian as an African chuckwalla.

FOOD: assorted fruits and vegetables with occasional lean dog food
SIZE: to 2 feet
TEMPERATURE: 85–95 degrees F.
CAGE: desert vivarium, heavily misted daily
PRICE: $75

14. Indian tree lizard

More readily available and about half the size of the agama is the Indian tree lizard *(Calotes versicolor)*. This is a light brown arboreal lizard whose body is compressed from side to side—just the opposite of a gecko. The males are more striking-looking than the females, having a red head. These are very social creatures that interact readily with both their kind and other forest lizards. Although they can be a bit aggressive toward something much smaller (as can most carnivores), they make good members of a vivarium community, bobbing and demonstrating to mark off their turf. These guys like to drink from wet leaves, so mist thoroughly; and don't forget plenty of branches for climbing.

FOOD: insects aplenty, and smaller lizards—so beware
SIZE: to 1 foot
TEMPERATURE: 80 degrees F.
CAGE: forest vivarium
PRICE: $15

15. Jackson's chameleon *(Chamaeleo jacksonii)*

Like tree lizards, the *true* (not to be confused with the American anole) chameleons are Old World forest and mountain dwellers who like life warm and wet. Famous for the ability to change color to suit

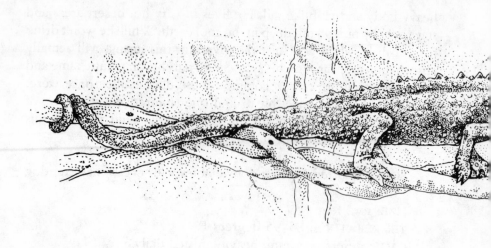

the mood or scenery, these animals are becoming increasingly rare in captivity. One of the larger chameleons is Jackson's chameleon. The law regarding these animals is becoming tougher, but enough specimens are being bred in captivity to show up occasionally for sale. In addition to changing color, the chameleon is odd in other ways. His eyes are on opposite sides of a body that is greatly compressed from side to side. Each eye is socketed in what looks like a machine-gun turret, and the eyes move independently. This means that the animal can look at you at the same time that he inspects his morning meal, a fly or moth. This slow, lumbering little beast with skin that blends into the foliage can grasp fingers or branches with his tails or feet.

Despite the sure grip they have on things, chameleons are not fast movers. You might well wonder how such a slow-motion dude catches buzzy insects in a fast-paced world. The answer? With his tongue! The tongue of the chameleon is often as long as or longer than his body. He is able to shoot it out of his mouth with astounding accuracy. At the end of the tongue is a sticky tip to which the poor bug adheres as he is rapidly drawn to the maw of the lizard and a meeting with his maker. These viviparous (see "Lizard Biology") lizards can give birth to up to thirty young. You can easily tell male from female as the male has three horns

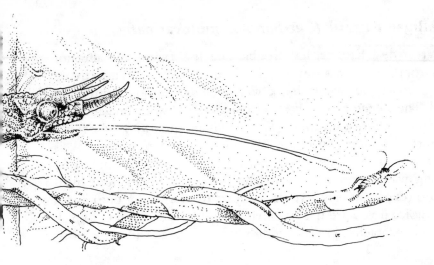

Jackson's chameleon

on his head like some prehistoric monster; the female has only one.

Although fascinating and a bit grotesque, these animals do not have great captive lifespans. Six months to a year is a good guess. I have found that they need lots of ultraviolet and do well out of doors if you live in the Sun Belt. Though they are from warm areas, they are used to a drop in nighttime temperature, so they can be left outside all the time in summer. If you do live in a warm area, try housing them outside in a screen or mesh cage. Indoors they can be kept uncaged on a piece of driftwood suspended from the ceiling by hooks and wire. My sense is that these animals, unlike most reptiles, genuinely resent confinement. If you do let them climb about, you must offer live insect food by hand and let them lap water from a dripping finger or leaf. Proffer a dusted cricket several inches from your lizard's head. The insect's waving about will attract your pet's attention, and his tongue will do the rest.

FOOD: a variety of insects
SIZE: to 1 foot
TEMPERATURE: 70–80 degrees F.
CAGE: unconfined on branches indoors or outside (when weather permits) in a wire enclosure to keep out predators
PRICE: $50

16. Alligator lizard *(Gerrhonotus multicarinatus)*

A great deal hardier, less trouble and less exotic, the alligator lizard from our own Southwest is a real little trucker. This insectivore even devours the deadly black widow spider without batting an eyelid. The alligator lizard comes from grass and woodland and thus does fine in a forest vivarium. This shuffling, burrowing fellow is a holy terror, though, on unpotted plants, so be sure everything is secure. Anchor his water bowl firmly too, as he likes to drink from standing water, only to spill it later! This is a tough, long-lived creature (expect at least five or six years from a young one) and a good choice if you are unsure of your sensitivity and ability to pick out subtle problems. He is a reddish brown or gray with dark cross-bands.

> FOOD: various insects and even pink mice for large adults
> SIZE: 11–18 inches
> TEMPERATURE: 80 degrees F.
> CAGE: forest vivarium with a water bowl and firmly anchored plants
> PRICE: $10

17. Sheltopusik *(Ophisaurus apodus)*

The tongue-twisting Slavic name is not the only thing that's strange about this animal! Also known as the "legless lizard," the sheltopusik is a burly, four-foot animal whose limbs have been evolutionarily reduced to nothing more than pimples on either side of the cloaca. Similar in overall demeanor and body form to the alligator lizard, the sheltopusik uses its strong body musculature to move through European and Central Asian scrub brush, hunting insect prey by day. This animal is popular with European herpetologists, and is known to commonly live twenty years in captivity. Not a living bridge to the snakes, but rather a very specialized lizard, the sheltopusik makes a fine terrarium inmate, but must be kept warm and dry.

> FOOD: insects of all types for young, mice and insects for adults
> SIZE: to 4 feet and as thick as a man's forearm
> TEMPERATURE: 75–80 degrees F.

CAGE: simple, but floored in shavings or corncob so that the
animal can indulge its love of burrowing
PRICE: $60

18. African plated lizard *(Gerrhosaurus validus)*

A broader, flatter version of the alligator lizard is the plated lizard
from the rocky hot areas of Africa. Though quite strong and sometimes difficult to hold, this big bruiser is one of my favorites because
it is so alert and tames down so well. The big brown fellow with
keeled scales and yellow stripes is attentive from the black "balls"
of his feet to the tip of his tongue and will never bore you. I wouldn't
be surprised if this hefty guy lived fifteen years or even more. This
is the type of creature who can become a responsive pet, even
learning where and when you feed him and learning to recognize
you.

FOOD: insects and tiny mice for young, adult mice for larger
animals
SIZE: to 2 feet
TEMPERATURE: 85 degrees F.
CAGE: simple
PRICE: $150

19. Emerald lacerta *(Lacerta viridis)*

Europe is the home of the green or emerald lacerta, a member of
an entirely different group from the plated lizard. This is a more
modest-sized animal that will live well in a forest vivarium. Emerald
lacertas are popular creatures on their native continent, mainly because their deep green bodies and aquamarine heads are so lovely
to look at.

FOOD: insects, lean dog food with a raw egg mixed in occasion-
ally
SIZE: 1 foot
TEMPERATURE: 80 degrees F.
CAGE: forest vivarium, misted heavily; no climbing branches
necessary, but lots of floor space
PRICE: $25–$35

20. Golden tegu *(Tupinambis nigropunctatus)*

If you are a real macho type, you will appreciate the golden tegu, for he is a real macho lizard. Most members of the South American group to which he belongs are small, insectivorous ground lizards that scurry through the litter of the tropical forest floor looking for prey and avoiding danger. The tegu, however, is a large, squat lizard that is eaten by local Indians. It is a true omnivore, eating fruits and meats and scavenging adeptly in the wild. This black lizard with shiny scales and gold banding is a tough, impressive fellow, hissing aggressively at the slightest provocation. The adults lay their eggs in termite nests so that the young will open their eyes to a veritable feast.

Golden tegus must be housed alone, as they will attack nearly anything small. Find yourself a young one and handle it regularly. You may wish to use gardening gloves, as the pinch from a bite can be painful. Adults are a poor choice, as they are just too difficult to tame. It takes no particular expertise, however, to feed a fascinating little baby and grow it into a mellow and hardy giant. This is a truly fearsome reptile that is small enough to be manageable and that adapts well to captivity. If a taste of the dinosaur era appeals to you, you may just have found a pet!

> FOOD: rodents of approximately the same size as the tegu's head
> SIZE: to 4 feet
> TEMPERATURE: 85 degrees F.; cool it down to 70 degrees prior
> to handling to improve attitude
> CAGE: simple
> PRICE: $65

21. African savannah monitor *(Varanus exanthematicus)*

Of all the large, predatory reptiles, this buff-colored and blotched lizard makes the most tractable pet. If the tegu's disposition is as spicy as Mexican food, the savannah monitor's is fettuccine in cream sauce. Start with the youngest animal you can find, work with him daily to make him lose his fear of your hands and he will become an absolute lap lizard.

This is a fitting last recommendation, for the absolute best reptile pet that I have ever been lucky enough to own was a savannah monitor (remember the story of Xan?). Suffice it to say you can expect that a lizard of this species will grow to know you and your habits and can even be kept out of a cage as long as he has a warm spot to run to when he gets cold. What I did when Xan was an adult was put some newspaper down in my walk-in closet and leave the door open. An infrared heat lamp and water bowl ensured that he could be found there almost all the time. I always gave him his meals in the closet except when he insisted upon climbing up my leg for a bit of what I was cooking in the kitchen.

This is one lizard worth raising like a puppy!

FOOD: rodents of appropriate size

SIZE: adults are 4–5 feet

TEMPERATURE: 85 degrees F. in a cage, 90 degrees under a lamp if uncaged

CAGE: simple, as an adult may be kept out of cage if heat and water are provided

PRICE: $75

TURTLES

Florida soft-shell turtles

When I was a kid, my grandfather took me to the circus. While daring and spectacular feats were going on below, vendors were walking up and down the aisles selling sparklers, circus caps with elephant heads and propellers affixed, candy, hot dogs, popcorn—and turtles. Yep, I distinctly remember a fellow walking by with a big red board, a turtle taped to it by the shell, legs kicking madly. "Baby turtles, seventy-five cents!" he yelled. What your seventy-five cents bought was a malnourished creature with a paper-thin shell who soon developed swollen eyes, stopped eating the crushed "ant eggs" you offered him and ended up being flushed you know where.

Not a very dignified fate, I think, for so venerable and tenacious a creature as the turtle. While pyramids, temples and cities have risen and fallen, while dinosaurs have ruled and been swept away and atomic bombs have shaken the earth, turtles have gone right on eating, swimming and lumbering about making baby turtles. You may have difficulty distinguishing between a salamander and a newt, or between a frog and a toad, but everyone knows a turtle on sight. If you have never really looked into the subject, though, chances are you are not aware of the amazing variety of these beasts we call turtles. They show up all over the globe, inhabiting the oceans, deserts, ponds, lakes and streams. They crawl through the litter of warm forests everywhere and burrow in the tepid mud beneath bogs you never even knew were there. Not only that, but their grasp on life is uncommonly tight. I have seen turtles with their shells cracked

125

and organs hanging out from an encounter with a tire stepping friskily along and sniffing out berries. I have seen giants with shells worn so smooth they have doubtless seen a hundred summers more than I. There is nothing quite like the turtle.

You've seen turtles, you say. They are nothing new; let's move onto something really exotic. Well, rid your mind of the image of the high-domed shell of the garden box turtle. Forget her red head and big brown eyes. Imagine an animal that weighs a hundred and fifty pounds and lurks at the bottom of a swiftly moving stream, waiting to exact his toll in careless ducks and curious fish. Or instead try to fathom the riddle of the green sea turtle, three feet long and capable of outrunning a ski boat using just two legs. Not only is she swift, she has a memory that puts the latest minicomputer to shame. She spends years cruising thousands of miles of tropical oceans, munching her way through myriad forests of kelp. Then nature calls her back not only to the same island on which she was born, but to the exact same strip of beach. Does she use the poles as internal compass headings, does she "taste" her way back or does she take her headings from the stars?

How about the soft-shelled turtles of the Nile and Ganges rivers, big flat creatures with no tough home on their back but a set of nails and jaws that more than make up for it in the protection department? How about the false map turtles with road routes on their shells, or the snake-necked, big-headed and snail-eating turtles?

If the charm of animals so unusual and ancient has not swayed you yet, I urge you to read this section. I'm sure that if you feel up to the challenges of turtle keeping, these droll pets will repay you for years to come.

TURTLE BIOLOGY

Do you know the difference between a turtle and a tortoise? Well, if you don't, this is a great place to start our discussion of "shelled reptile" biology. "Turtle" is the big, all-inclusive, general name. It is always correct. If you see what looks like a turtle, call it a turtle and you are okay. It doesn't matter where this shelled reptile lives, whether it swims or sinks, whether it is green with purple polka dots or slate gray with a bored look in its eye. A reptile with a shell is a turtle, period.

Green anole

Haitian curly-tailed lizard

Chain kingsnake

Bull snake

Indigo snake

Rainbow boa

Carpet python

Musk turtle

False map turtle

Red-eared slider

Painted turtle

Bell's African hingeback tortoise

Sulphur-crested cockatoo

African grey parrot

Sun conure

Janday conure

Within this vast, all-inclusive group we find the tortoises and the terrapins. "Tortoise" refers to any of several genera of specialized turtles that spend their entire life on land. Because they don't need to cut neatly through the water, the shells of tortoises need not be streamlined. Instead they are heavy, domed, thick and durable; excellent at resisting the jaws of a fox or the talons of an eagle.

Tortoises don't have to be capable of paddling around, either. As a result, their limbs are not designed for swimming; they're designed for lifting the shell and moving along with a minimum of fuss. When a tortoise walks, his limbs lift his body off the ground like great pillars. A tortoise undershell (plastron) never hits the dirt when he is moving—unlike that of an aquatic turtle, who drags himself along in a most undignified manner.

The word "terrapin" properly refers to only one particular species *(Malaclemmys terrapin)* of turtle. This is a domestic animal, frequenting our Eastern Seaboard. Its complete name is "diamondback terrapin," and it is best known for its contribution to canned turtle soup.

Now that the confusion is cleared up, let's talk more about the shell. There are two parts to the shells of most turtles. The underlying layer is of bone and covers and adheres to the ribs. It is divided into plates, each abutting the next, like sections of a map. Over this layer of bone another, the second shell layer, is deposited by special cells. This is the tough, horny outer layer that we generally refer to when we speak of the shell. Although this tough, keratinous layer is dead (much like our hair), it is continuously being replaced from underneath to compensate for wear and tear. The divisions, or scutes, that we see when we look at a turtle's shell do not directly correspond to the divisions of the bony layer, but rather form a pattern all their own. In some turtles the horny shell is paper-thin; in others it has the thickness of a cookie. We call the top of the shell the "carapace" and the bottom the "plastron." Try to remember these terms, as you will see them a lot from here on in.

Many people want to know whether you can tell the age of the turtle by looking at the rings in each scute and counting them. In the wild, turtles grow appreciably only when it is warm. Thus turtle growth is seasonal, and the lines that look like rings are "dead times" in the growth of the shell. In young turtles that have lived in the wild, "reading" the rings tells you something. There are not too many lines in a young animal, and the pattern of growth is pretty idealized. In older turtles there are just too many rings to really count; they all just mush together. In turtles that have been kept in captivity, the growing takes place steadily, since most of us won't let our animals get so cold they all but stop growing.

Now that we are on the subject of growth and longevity, what are we to make of the occasional turtle we find in the woods with "DEBBIE AND FRED—1634 A.D." carved into the shell? This sort of thing is funny and interesting, but of course is scientifically worthless. There is nothing to stop anyone from writing whatever he pleases on the back of a turtle, so I guess you will just have to make up your own mind whether to believe everything you read.

The snake biology section contains basic information common to all reptiles. It is there that I explain a bit about the way the reptile machine exchanges energy, runs and grows. However, turtles, while reptiles, are different from snakes in more than just the obvious ways. There are some things about the biology of the turtle that are special and worth looking at here.

Can you think of some special problems (besides maintaining a sense of humor) that might arise from carrying your home around on your back all the time? Your movements are very limited, remember. Turtles don't make good yoga teachers. Their bodies are encased in an incompressible and inexpansible shell. To see where this might get rough, put your chin to your chest and watch your upper body as you take a deep breath. Your whole torso, of course, expands. Now have a friend squeeze you tight while you try to inhale. A different kettle of fish, eh? (Now ask your friend nicely to let go.)

A turtle can't puff out his chest like Mr. America, but he can do some pretty interesting things instead. By moving his innards around a bit and by pushing out his legs, he makes room for air to come in. When it is time to breathe out, he does just the opposite.

If you stop and think about this a minute, you will realize that the turtle is in for trouble. Consider the following scenario. Rita, the neighborhood box turtle, is out in the forest, munching on some earthworms and berries. All of a sudden, a big, red turtle-eating fox appears and makes a run for Rita's face. Rita spits out a berry and quickly pulls into her shell. In doing so, she exhales, giving the little hiss we sometimes hear when a turtle closes up. So there she is, without any air in her lungs and with the sly, patient fox waiting for her to open up again and breathe so he can have her for lunch.

If *you* try being patient and waiting for something with no air in your lungs, you will either pass out or give up. A little gland near the brain monitors your blood for telltale signs that you need to breathe. Poisons build up in the blood, you see, and when it is time to get rid of these by exhaling and inhaling again, we do so. A turtle, however, has no worries in this regard, since it is specially suited to withstand the presence of these poisons without kicking off. Exactly how long a turtle can hold his breath depends upon the temperature and the type of turtle, but it is certainly a lot longer than we can hold ours! As a matter of fact, some turtles may be able to breathe through special tissues in the throat and cloaca. I have caught musk *(Sternotherus odoratus)* and painted *(Chrysemys picta)* turtles paddling sluggishly under the ice in frozen ponds in New England with no apparent way to reach the surface. This is a special circumstance, of course, for when the water is cold the body machinery is slowed down and metabolic need for air is slight. By no means attempt to demonstrate this ability with a pet turtle, as he will simply drown!

Speaking of swimming under the ice, remember that this is not the typical course. Turtles, like all reptiles, slow down when the temperature drops. In parts of the world where there is a cold season, turtles overwinter as all reptiles do; they go to sleep. While hibernating is a fact of existence to the Temperate Zone turtle in the wild, it is of no importance to you as a beginning turtle keeper. *Do not attempt to force your pet into hibernation!* Instead, keep your turtle warm as discussed below and you will enjoy his active good health the year around.

Like most other reptiles, the majority of turtles are carnivores. Yet most meat-eating turtles eat vegetation too, and most vegetarian turtles enjoy a bite of meat now and then. To lay down hard-and-fast rules about any chelonian (from the Latin for the turtles, *Chelonia*) diet is to entirely miss the point. The typical turtle is a wanton opportunist, a scavenger rather than a predator. You can see why this might be. Although hardy, tough and durable for their size, most turtles are slow-moving animals that have a hard time catching prey. Certainly turtles do hunt—at least some of the swifter aquatic types do—but they derive much of their nutrition from offal and carnage. Probably the best way to describe a turtle's dietary preferences is to call him an "omnivore."

Turtles, unlike lizards and snakes, do not have teeth to help them with the business of hunting and eating. Instead they have a horny bill (sometimes drawn to a point) and strong jaws to go with it. Some of the large, predatory varieties (in the distinct minority) can give you quite a nip. A turtle bite is a less-than-romantic wound to nurse.

While lacking teeth, the turtle does have a manipulable tongue, anchored to the bottom of the mouth by most of its length. Tongue movement is quite limited, however, and aquatic species need to be able to submerge the head and fill up the mouth with water in order to chew and swallow properly. Tortoise tongues are more mobile, so this type of turtle can do it in the dirt.

Speaking of "doing it," turtle reproduction follows the reptilian pattern of internal fertilization and the laying and leaving of eggs. There is no parental involvement with the young after they emerge from the egg. When we discussed squamates (science-speak for lizards and snakes), I said that there were two reproductive strategies: oviparity, or the laying of eggs, and viviparity, or the bearing of live young. Turtles, alas, haven't such imaginative and creative sex lives. All they do, epoch after epoch, is lay eggs and forget all about them. The part before egg laying, though, is a bit spicier. The male has a penis, which unlike the divided organ of snakes and lizards is a single, well-formed affair with a groove down the middle through which the sperm runs. The female has the usual gamut of internal reproductive organs, including a clitoris. Both the penis and the clitoris arise from the cloaca, a combined excretory and reproductive organ present in both sexes at the base of the tail. When copulation occurs, the male must climb onto the female and insert his penis into her cloaca directly.

Prior to this rather cut-and-dried climax, some really wild things go on. The male, who is distinguished by his concave plastron and long front claws, may actually engage in a courtship dance with the female. If this occurs in the water he may approach her and wave his claws in front of her face, thereby titillating her (at least, I'm told she finds it titillating). Prior to the climax of a pair of *tortoises*, males may war over a female by butting each other, shell to shell. While this might seem cute in a couple of four-inch Russian tortoises, it is downright spectacular if the combatants are Galapagos giants that weigh five hundred pounds or more!

In order to insert his penis into the female, the male has to cope with the fact that there are two shells keeping them apart, his and hers. That is why the male's carapace is often indented or concave at the bottom. This feature allows him to accommodate the swell of her shell. If the shell is highly domed, as it is in the box turtle, the male must enter the female more from behind than from above.

From here on the rest is more typical birds-and-bees stuff, except for one thing. A female turtle may retain some of the male's sperm in her system for years! That means that the result of two turtles' passing in the night can be forthcoming for years on end. Naturally, each year the number of fertile eggs that a female lays will decrease (assuming she doesn't hook up with another guy!).

Now that you have some natural history under your belt, let's talk about one of the most important questions a prospective pet owner wants answered. How smart are turtles, and what information do they receive from the outside world on which to base their thoughts? If you have read other sections of this book, you know that I feel intelligence is a difficult thing to evaluate, even in a person! Difficulties notwithstanding, I have to say what my experience has shown me: Turtles are the cleverest reptiles around!

Because this is such an unscientific, purely subjective remark, I wince to think of what my colleagues will murmur when they read this. Yet I'll say it again: I think turtles are downright brilliant, at least for reptiles. They can rely on senses similar to those of lizards, their close-up (and in some cases, color) vision being particularly good. They can learn to run mazes and display a wide variety of responses to stimuli. Turtles can learn to expect food at certain times and even to recognize their keeper!

Many years ago, my little brother purchased a baby three-toed box turtle *(Terrapene carolina triunguis)*. Little Samantha was an alert creature who seemed to recognize me and my family. She would waddle over for crickets and fruit whenever we approached her tank. I used her for years in lectures because her appetite was so voracious that she could be depended upon to eat, even with scores of people watching. On more than one occasion she munched goldfish in half at the same time that a five-year-old child was turning her upside down!

After a while my brother grew tired of her and I took her to my place. She had the run of the bathroom (a good idea only if you live in a warm area and are diligent about cleanup) and I put her into the sink once a day to have a soak and a drink. Samantha loved berries and crickets as well as bananas and spinach. Never once did I enter the room and fail to elicit a greeting. She would waddle across the floor in my direction, head craning for a look, eyes bright. If I had no food to offer she would bite at my toes until a repast was forthcoming. These were turtle love-nips. They didn't hurt, but they told me she was hungry. Sam comes to mind because, in my world, her alertness was legend.

One of my very first turtles was a Western painted turtle *(Pseudemys picta belli).* He was a lovely-looking olive green fellow with beautiful markings on his shell and yellow stripes on his head and limbs. He lived in a community tank with some other turtles. Whenever I walked into the room, he would spy me and swim up to the front of the tank. Finding a hole through which he could stick his neck, he would follow my every move. When I approached the tank, he would swim not to me, but to the other turtles sitting on a rock. Gaping and thrashing, he alerted them all to the fact that food was coming! As a pack leader, he drew the lot of them to my fingers and then shot across the tank to an isolated corner and waited, mouth agape, not wishing to share.

I have a friend with a desert tortoise that she has had for years. It lives in her home, sleeps by her bed and follows her all about the house, standing on her foot when it is hungry and gazing up at her.

There are more brilliant turtles I know. This is just a taster. Hopefully, you are interested enough to want to know what exactly turtle care entails. Read the next section!

A HOME FOR YOUR TURTLE

Housing turtles can be a sticky wicket. The same diversity and uniqueness that make different types of turtles attractive to us make it difficult to generalize about their care. You can't, for example, put a desert tortoise in a cage with a painted turtle and expect both to thrive. There are some turtles that live only in the water and never come out, and there are some turtles that live in the desert and quite possibly never see water unless it rains, getting all the fluid they need from the food they eat. The great majority of forms, however, are somewhere in between. They swim, but like to climb around a lot. Or they may climb around a lot and like to get their feet wet sometimes. There are nearly three hundred species of turtles and just as many special and unique lifestyles that they choose. How can we deal with all this creativity using simple equipment in the home?

The answer is, we *approximate.* As long as we are careful to provide everything an individual *does* need, we don't have to worry about also providing something it does *not* need. We have to know something about our particular pet, and we have to be careful not to mix (in the same cage) turtles that have vastly different preferences.

I have divided this section into two parts: the water cage and the land cage. Each section will discuss setting up and maintaining your pet's home. Within each section I will also discuss how the basic cage can and should be modified a little here and there to suit the exact shelled friend you choose. By the end of this little treatise I hope you will have a concrete idea of how to prepare your chosen pet's home.

The Water Cage

As for so many animals that we consider in this book, the aquarium is probably the most readily available and easy-to-use item for a cage. Since turtles need surface area rather than depth, choose a shape that is long and wide but not necessarily deep. A fifteen- or twenty-gallon tank is a good size for most applications. If you have only one turtle and are sure that you won't be getting any more, you can get by with a tank as small as five or ten gallons. Just remember, though, once you start learning about these exotic pets you will undoubtedly become fascinated. If you want a couple of turtles a few months down the line, you will just end up putting your ten-gallon tank in the closet and buying a twenty for your clan. I started with a painted turtle in a five-gallon tank when I was ten years old. I promised my mother that I wouldn't get any more. Five years later I had one hundred and thirty turtles in tanks and pools all through the room! (Plastic kiddie pools are another "cage" option if you have loads of space and loads of turtles. The very largest of these plastic pools can hold ten six-inch aquatic turtles. If you are reading this book, you are not quite ready for turtle heaven in your home.) Don't go wild and overextend yourself in time and money, but do consider the small difference in price between aquaria of similar sizes and opt for the larger tank when you can afford it. This tactic beats having a closet full of tanks too small to use.

How Much Water?

Okay, you have a long, low aquarium of, say, twenty gallons. You know that it is intended to hold water for an aquatic turtle, so one of the first questions that should pop to mind is how much water to put in it. Should you fill it completely, leave it half-empty, put an inch of water in it? Naturally, this depends upon the size of the turtle you are putting in. It also depends upon how well the animal can swim. To get some idea of your pet's swimming abilities, take a look at his feet. Spread his little toes apart and see how much webbing there is. If the nails are very thick, and the toes distinct and poorly webbed, as in our native American box turtle *(Terrapene carolina),* you have a poor swimmer on your hands who needs shallow water lest he tire and drown. If, on the other hand, the webbing is extensive and makes the foot a real paddle, as in our soft-shelled turtles (*Trionyx* sp.), your pet probably swims well and would enjoy water of some depth for frolicking. Another clue to how aquatic a turtle is can be found in the shape of his shell. High-domed shells don't cut through the water very well and can be so heavy that the turtle sinks like a stone. Low, streamlined shells, conversely, are lightweight and cut through the water readily.

If your turtle is a really good swimmer, you can give him water that's twice as deep as his shell is long. Put him up against the glass and make a mark where two shell lengths measure off. You can safely fill the water this high. Painted turtles and sliders (*Pseudemys* sp.) as well as map turtles (*Graptemys* sp.) are examples of turtles that can take pretty deep water in stride.

Less good swimmers with heavier shells and less webbing don't, as I have indicated, want such deep water. For these turtles a good rule of thumb is to give them water as deep as their shell is wide. Put your pet's belly against the glass and put his left side down at the bottom edge of the tank. Make a mark where the right edge of his shell meets the glass and fill the water to there. Asian box turtles (*Cuora* sp.), leaf turtles (*Geomyda* and *Heosemys* sp.) and our native spotted turtles *(Clemmys gutatta)* are types that like water but are not especially gifted swimmers.

There are two groups of aquatic turtles that are exceptions to my rules of thumb. The soft-shelled turtles are the first. These are great swimmers, among the very best, yet they prefer to have water that's fairly shallow. They lie covered with sand on the bottom of the tank and stick their long necks up toward the surface. Breathing through their snorkel-like noses, they can rush through the water like minia-ture bullet trains.

The second exceptional group is composed of the musk, mud and snapping turtles. These paradoxical creatures don't swim very well at all, their shells being bulky and their limbs short. Yet these fellows can remain submerged for long periods of time and scavenge the bottom for dinner. You can fill an aquarium all the way to the top and nearly any of these beasts will do fine. Beware, of course, of very small turtles in huge tanks. An inch-long musk turtle hatchling will naturally exhaust himself trying to reach the top of a seventy-gallon tall-style aquarium. Watch your pet's efforts to get to the surface and breathe. Use common sense.

On Drying Off

Musk, mud and snapping turtles are content to while away the hours at the bottom of the tank. For these species I recommend what I call a "clinging" rock—nothing more than a moderate-sized rock that need not break the surface and is there only to give the little fellows something to grab on to. These species are big clingers. While they may occasionally utilize a dry spot, they can get by without one, as long as the water is not so deep that they struggle for every breath.

Most other types of turtles, however, must have a place on which they can climb out to rest or bask in the warmth of a lamp you provide. Swimming is fun, but one needs a break! If you get a sense of what the preferences of your animal are, you will be able to deduce how much land he needs. The totally aquatic forms need little or none (perhaps a fifth of the surface area of the tank), the moderately aquatic animals need some (a third of the tank's surface) and the slightly aquatic forms need lots (half of the tank's surface area) of turf.

There are different ways to provide land space. One way is to simply stick a large rock into the tank. It should be sizable enough so that some protrudes from the water and there is a completely dry spot for the turtle that he can easily reach. If a turtle's shell cannot totally dry out, it is subject to infection and fungus.

If the natural look appeals to you, go ahead and use rocks. Do be aware, though, that there are disadvantages. One problem is that using a big rock takes up swimming space in the tank. I also find that dirt tends to accumulate under and behind the rock where the flow of water is reduced. While a single rock of the exact right dimensions can be Gibraltar-stable, a stacking of stones can be dangerous. Turtles are strong and can move the rocks with their legs. Years ago I had a fifty-five-gallon tank full of small turtles from South America.

One day I brought home a hatchling to add to the community. I had rocks stacked all through the aquarium and powerful filters going day and night to keep it clean. Nonetheless, I had to break down the tank once a month and totally clean it out (best done by scrubbing with salt and then rinsing thoroughly). When I restacked the rocks, I was always careful to make the arrangements secure and stable. The new addition was overjoyed with his accommodations and dived eagerly through the holes and cracks. I watched him for a while and then left him alone to get used to his new life. The sad ending to this story is that I found him late that day, wedged between the front glass and a red stone. He was pressed tightly into a grotesque gulping posture and was submerged, lifeless and alone. Heed the lesson well. Even a little turtle, if he has enough leverage, can move mountains enough to get himself into trouble.

Wood provides a safer dry-out haven, though it too presents problems. A flat piece of board will float for a while and provide a good platform. Sooner or later, though, it will become waterlogged and start to sink. If you wedge it in, it should stay, but will encourage the growth of algae. (Algae, incidentally, are fine if you don't mind the look of them. Many turtles will even relish grazing on them a bit.) If you wish to use wood, a gnarled old piece of hardwood such as manzanita or grape will resist decay the longest and stay smooth. If your turtles are small enough, you can even use a branch, for the natural effect.

A third possibility for a basking platform is Styrofoam. It is inexpensive, stays on the surface, does not decay or grow too much algae and waterlogs slowly. Go to the florist and purchase a slab of the thick green material that is used to set flowers. Cut it to a width slightly greater than your tank and wedge it in. With time the Styrofoam may compress and ultimately have to be replaced. No matter —it is inexpensive and easy to find. A Styrofoam platform doesn't take up space under the water either, so there is more swimming space for your pets.

As I have indicated, wood and Styrofoam can be wedged. Wedging brings up an important point, believe it or not. The basking platform, whatever, the material that forms it, *must be tipped into the water* so that your pets can climb up onto it. Little turtles in particular have problems heaving themselves up and over the edge of a land space that is just flush and parallel with the surface of the water. You have gone to some time and trouble to set up dry quarters for your pet. Watch and be sure he can reach it!

Keeping the Cage Clean

You have a medium-sized aquarium with a turtle or two in it. Your pets are happily swimming about, growing, eating and excreting. This is what is called a "closed" system. There is no place for waste to go. Your pets just keep eating and excreting, eating and excreting. . . . If you have but one small turtle in a five- or ten-gallon aquarium, there should be no problem just taking the tank to the tub, tossing out the water and replenishing it every couple of days. At one point in my eternal quest for better turtle maintenance I put all my fancy equipment in the closet and used fifteen or sixteen little tanks, each with a couple of inches of water and a rock. I heated the whole room instead of individual tanks. I took each turtle out to feed it, running a sort of round robin between turtles, special diets, tanks and feeding bowls. Within a week I had developed a bad back, dirty tanks and malnourished turtles. To avoid all this and save lots of work, you should invest in a filtering system.

We chelonophiles (turtle lovers) must suffer somewhat at the hands of the fish-loving public. Apparently turtles are not big business, for everything available for aquaria is designed with fish in mind. Sometimes equipment must be modified a bit in order to be of any use. In the case of filters, most types that are used for filtering fish water just cannot cope with the volume or size of the waste that a turtle puts out. Turtles, to put it succinctly, are bigger and dirtier than fish! There is, however, one type of mechanism that works quite well with little or no alteration. This is an outside filter that draws the water up from the tank by suction. Most "outside-box" filters depend upon the siphon effect to draw dirty water from the tank into the filter and pass it through filtering materials. For the siphon effect to operate, the water in the tank must be higher than that in the filter. An air pump or motor then returns the clean water to the aquarium. The unit I recommend, however, is called a "power filter" because the motor both pulls water into the filter and pumps it out. Since the siphon effect is not required for the water to be drawn into the filter, the level of water in the tank is irrelevant. This lets us fill the tank with as much water or as little as we please and not worry about the filter's not functioning! Several companies now produce filters with this design. Hagen even has a line of such machines in a variety of sizes to fit virtually any size aquarium. They are called Aquaclear aquarium filters. Even as you read this, more companies are coming out with similar designs (the Whisper Power Filter is another good product), so keep your eyes open when you shop.

As far as turtle keeping goes, these "power filters" are an absolute breakthrough. They are powerful enough to suck feces right out of the tank as well as to purify many gallons in a short time. Fouled water enters the filter box through plastic tubes. First it passes through either cotton or spun glass (so called "glass wool") to remove detritus. Next the water is further purified by passing through charcoal. Charcoal removes chemical waste, leaving the water almost fresh enough to drink. (It doesn't taste great, though, so just take my word for it.) These machines come with a plastic tube just six or seven inches long. If this tube does not reach to the water level in your aquarium, ask your pet shop for a longer tube. If none is available, you can buy an extension, which should work fine. If air leaks into the extension tube you can seal the tubes together for an airtight fit. Heat a screwdriver over an open flame or on your electric stove. Use the hot tip to melt the tubes together. One word of caution: Don't inhale the fumes as you melt this plastic; they can be toxic.

The manufacturers of power filters suggest what size filter to use with what size tank. They are "thinking fish," though, not turtles. A handy way to know which unit to choose is to take one size bigger than recommended by the company. The larger the filter, the more powerful the motor. A powerful motor does a better job of keeping your tank clean. Too big a filter, on the other hand, can buffet your pet around by creating a strong current in the tank. Large filters, I am afraid, can also kill small turtles. It doesn't happen often—in fact, it is rather a freak occurrence—but happen it does. Now and again a curious turtle will poke his head up a suction tube just to see what is going on. (Curiosity is a sign of intellect, remember.) A very powerful current will keep his unfortunate head there until he dies of suffocation, unable to reach the surface for a breath. To avoid this, position the opening of the tube within a half-inch of the bottom of the tank. Doing this leaves enough room for the filter to suck up dirt but not turtle heads.

An outside filter performs all the water cleaning necessary to the system. If you wish to additionally freshen the water, you have the option of pumping bubbles through it. Bubbles hasten the flow of the current, and adding oxygen to the water in this manner also makes life easy on those turtles that like to breathe by extracting air from water while sleeping submerged. Bubbling all but eliminates turtle odors too, but aquatic turtles don't smell much anyway. To pump air into the water, all you need is an air pump (available at any pet shop for less than $10) and an "airstone." The latter is nothing more than a porous piece of ceramic or rock that emits tiny bubbles when air is forced through it. This is common fish-keeping equipment and readily available.

Warmth for the Water Turtle

Like all reptiles, turtles rely on outside heat sources to keep warm and keep going. (For a full discussion of temperature and its importance to the reptile, see the snake biology section.) Typically an aquatic turtle will either live in warm water or come out of brisk water to bask in the hot sun. The best that we can do for our pets is to heat both the water and the land so that they need not work too hard to stay at a comfortable temperature. Naturally, if your pet is one of the species (say, a mud or snapping turtle) that needs no basking platform, you must heat only the water.

Seventy-five to 80 degrees is a good temperature range for the water in your pet's home. To achieve this, we must again lean on technology developed for the fish market. Aquarium heaters are inexpensive and reliable these days, but not all are suitable for use in a turtle tank. As with outside filters, many heaters will operate only if the water level in the tank is at or near the very top. That does not help you if you have only three inches of water in the tank for your soft-shelled or leaf turtle. For low water levels you must use a fully submersible heater that may be stuck with suction cups to the bottom of the tank instead of clipped onto the aquarium's edge. Ebo Jaeger makes a good unit available in various wattages depending upon the size of the tank. Fifty to 75 watts is more than adequate for most applications. If you have a very small tank or a very big one, your pet shop can help you assess the correct wattage. (Other acceptable brands of submersible heaters include the Rena Model F, the Neptune from Aqua Marine Technology and the Thermal Compact.)

Turtles require both a fluorescent bulb to mimic the sun (more on this below) and an incandescent bulb to heat the basking platform. To keep his dry spot warm, all you need is a clamp-type fixture, with a porcelain socket to accommodate the high heat from some bulbs, and a small spotlight. Even a gooseneck desk lamp will serve, provided you can adjust it to shine directly on your turtle's basking spot. Play around with the lamp, changing the wattage of the bulb and the distance between bulb and turtle until a thermometer tells you the basking platform is at about 80 degrees. What size bulb you will need and how close the lamp must be to the tank will depend upon many factors, including the temperature of your turtle room. A thermometer placed on the platform directly where the turtle will bask should read about 90 degrees.

Lighting the Water Cage

A healthy shell needs calcium, and a turtle can properly use calcium in its diet only if it receives some sunlight. Adequate sunlight, of course, is not always available, particularly if you live in an apartment and it is wintertime. For years, hobbyists tried to raise baby turtles indoors and failed. Even certain types of adult turtles just seemed to fade when kept out of the sun. Nobody realized what was going on for a long while. When I was a boy I was frustrated and disheartened in my failed attempts to keep certain exotic types. All that has changed! As I indicated in the snake chapter, "fake sunlight" is now available from certain kinds of fluorescent bulbs. These bulbs mimic the ultraviolet rays of the sun and make all the difference in the world to certain kinds of turtles. If you know something of the natural history of your pet, you can almost predict its need for sunlight. While no turtle can stand constant sun without shade for long periods of time, such turtles as sliders and maps bask often and need ultraviolet light to stay healthy. Species such as soft-shells, mud turtles and snappers, on the other hand, need little, as they spend most of their natural life away from the sun. As I have indicated in the lizard chapter, "Vita-Lite" and "Chromalux" are the fluorescent models of choice. They come in a variety of sizes and can be burned in a standard fluorescent fixture. Opt for the biggest one that you can fit over your tank and leave it on all day. Eight or nine hours without light at night is good for your pets, provided the water is warm.

Mistakes Not to Make

1. Don't include live plants. Turtles will shred and eat them and foul the tank.

2. Don't overcomplicate. You will end up cleaning more and enjoying your pet less.

3. Don't overcrowd a tank. *For turtles less than four inches long, five gallons per turtle is a handy rule. Bigger turtles require as much as ten gallons apiece.*

4. Be careful when mixing turtles to avoid widely disparate sizes. A six-inch turtle will gladly make a meal of a three-incher. *Never, never* put snapping turtles in with other turtles, and be wary of musk and mud turtles too. Watch any new setup closely for a few days; you may save a neck!

The Land Cage

When we discussed aquatics, I stressed that there is quite a variety of turtles that like water. The same is true, to a lesser extent, of the land turtles. There are tortoises that prefer no water at all (save a dribble to drink) and box turtles that live to wallow in the muck and mire. In the water cage, we took account of the preferences by adjusting the ratio of water to land. In the land cage we will do much the same thing. When you envision the enclosure for a land turtle, think mainly of tortoises and box turtles, as these are typical inhabitants.

You will be happy to know that it is very simple and inexpensive to set up even the best terrestrial turtle pen. No heaters or filtering devices are called for. In essence, all you need is a box. A plywood unit that you knock together will serve. In a pinch you can even get away with a grocery carton, provided you are willing to replace it every so often as it soils. An old steamer trunk from an army–navy outlet works well, as does a long and low used fish tank. I once used an old chest turned on its back, with all the drawers taken out and the cross braces removed. As long as the container has sides that won't allow your pet to escape and is of sufficient size to permit strolling (tortoises especially are browsers and grazers, often covering some serious territory in the span of a day), just about anything goes. If you do use wood or paper, be sure and line it with a large garbage bag to protect it from spillage.

The Cage Floor and the Hiding Place

There are two alternatives when it comes to flooring. You can use either newspaper or dried corncob. While newspaper is cheap and functional, corncob bits look better and absorb more. The choice is yours, but do stay with these two floorings. Gravel and sand (except in the case of Horsefield's and pancake tortoises) tend to be inadvertently swallowed when a turtle is eating and to cause digestive problems. Rocks and stones, moreover, are abrasive and can damage a turtle's plastron. Additionally, the cage should be devoid of decorative plants. Offer your turtle food only in his food bowl as discussed below. Many house plants (*Coleus* is a prime example) are poisonous and will just be uprooted and trampled anyway.

Like lizards and snakes, land turtles are secretive customers. To make your pet really feel at home, you should provide a hiding place. An inverted shoe box in one corner is good for small turtles. A larger carton in the same position will serve bigger animals. Cut a turtle-sized hole in one end of the container, just big enough to allow your pet to enter and small enough to keep the inside attractively dark.

The Watering Hole

All land turtles should have a small bowl of water available that is strictly for drinking. Even tortoises that naturally get their water only from their food will avail themselves of standing water when it is offered. The drinking bowl should be big enough not to tip over when your turtle puts his leg up on it, but too small to encourage a bath. Speaking of a bath, a soak is a virtual necessity for all land turtles, though steppe dwellers such as Horsefield's tortoise require soaking no more than once every two weeks. Forest and field dwellers such as the box turtle and red-footed tortoise, on the other hand, can use a twice-weekly soak. The best plan is to put the tortoises in your bathtub, although a pie pan placed in the cage for half a day will serve. *In no case should the water be deeper than half the height of the shell!* If the fleshy parts of the animal are covered, the depth is sufficient.

Lighting and Heating the Land Cage

In a sense, a land cage can be treated like an aquatic turtle's basking spot when it comes to light and heat. The incandescent spotlight of appropriate wattage to get the cage directly beneath it up to 90 degrees is the best heating tool. It should be placed at one end of the tank. The rest of the cage can be allowed to be somewhat cooler, the end farthest from the heat lamp falling to room temperature. Remember that turtles, like all reptiles, must regulate their body temperature by moving into and out of the heat. The cage must be set up to allow them to do this, just like the lizard cage.

Many years ago, I had a baby Indian starred tortoise *(Geochelone elegans)*. The little fellow was in miserable shape when I got him. All the warming and cajoling, all the succulent greens and luscious fruits I proffered barely got him to nod his head. He drank rarely and ate less than a meditating yogi. I was about to give up on him when it occurred to me to try some ultraviolet. I moved a large bank of full-wave bulbs over his tank and turned them on. Within three days he was transformed from something resembling a mushroom into an active fellow who couldn't get enough pears and spinach. The moral of the story is very simply that while a spotlight serves to heat the land-turtle pen, it does not provide the ultraviolet that land turtles, like aquatics, need so badly. For details on providing as much in the way of artificial sunlight as possible, see the information in the aquatics section.

FEEDING YOUR TURTLE

You already know that turtles frequent a wide variety of habitats and show lots of different preferences when it comes to land or water. Chelonian dietary tastes and habits are equally electic. Some turtles enjoy fruits and vegetables, some crave meat. Some relish fish, others fowl. I have even kept animals that would refuse anything but whole, live, snails! All this individuality makes it a bit difficult to generalize. For starters, I am going to have to treat land turtles and aquatics separately.

Feeding Aquatics

Feeding a water turtle can be either a straightforward, hassle-free process or a terrible chore. Water turtles, you see, are absolute slobs. They rip and tear, bite and spit out, eviscerate and claw even the smallest, nearest morsel offered them. Even if you kept a solitary three-inch turtle in a one-hundred-gallon tank, feeding him there would turn the tank into a foul and reeking mess in short order. To make life easy, you must therefore take this cardinal rule to heart: *Never feed your turtle in his tank!* Instead, you must remove the animal from his home and provide him with a feeding container from which he cannot escape and which is still small enough to be manageable. Aluminum dog dishes, Tupperware boxes and even the bathroom sink can be acceptable dining quarters. To prepare the dining area, first fill it with water just a bit warmer than what the turtle lives in. (Remember that the speed of a turtle's bodily processes is intimately linked, as in all reptiles, with temperature. Warming the water "speeds him up" and whets his appetite.) Next place the turtle in it, and then the food. When he stops eating, return him to his clean, unfouled home. (Water in a small container cools fast. This will slow your pet down again, retarding digestion and making food putrify in the gut. Return him to his home when the feed container cools to room temperature.)

Because the tongues of aquatic turtles are not the best at drawing food into the mouth, moving it into the right position and then shoving it down the throat, most water turtles drink some as they eat, using water to help swallow. When you fill the feeding container with warm water, fill it to a depth that just covers your pet's head. This will allow him to perceive and swallow his food while not giving him so much warm, deep water that he thinks he's on vacation!

Adult and almost-adult turtles do fine on a schedule of two feedings per week. Young turtles should be fed every other day. If you have somehow procured a hatchling (turtles under four inches long are illegal to sell), you will need to feed it every day.

You know where, why and how often, but you still don't know exactly what you should be feeding your pet. I have prepared a list below. The best course of action is to try a bit of everything in hopes of discovering what your pet's preferences are. Of the items I have listed, fresh, live goldfish or guppies are the most nutritionally complete, as they include all the various parts of the animal. Many aquatic turtles will kill and devour such aquarium fish, and this should be encouraged. When purchasing these fish for food, be sure to tell the shopkeeper your intent. You will pay less that way! Raw, sliced fish, by the way, can be cut into meal-sized bits and put in the freezer. This will allow you to remove one meal at a time and store the rest indefinitely.

1. raw smelt
2. raw carp
3. raw shrimp
4. raw halibut or scrod
5. live goldfish
6. live guppies
7. lean beef (turtles have a hard time digesting fat)
8. fresh spinach
9. fresh berries
10. banana
11. fresh peach
12. canned cat food (no visible fat)
13. earthworms
14. crickets

Many turtles, particularly if they are exotic, are not terribly well known to science. If we don't know exactly what they eat in the wild, it is hard to know whether they are getting what they need in captivity. To maximize the chances that you are providing what your pet requires, vary his diet as much as possible. *The greater the variety of food your pet accepts, the healthier he will be!* The list above is a jumping-off point. Your creativity is called for here. There are just a few food items that you should stay away from. Lettuce is a no-no, as it has no nutritional value and causes diarrhea. Hamburger meat should not be used, as it is too high in fat (which turtles digest poorly). Commercial "turtle diets" are also not recommended, as these contain no substantive nutrition.

If you could provide an ideal, balanced diet, vitamin and mineral supplements would be unnecessary. I have explained, though, that half the time we don't even know what a balanced diet is! Thus a multivitamin powder made for puppies or kittens can help if sprinkled lightly on the food. Cod-liver oil is also helpful, as it contains a lot of vitamins A and D. Vitamin A keeps your turtle's eyes healthy. Vitamin D helps young turtles use calcium properly in developing their shell and bones.

Speaking of calcium, a bit extra in the diet of (especially young) turtles is helpful. You don't have to be a chemist, though, to keep your pet up to snuff in the calcium department. Just leave a piece of plaster of Paris in the tank all the time. As it slowly dissolves, your pet will drink it!

Copper is another important mineral that is easy to provide. It fights fungus, to which aquatic turtles are sometimes prone. All you need do to ensure that your pet is getting enough copper is drop a couple of pennies in the home tank and let them lie there, releasing tiny amounts of copper into the water!

Feeding Land Turtles

Land turtles, particularly tortoises, are big on grazing. They munch a bit here, meander a bit and munch a bit there. They can also use their tongues a lot better than their aquatic cousins. I wouldn't enter one in a French-kissing contest, mind you, but when it comes to moving food around in the oral cavity, they do a pretty fair job. With these habits and abilities, you can see that a feeding container is unnecessary. Instead, a paper plate or a pie tin piled high with the daily fare is all that is called for.

Land-turtle feeding took a giant step the day the food processor was invented. If you own a blender or a food processor, preparing food for your pet becomes a lot of fun. Here is a list of foods from which you can choose. A mélange of many, just as for aquatics, increases the chance that you are covering all the nutritional bases. Just toss a bunch of these into your kitchen machine and stop blending when you reach the lumpy-mush stage. There should still be recognizable bits in the mix, but it should be fairly well pureed.

1. fresh spinach
2. kale
3. squash (yellow, acorn or zucchini)
4. berries of all types
5. dandelions and other flowers
6. melons of all types
7. oranges

8. peaches
9. tangerines
11. nectarines
11. grapes
12. plums
13. bananas
14. apples
15. carrots
16. worms of various types
17. *lean* dog or cat food

Again, your imagination is the only limiting factor, but remember that these animals *generally* need more vegetable matter than meat. The only exceptions are the box and wood turtles (general *Clemmys, Geomyda, Heosemys, Cuora, Terrepene*), which are big eaters of lean dog or cat food and insects such as crickets. Meat requirements of tortoises, especially young ones, is a hotly debated topic among experts. Until we know precisely how much meat they need, I would give tortoises meat once a week to be on the safe side.

All this variety is well and good, but what do you do if your pet refuses anything but, say, apple? Well, that is where the blender *really* earns its keep. Take a couple of apples and toss them (cored of course, as the seeds are poisonous) into the blender along with a small amount of some other items you want your pet to munch. You might add some kale, for example, and some cat food. Punch the blender and, voilà! you have apple-flavored health mix! With any luck, your pet will eat the meal and not even know he is eating some things he has previously disdained. I have used this method to wean land turtles from an addiction to lettuce. Lettuce is relished by many herbivores, but contains nothing of any value except water and a pleasant taste. If your land turtle is stubborn and refuses some of the hardier items on the menu, use the blender to make a lettuce-flavored mix that will be more nutritious. Gradually reduce the lettuce content of the mix until your pet is eating just what you want him to.

Using the blender or food processor it is possible to entice your pet into eating many things. Remember to enrich the diet by introducing as many different food items as possible. The same vitamins I recommend for aquatics should be added to the puree as well. Calcium is as important for land turtles (particularly young ones) as it is for aquatics. Since you can't dissolve a piece of plaster in your tortoise pen, add calcium in the form of calcium phosphate (available from your pharmacy without a prescription). Land turtles are not especially prone to fungus, so you can forget throwing pennies into the cage. Just keeping a turtle is enough to bring you luck!

ACQUIRING A TURTLE

Picking your way through the world of differently shaped and colored turtles can be a bit overwhelming. I suggest that you read this section and then go out and *see* some turtles, either in a zoo or in a pet shop. After you know what you want, the next step is to shop for it. I have provided lots of information about where to buy your reptile in the snake chapter, and you should review that section now. Snakes, lizards and turtles are all reptiles, as you know, and are thus handled by the same dealers. As a brief reminder, recall that while mail-order houses may offer lower prices, your local pet shop is probably the place to buy your pet. You can gain valuable information from a pet shop regarding specifics of care, diet and the age and sex of the animal. You can also perform a basic "physical" on your prospective pet when he is there at hand rather than a number on a price list.

In certain parts of the country you may be able to just walk out and catch a turtle, either crossing the road or sunning itself on a rock. If you do go out "turtle hunting," be sure to carry a field guide along so that you know what type of animal you have caught. Go through the guide briefly *before* you go out. Research things a bit. It is not fair to the animal to simply pluck it from the wild and then toss it out the back door when it turns out not to be the kind you want.

Age, Sex and Eggs

When we discussed lizards and snakes, I made the point that starting with a young animal was important for a number of reasons. When it comes to turtles, everything changes. Turtles live forever (or at least as long as you let them), they are not vicious and they usually eat readily and with gusto. This makes our job a lot easier, for a turtle of virtually any age will do. The situation that might mandate a younger turtle is one in which your space and budget limit you to a small cage (bearing in mind, of course, that turtles less than four inches long are banned from sale by law in most states). Like all reptiles, turtles grow throughout their lives, so a well-fed older turtle is generally a larger turtle and his age may thus indirectly become a factor. Fortunately, most turtles grow slowly enough that you should be able to cope with your pet's changing size should you start small.

Size is also the only factor that might bear on your preferring one sex over the other. In most species one gender or other is the larger. Most often the female exceeds the male in size. (Naturally, I cannot give you information for every species, but field guides and your local pet shop may be able to help.) You can have your choice without too much difficulty, because unlike lizards and snakes, turtles are not cryptic about their sex. A male's plastron (lower shell) is usually concave to accommodate the swell of the female's carapace (upper shell) during copulation. A female turtle usually has a flat or even slightly convex plastron. The tail can be another characteristic for distinguishing between the sexes. Since the base of the tail houses the penis, the male's tail is usually the more robust.

A newly procured male can do relatively little in a biological way to surprise you. A new female, however, may have quite a treat in store! Though the chance is but minuscule, your new female pet may just be gravid (pregnant) and lay some eggs (see the turtle biology section for more about turtle reproduction) on your doorstep. Hatching turtle eggs is an involved and tricky business. The best plan is to take the eggs and bury them two-thirds of the way in sterile earth (available in garden shops as "Redi-Earth"). Keep them enclosed in a plastic sweater box or the like. They should be moist but not damp. Generally the incubation period is approximately two months, but be sure to contact your local zoo for further hatching information and advice. Hatching turtle eggs is well worth the trouble just for the experience it provides!

Healthy or Sickly?

I have said already that turtles can hang on to life with a tough and lasting grasp. A sick individual is slow to weaken, so an animal that shows obvious signs of illness is probably in an advanced state of decline. While I cannot go into the treatment of ailing chelonians here, I can give you a checklist to run through just to make sure that your prospective pet is a healthy one:

1. Are the eyes open, clear and bright? If not, will the turtle open his eyes if you tap the shell with your fingernail? Swollen or puffy eyes are nearly always a sign of disease or malnutrition. In some cases an otherwise healthy tortoise cannot open his eyes because he is dehydrated. If the limbs look a bit shrunken and there is no water in the pen, the animal could simply be too "dried out." To tell whether lack of water is the culprit, offer the turtle a drink. If he drinks instantly and deeply, an abnormal thing to do when you are in the hands of a giant with uncertain intent (you), he may be okay.

2. Does the turtle have all his limbs and toes? A "handicapped" turtle, like a three-legged dog, will adapt well to his loss and may not show a problem when he walks. Pick up the animal and look it over carefully. A terrestrial turtle may retreat into his shell. If he does so, put him down and wait. If no action is forthcoming, place the animal in a shallow tin of cool water. Try offering a tasty food item. If none of this works, come back another time. Don't buy a turtle you can't really see!

3. Is the shell firm and whole? With the exception of the soft-shelled turtles (*Trionyx* sp.) and hatchlings of any species, the animal should have a tough coat of armor. Take the rear margins of the shell between your fingers and try to wiggle them up and down. There should be little or no flex. Next, position your thumb in the center of the plastron and press firmly. The shell should feel firm. If there are scars, breaks or pits in the shell, pick at them with your fingernail. They should not flake or chip. If they do, reject the animal, as he is likely suffering from a fungus.

4. Is the animal alert; does it respond to you? I don't mean to suggest that a turtle should run at you, tail wagging and tongue hanging out. A response can be a sharp exhalation and retreat into the shell. Any type of response is okay, but ignore a turtle who ignores you!

5. Is the turtle strong? When you grasp a limb and pull gently, the turtle should pull back with surprising strength. Turtles are *powerful* little creatures. All that shell conceals a lot of muscle. If the animal seems flaccid or limp, don't buy it.

6. Is the skin free of sores and parasites? Sores heal (it helps to

paint them with an antiseptic scrub such as Betadine), but scars and abrasions can tell you that the animal has been mistreated. Parasites on the animal's external surfaces can be plucked off without further ado, but may indicate that the turtle came from an area where *internal* parasites such as tapeworms were also a problem. Parasites living inside an animal can be a real threat to your pet.

The overall sense you should get from your prospective pet is one of alertness and vigor. He may be stubborn, but his heart is in whatever he does. When you find the right turtle, using the guidelines I have given, you will know it. It will "feel" right!

TURTLES I RECOMMEND

Since there are only about three hundred species of turtles in the world, it is easy to love the whole group. Still, I can't very well recommend *all* turtles, as many are simply not feasible pets. A seven-foot, twelve-hundred-pound leatherback sea turtle, for instance, wouldn't fit in your apartment, while a two-foot-long Ganges soft-shell would be too feisty to handle and too tough to procure.

As usual in choosing the species to recommend, I have picked hardy, available animals that shouldn't break the bank. Yet I also wanted to be sure to come up with a group that did a good job of emphasizing the true diversity of turtles. To ensure that I have included turtles from all walks (and swims) of life, I have begun my offerings with the most water-loving turtles and moved to the confirmed landlubbers.

1. Common musk turtle *(Sternotherus odoratus)*

Our Eastern states are the home of the first turtle on the list. The common musk turtle, or "stinkpot" is a truly diminutive species. The carapace is black or dark brown and the plastron is reduced (meaning that it is small and leaves a lot of flesh exposed). Although lines on the head and little, wartlike barbels under the chin are the only markings, the musk turtle manages to be really cute. The hatchlings are less than an inch long, making them among the very smallest of turtles. Back in the days when one could legally buy hatchlings, I happened across a baby musk turtle in a pet shop. The little fellow was so small he was barely distinguishable as a turtle. I brought him

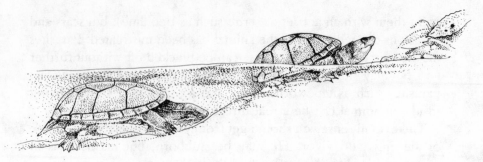

Common musk turtle; common mud turtle

home and put him into a community tank with some other very young animals. He immediately went for the bottom, where he hid behind a rock for a time. Once he was used to the enclosure, he came out and started cruising around the tank, beating up on everybody. The little creature was the ruler of the cage!

Sometimes if you are out turtle hunting in very clear, shallow water, you can see one of these spunky little devils prowling the bottom of a lake, stream or pond, looking for food. If you make a grab for him, you will soon learn where he gets his various nicknames. The musk turtle has a set of glands in the soft flesh of his body, toward the rear. When handled roughly, especially when first caught, he emits a foul-smelling substance. Fortunately for those of us who love him, the musk turtle gives up this habit when he settles into a captive situation.

Musk turtles are very hardy in captivity, but because they become quite sedentary they may grow algae on their shells. This is easily removed with the gentle use of a toothbrush (I wouldn't brush my teeth with it again if I were you) and some vinegar. Aside from this extra bit of attention, the common as well as our other musk turtles are the easiest of all aquatic turtles to deal with in captivity.

> FOOD: bugs, cat food, chopped crayfish or other frozen shellfish sold for fish food in pet shops, leafy greens once a week, minnows, guppies and goldfish (You may have to stun them with a quick whack first, as not all musk turtles are agile enough to catch a live one.)
>
> SIZE: to 4 inches (Despite the fact that all but large adults are under the legal size limit, these turtles are available.)

TEMPERATURE: 75 degrees F.

CAGE: a straight-sided aquarium of 5 to 10 gallons as a minimum, water to the level suggested by the shell rule given
above. A basking spot is optional, but you should provide a
clinging rock.

PRICE: $5–$6

2. Eastern mud turtle *(Kinosternon subrubum subrubum)*

The Eastern mud turtle is another species that spends a great deal
of time scavenging the bottom of shallow ponds and ditches. Mud
turtles can tolerate some salt in the water and are sometimes found
in or near estuaries, though they seem to prefer ditches. Unlike the
musk turtle, these animals like to walk about on land and do so quite
well. The plain Jane mud turtle has barbels on his chin just like the
musk. These protuberances differ in size, location and number from
one species of mud turtle to the next, providing a handy classifying
tool for scientists. While a mud turtle will never win a beauty contest,
it *is* a hardy, long-lived (twenty years) aquatic pet that has a definite
personality.

FOOD: as for the musk turtle

SIZE: 3–4 inches

TEMPERATURE: 75 degrees F.

CAGE: water cage of approximately 10 gallons with no basking
platform. These animals do like to dry off and walk a bit, so
they should be allowed to do so once a week. For some
reason, they rarely avail themselves of an in-tank platform,
but will relish a clinging rock.

PRICE: $5–$6

3. Matamata *(Chelus fimbriatus)*

Just in case you are getting tired of hardy, inexpensive, plain
domestic bottom crawlers, I am going to throw a delicate, expensive,
exotic and bizzare-looking bottom crawler into the fray. The freakish
matamata is one of the strangest creatures ever to prowl the Amazon
or any other water system. This animal largely defies description. I
have had friends who were familiar with my interests and eccentrici-
ties look me straight in the face and ask me what the matamata was

and if it was alive! The best I can say is that it resembles nothing so much as a piece of rotting wood. The matamata sits motionless on the bottom of a placid, shallow tributary, occasionally reaching toward the surface for a breath of air using its snorkel-like neck and nose. Looking utterly inanimate, it has flaps on its head and neck that wave in the current like strands of algae. These flaps serve a dual function. First, they lure unsuspecting fish close to the turtle in hopes of a meal. Second, they provide sensory information to the turtle, as they respond to the tiny changes in current caused by the approaching fish. In short, they bring the fish in close and then tell the turtle that the fish is there. As soon as the fish swims in for a mouthful of "algae," the turtle makes his move. In the blink of an eye, his curled, S-shaped neck is extended. The sudden shooting out of the neck and a simultaneous opening of the large mouth sucks up the fish like an underwater vacuum cleaner. Once the hapless fish is inside, the turtle expels the water and settles in to wait again.

If you really want a turtle, but feel that the chore of removing your pet from his living quarters twice a week for feeding is too

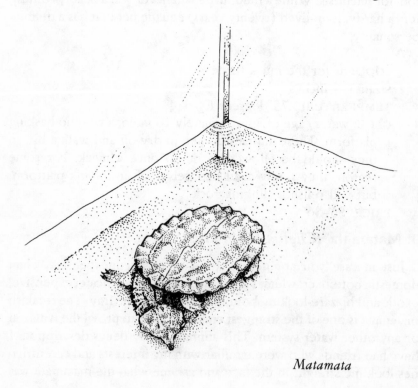

Matamata

much of an ordeal, the matamata is for you. This turtle provides
the sole exception to the golden rule, for you can feed this creature
in its home tank. In fact, I strongly advise that you do so. While its
quiet routine must be periodically punctuated with the violence of
feeding on live goldfish, this is essentially a placid creature who
cherishes the status quo. Regular handling and moving is not desirable here.

If you are a photography buff, you may wish to photograph the
matamata's mealtime activities. Don't use bright lights, though, as
the matamata comes from murky waters and likes a dimly lit environment. Like any young turtle (adult matamatas are very scarce in the
marketplace), the juvenile matamata will benefit from ultraviolet,
but keep the intensity low.

> FOOD: live aquarium fishes (goldfish, guppies) or minnows
> SIZE: to 16 inches
> TEMPERATURE: 80 degrees F.
> CAGE: aquarium without basking platform and with water suffi-
> ciently shallow that the turtle may reach the surface with its
> snorkel nose while resting on the bottom. A clinging rock is
> advisable too.
> PRICE: $100

4. Alligator snapping turtle *(Macroclemys temmincki)*

The camouflage and lure strategy practiced by the matamata is not
unique in the turtle world. In fact, there is another beast on our
master list that does precisely the same thing. The alligator snapping
turtle is another fascinating schemer and hails from river systems of
the South. Do not take my use of the word "beast" lightly, for the
alligator snapper is the world's largest freshwater turtle! A specimen
at the Brookfield Zoo in Chicago reached a length of three feet and
a weight of 263 pounds.

Unlike the delicate matamata, the alligator snapper is a robust,
indeed fearsome animal that both prowls the bottom of river water
looking for a meal and practices matamatalike deception. Lying on
the bottom, its rugose shell looking like a rock, the master snapper
opens its prodigious maw and waits. A small bit of flesh on the tip
of its tongue is visible, wiggling just like a worm. A hungry fish darts
in for the bait and, *poof!* itself becomes a meal.

The alligator snapper is well named. The massive carapace adjoins

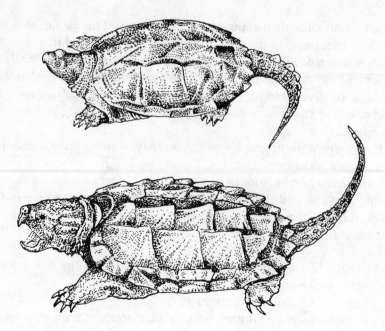

Common snapper; alligator snapping turtle

a large muscular head and long neck. Although the half-dozen specimens that I have kept over the years have never dealt me any dirt,
this animal can deliver a really serious bite if it has reached a substantial size. (Even a six-inch individual can hurt you, as the upper beak
possesses a sharp tip.) An alligator snapper can reach much of the
way around its shell, so the best place to hold on is the rear margin
of the carapace.

Between the massive head, strong, well-developed limbs and long
armored tail, the plastron of the giant snapper is almost lost. This
illustrates a general turtle trend that is quite remarkable. If you were
to look closely at a large number of different types of turtles, you
would notice that the mellow, lethargic, "laid-back" species have
thick, well-developed shells into which they can retreat in the face
of trouble. Creatures like the alligator snapper, the musk turtle and
a few others listed below, however, are energetic, argumentative and
quite capable of defending themselves. They also have poorly devel-

oped undershells that don't cover their vitals too well should they be challenged to open combat. The moral of the story is: If a turtle has a tiny plastron, he is probably a martial artist!

FOOD: Live fish are best, though this is an omnivorous creature that will eat most anything.

SIZE: potentially giant, though most in the pet trade are about 4 inches

TEMPERATURE: 80 degrees F.

CAGE: an aquarium with no basking platform but with a clinging rock

PRICE: $60

5. Florida soft-shell turtle *(Trionyx ferox)*

The Florida soft-shell is another domestic species with a reduced plastron. As you may recall, the normal turtle shell is made of bone overlaid with a tough horny material. In the case of the soft-shell, the horny material is replaced by a leathery skin. The shell is poorly adapted to protect what is inside it, but is low-slung and streamlined, perfect for cutting through the water at great speed. The limbs are well developed and powerful with pronounced webbing, allowing it to paddle strongly and run well. If you think about it, this turtle is another example of nature's evenhandedness. Like the alligator snapper, it too has its deficits (a thin, weak shell) and its strengths (great speed and a quick bite).

The lifestyle of the soft-shell turtle, despite its ability to run quickly on land and zip through the water, is relaxed. Extending its long neck, the softshell enjoys basking in shallow water, mostly buried in silt or sand. Different types of soft-shells occur in warm rivers and lakes in this country and in the tropics. When young, the Florida species has an olive carapace, with gray striping and yellowish lines tracing the outside of the shell and head. As the animal matures, the colors are lost and it becomes a dull greenish brown.

FOOD: guppies, goldfish, lean cat food, some dark greens

SIZE: to 20 inches

TEMPERATURE: 80 degrees F.

CAGE: a water cage with a *smooth* basking platform. Water should be shallow enough for the turtle to be able to reach the surface with its snorkel nose when lying on the bottom. The substrate should be very fine sand to an adequate depth to cover the turtle.

PRICE: $12

6. False map turtle *(Graptemys pseudogeographica)*

Let's leave the world of the unusual and bizarre and take a look at three common native turtles that are hardy and make good pets. The first of these is the very aquatic false map turtle, named for the fine wavy lines on its head and gray-brown shell. This beast, a member of the so-called "sawback" group, is found in rivers feeding the Gulf of Mexico. Sawbacks are so named for the serrated, raised scutes that run down the center of the carapace. Many of the sawbacks are endangered and as such protected by law. The false map, however, is in good shape in the wild. Many people consider this to be the most beautiful of the North American species.

FOOD: goldfish, guppies, lean catfood and dark greens
SIZE: female to 10 inches, males to just under 6 inches
TEMPERATURE: 80 degrees F.
CAGE: water cage with accessible dry basking area
PRICE: $10

False map turtle

7. Red-eared slider *(Chrysemys scripta elegans)*

There is probably no more widely kept turtle pet than the red-eared slider. This tough species is everybody's first turtle and most people's last. Too bad, since if properly cared for, the quarter-sized green buddy you barely remember might still be alive today. The male of this Southern species has long claws that he uses to titillate the female during the courtship dance. These green-and-brown animals are characterized by always having the red stripe by the ear and a buff-colored underside sometimes marked with dark blotches.

> FOOD: goldfish, guppies, lean dog or cat food and green vegetables. As the animal ages, its taste for vegetable matter heightens.
> SIZE: female to 8 inches, the male somewhat smaller
> TEMPERATURE: 75–80 degrees F.
> CAGE: standard water cage with basking platform
> PRICE: $5

8. Painted turtle *(Chrysemys picta belli)*

Along the same line as the red-eared slider is the painted turtle, another aquatic denizen of our nation's ponds, lakes and rivers. There are four races of the painted turtle distributed throughout the country. They differ subtly in their hues and patterns but are really the same turtle. The Western variety is to my eye the prettiest. This animal has an olive carapace with red and yellow markings. There is a reticulated pattern of yellow lines on the limbs and head. The plastron has dark blotches. Where the markings of the map turtle are suggestive and refined, those of the painted turtles are so vibrant that they border on being gaudy. Because they range farther north in the wild, the painted turtles can tolerate cold a bit better than sliders. If you keep your house brisk in the winter to save on heating bills, this might be a good choice in a pet turtle.

I owe a considerable debt to a painted turtle in my past. When I was a small boy who did not know the difference between a turtle and a tortoise, I was canoeing on a lake in Connecticut and spied something with a shell swimming by the boat. I stuck my paddle into the water beneath him and flipped him up and into the canoe. I kept him in a five-gallon aquarium and soon started adding all the turtles that an eleven-year-old boy's budget would allow. If not for that painted turtle you would not be reading this book!

> FOOD: as for the slider
> SIZE: to 7 inches
> TEMPERATURE: 70–80 degrees F.
> CAGE: standard water cage with basking platform
> PRICE: $10 or less

9. Reeve's turtle *(Chinemys reevesi)*

Similar in habits to our sliders and painted turtles is a species that is brought to us from the Orient. Reeve's turtle is a drably colored species (gray-brown shell, gray limbs, head gray marked with yellow) whose behavior can only be described as droll. Beginners and advanced hobbyists alike treasure this inexpensive and hardy animal whose calm and flexible temperament make it a perfect denizen of a community tank. Do watch for other species that might be aggressive toward your Reeve's, though, as his long tail is delicate and easily bitten off.

> FOOD: guppies, goldfish, lean dog or cat food and some dark
>   greens
> SIZE: to 5 or 6 inches
> TEMPERATURE: 80 degrees F.
> CAGE: standard water cage with basking platform
> PRICE: $8

10. Malayan box turtle *(Cuora amboinensis)*

Another Asian turtle commonly imported is the Malayan box turtle. This is an attractive turtle with a high, domed shell and yellow markings. The shell closes tightly, just like that of our native box turtle, making things difficult for a predator. Such complete protection is cumbersome, however, and the shape and weight of the shell dictate that this turtle must spend most of its time in shallow water or on land.

The Malayan box turtle is hardy and voracious. When I was in college, I gave my girlfriend a young male. She liked him so much, she aquired a female to keep him company. Both grew to dinner-dish proportions on a steady diet of Alpo and lived for years in a twenty-gallon tank. Recently I had an opportunity to inquire after them and learned that although the female was still going strong, the male had disappeared.

"Disappeared," I said. "You mean it died."

"No," my friend answered hesitatingly, "it got loose."

When I pressed the point, it came to light that the turtle tank had been placed on an open windowsill and left there while their owner went to work. Somehow the male had climbed out and plummeted four stories to the yard below. My old friend presumes that it survived, as there was no corpse but there were tiny turtle tracks leading to an inviting pond at the back of the garden!

FOOD: lean dog food

SIZE: to 8 inches

TEMPERATURE: 80 degrees F.

CAGE: a shallow-water cage (no deeper than the height of the shell) with a large walk-about platform—and a good screen top to keep your pet in!

PRICE: $20

11. Helmeted terrapin (Pelomedusa subrufa)

A geographic giant step from Malaysia takes us to the continent of Africa, home of the helmeted terrapin. This is a flattened, brown animal with piercing and protruding eyes and well-developed claws. He is only semiaquatic, taking great journeys in search of water when the temporary pools he frequents dry up. His wide mouth appearing to be in a constant grin, this turtle walks in a manner more characteristic of tortoises than other turtles, lifting himself off the ground with columnar limbs (see "Turtle Biology"). Caught too far from water, he will estivate (burrow and sleep) until it rains.

The helmeted terrapin is interesting for yet another reason. When he pulls his head into his shell, instead of yanking it straight back, he pulls it sideways! With him thus closed up, one eye surveys the world while the other surveys the armpit. So-called side-necked turtles are not rare; the matamata is one, as are many other species in the Old and New Worlds. Turtles that pull their heads in this way don't live in this country, so you may never have seen one.

FOOD: goldfish, guppies (you may have to stun them first, as this is not a speedy turtle), other filleted fish, lean dog food or cat food, crickets and other insects.

SIZE: to 12 inches

TEMPERATURE: 80 degrees F.

CAGE: shallow-water cage (no deeper than the *width* of the carapace) with extensive land area. This can be an aggressive turtle, so watch him carefully in a community tank.

PRICE: $30

12. Chinese big-headed turtle *(Platysternon megacephalum)*

Let's go back to Asia for the next step down the aquatic ladder for a look at one of my all-time favorites, the Chinese big-headed turtle. You can think of this as a small Asian snapping turtle that likes the cold. Frequenting swift-running mountain streams brimming with chilly water, this animal has a long, heavily armored tail and a strong, slightly depressed shell and is good at scaling branches. Big-heads have been seen way up in trees that overhang a stream, leaping off at the slightest provocation into the icy waters below. This fellow isn't called "big-head" for nothing, and his appetite and jaws are prodigious. Though only five or six inches long, he can deliver quite a pinch to a careless finger.

Turtles are a silent lot, but the big-headed turtle emits a strange squeak when bothered. It does get bothered a lot in its native land, as it is often captured for food.

FOOD: live goldfish, lean cat food or dog food

SIZE: to 6 inches

TEMPERATURE: 60–70 degrees F.

CAGE: a water cage with a thick branch on which to climb, and robust screening up top to prevent escape

PRICE: $45

13. Eastern box turtle *(Terrapene carolina)*

The turtles on the list are becoming progressively terrestrial. At the beginning we saw the musk turtles and snappers, which rarely leave the water. The Asian box turtles and big-heads as well as the helmeted terrapin spend a great deal of time on land. The next turtle is the consummate example of a turtle in transition. Our native box turtle likes moist areas with bogs and streams, but is almost completely terrestrial. This animal can close its shell so completely that nary a knife blade can fit in. There is a hinge on the lower shell that allows it to fold up to meet the strongly domed upper carapace and effectively protect head and limbs. There are several races of the box turtle in this country, but the one most often offered for sale is the common or Eastern variety. In coloration this is a highly variable turtle. A typical example might be dark in shell with lots of yellow and red on the limbs and head. Another might be tan of shell and dark of foot. Whatever the color of skin and shell, however, males always have red eyes and females brown.

This living bridge between aquatic turtles and true tortoises is a tractable, almost cuddly creature that shows a responsiveness not seen in a lot of other turtle species. Box turtles have good memories and can even learn to come to the sound of their name. If you are looking for a dog in your turtle, this might just be the animal for you. As a final enticement, box turtles have been known to live more than one hundred years. If you get a young one, he will live *plenty* long enough!

FOOD: lean dog food, assorted fruits and dark greens such as kale

SIZE: to 6 inches

TEMPERATURE: 70–80 degrees F.

CAGE: If you wish the pet confined, a spare land-turtle cage with a large pan of water will do. You can also let the animal free in your home during the warm months, provided you remember to feed and soak him twice a week.

PRICE: $15

14. Red-footed tortoise *(Geochelone carbonaria)*

As I have said, while highly terrestrial, the box turtle is still in the process of becoming free of the water. The last four turtles on the list, however, have taken that step. These are true tortoises, bound to the *land* by their heavy shells and columnar limbs (see the turtle biology section). They need water only for occasional drinking and soaking. Although they are more delicate than their aquatic counterparts, their firm needs are more easily met. These animals, like the others, are listed in order of decreasing need for an aquatic environment, the first being a forest tortoise and the rest savannah and desert species.

The red-footed tortoise from South America is a large black animal with a yellow spot in the center of each of the divisions of the upper shell. The head is marked with yellow scales, and the limbs often have a good bit of red on them, whence the name. You might well wonder what a helpless, slow-moving animal like a tortoise is doing walking around looking like a neon sign. I wonder too, because I have observed redfoots in the wild, shifting around in the leaf mulch on the forest floor, completely covered by dirt, as drab and camouflaged as could be! In captivity, a bit of mineral oil applied to the carapace, limbs and head (watch out for the eyes) will keep the colors bright.

Redfoots are sensitive to drafts, so keep yours away from windows and doors. Being denizens of tropical forests, these animals also like humidity, so mist the cage and turtle a couple of times a week to keep the creature's skin supple.

> FOOD: fruits and vegetables of all kinds, lean dog food once a week.
> SIZE: to 12 inches
> TEMPERATURE: 70–90 degrees F.
> CAGE: land cage with large, shallow (2-inch) tin for drinking and soaking
> PRICE: $50

15. Pancake tortoise *(Malochersus tornieri)*

When we looked at the aquatic turtles, you will no doubt recall that there were some oddballs in the bunch. Well, of our group of four tortoises, the pancake tortoise is doubtless the most peculiar. He is flat as a dinner plate (hence his name), and his shell, even when he is as healthy as garden peas, is soft and flexible! When it comes to judging the health of one of these turtles, forget the guidelines about shell. If you go looking for a pancake tortoise with a hard shell, you will be looking a long time. You may actually have trouble finding this turtle, as new legislation is constantly being enacted to protect some tortoise species. As I write this, the species is still available.

The pancake tortoise uses his flexible body to help him scale vertical crevices by wedging himself in and pushing against both walls. He can expand and contract his shell somewhat, and this aids him in his climbing efforts. The shell is usually tan, sometimes brown, and the pattern is indistinct.

> FOOD: a variety of fruits, vegetables and flowers, lean dog food once weekly if he will eat it
> SIZE: to 6 inches
> TEMPERATURE: 80–90 degrees F.
> CAGE: land cage with some rocks for wedging and hiding and a water bowl for drinking.
> PRICE: $150

16. Bell's African hingeback tortoise *(Kinixys belliang)*

The last two turtles on this list are intense water-haters. Bell's African hingeback tortoise is one of several species of hingeback tortoises, hailing from multitudinous locales on the African continent. The present species is the smallest in the genus and perhaps the most commonly available. This mottled brown and sometimes lightly patterned tortoise is named for a hinge at the rear of the carapace that allows the aft portion to fold down and protect the legs and tail when the turtle is molested. Hingebacks are moderately sized forest animals, and require a great deal of drinking water and high humidity. If their simple requirements are attended to, they do well and live a long time. Tortoises, perhaps because of their longevity and slow life pace, develop a definite personality in the eyes of their keeper after a time, and can become quite tame and responsive.

> FOOD: fruits and vegetables of all kinds, lean cat or dog food once a week
> SIZE: to 8 inches
> TEMPERATURE: 85 degrees F., with a cooler end to the tank, say 75 degrees; nightly drops of tank to 75 degrees permissible
> CAGE: very humid land cage with drinking and soaking water always available
> PRICE: $50–$70

17. Leopard tortoise *(Geochelone pardalis babcocki)*

The leopard tortoise is a large, hardy animal that frequents the brushlands of South and East Africa. It features the blotched black-and-brown patterning of the cat for which it is named. Leopard tortoises in the bush blend in handily with the surrounding vegetation, whiling away the hot African day browsing on indigenous plants. If one accidentally tips over, he is easily able to right himself by maneuvering his highly domed shell to an advantageous position. There is an element of comedy to this action, instilled no doubt by the knowledge that success is only moments away.

The young leopard tortoises in my collection are eating machines, consuming melon, various dark greens and fruits with evident gusto. These animals can tolerate tremendous heat, but unlike the hinge-back must not be kept in a humid environment. Ultraviolet lighting in the form of a Vita-Lite fluorescent bulb is essential, and sunlight very beneficial if you have a secure area. A small water bowl for drinking is adequate, with a weekly soak to remove dead skin and prevent constipation a good idea. Leopard tortoises have always been, and continue to be, a very popular pet, and for good reason. If you fall in love with yours, it is unlikely that you will have your heart broken, as the leopard tortoise has been known to survive seventy-five years in captivity.

> FOOD: fruits and vegetables of all kinds, including backyard grasses and dandelions, meat perhaps once monthly, in the form of lean dog or cat food
> SIZE: to about 2 feet (rarely) and 70 pounds (extremely rarely)
> TEMPERATURE: 95 degrees F. at one end of the cage, 75 degrees at the other, with nightly drops to 70 degrees permissible
> CAGE: large, simple land cage
> PRICE: $65 for captive-hatched babies; prices rise into the $100s with increasing size

PARROTS

Blue-and-gold macaw

B leary-eyed, I locked the car and shuffled to the front door, books in hand. It had been a long night at the library, and I had an exam bright and early in the morning. I dreaded going into the house, for fear of what I was bound to find there. My ten-week-old whippet puppy had been left far too long unsupervised, and I expected a mess.

I turned the key and opened the door and the little dog rushed up to meet me. I petted her and surveyed the house with satisfaction, seeing no "mistakes." Suddenly, to my shock and horror, the little dog crouched and relieved herself right in front of me. I knew it was my own fault for leaving her for so long, yet I could not let the act go unpunished.

"You repulsive, miserable little dog!" I shouted. "You make me sick. Look at that floor—just look at that floor!" I pushed her outside and took off my coat. A few minutes later I let her back in and she climbed into her bed in the darkened house.

On my way up the stairs to my bedroom, it happened: an event that made my hair stand on end. A strange, but oddly familiar voice was talking. "You repulsive, miserable little dog!" it cried. "You make me *sick*. Look at that floor—just look at that floor!" it ranted over and over again.

Laughing so hard that I could barely walk, I went to the back room to see Greta, my African gray parrot *(Psittacus erithacus)*, leering over the quivering little pup from the perch atop her cage, imitating me perfectly.

The dog never wet the floor again.

Greta's level of ability is rare. While pet parrots are highly acclaimed for their ability to mimic human speech, not all individuals desire or are able to exercise this peculiar talent. There is, however, far more to parrot keeping than listening to a nasal rendition of yourself chastising your dog. Parrots, more properly called "hookbills" for the characteristic shape of their bill, are a group of some three hundred and thirty species of birds from warm areas of Central and South America, Africa and Australasia. For sheer diversity of size, color and personality no other group can match them.

Despite the fact that I am filled with boundless affection for all exotic creatures, despite the fact that I live in a house full of turtles, snakes, finches, fish, frogs, salamanders, dogs, cats, ferrets, lizards, spiders and toads, I must confess a prejudice: I think parrots are the ultimate pets. If circumstances forced me to part with all my pets, the parrots would be the last to go. Dogs and cats, terrific companions though they are, bring little of the wild into our homes. Reptiles and fish are fascinating and unusual, but not always responsive. Amphibians, moreover, are living treasures that should be appropriately prized, but have no clue that we exist. Yet if there is one sharp intellect that bridges the gap between our world and what is left of the wild, it must be that of the parrot.

In terms of expressiveness, parrots are all but bereft of ways of showing us what is on their minds. Their faces are fixed, immobile masks, and they spend life confined behind bars. Yet being able to play with toys, perform acrobatics and yell phrases is enough to convey alertness and intellect.

Acquiring a parrot, especially a young one (more on this later), will probably change your life in strange and mysterious ways. More than any other creature a parrot is like a child. When pleased with you it will coo and make happy sounds; when annoyed it will fling its toys every which way and figure a way out of its cage just so that it can mess your floor. Your parrot may develop into a brilliant and entertaining conversationalist, learning all that you want it to and much that you *don't,* but even if it never learns to talk, it will amuse you in countless other ways.

Like any romance, America's love affair with the parrot has undergone some good times and some bad. It seems to me that we are in the midst of a parrot boom. This is a mixed blessing, as is always the case when an animal becomes popular. Many people buy a parrot

African grey parrot

only to find that it makes too much noise, may nip when provoked or is in some other way not what they expected. The ill-fated creature is then shuffled from home to home, getting more and more insecure and unfriendly with every turn. On the other hand, a large and ever-growing number of enthusiasts are learning to breed these gorgeous animals with great success. This aspect of parrot keeping is of the utmost importance, as the forest and jungle habitat of the wild parrot is sadly shrinking by the day. Tragically, it may in the end come to pass that these magnificent birds are alive and reproducing only in zoos and the yards of the zealous and committed.

A number of recent restrictions have come from health officials who are trying to protect us and our livestock from a number of diseases that parrots may carry. You may even have considered a pet parrot and rejected the idea because of fear of the parrot as a carrier of disease. "Parrot fever," or psittacosis, is actually an organism that may be carried by all kinds of birds. A better name for it is ornithosis, or "bird fever." It can lead to respiratory problems in people but is easily controlled in both man and beast. In fact, quarantine regulations are now in effect that have all but eradicated the problem. What used to be a minor but real danger from pet birds of all types is now really nothing to worry about. Frankly, you have a much greater chance of getting smothered by ivy in your living room than of getting sick from a parrot obtained from a reputable dealer.

Below you will find out what makes a parrot tick. You will also learn how to feed and shelter your pet. Don't make the mistake of thinking that just because an animal lives in a cage and eats seed it is any less of a responsibility than a pet that purrs or barks. Parrots live a long time, sometimes seventy-five years or more, have a formidable memory and in many cases have emotions and an intellect to contend with. If undertaken in a responsible way, acquiring such a pet is a move that can bring you years of pleasure and companionship.

PARROT BIOLOGY

You already know that there are about three hundred and thirty different species of parrots, but a number like that doesn't tell you all that much. I bet you don't realize all the different kinds of birds that belong to the parrot family. That most popular of all winged pets, the Australian budgerigar, is a small parrot, as are the huge, colorful macaws you may have seen in a zoo. Stately cockatoos like Fred from the popular television series *Baretta* are parrots as well. Lovebirds are also parrots, as are the brilliantly colored, nectar-feeding lories. Speaking of color, this is another parrot strong point. Parrot plumage ranges from subtle hues to electric shades you would swear were neon.

Unlike that of swimming, wading and ground birds, the parrot physique is a masterpiece of flight engineering. The whole bird is designed with efficiency in mind. The parrot's lungs, for instance, work like a pump rather than a reservoir. To understand what I am getting at here, think about the way you breathe. When your body is hungry for oxygen, you breathe in. Air fills your lungs, oxygen is extracted and you breathe out the carbon dioxide that is left. In a parrot, air is moved across the respiratory surfaces of the lungs during both inspiration and exhalation, nearly doubling the efficiency of breathing! As a matter of fact, parrots even store air in their bones! This provides an extra reservoir of oxygen and also lightens the load they must carry aloft.

The parrot heart is an efficient, four-chambered device like our own, but it pumps three or four times as fast. When you think about a creature whose heart races so, whose bones hold reserve air and who goes dashing through the treetops, you can't help wondering how long such living in the "fast lane" can persist. Paradoxically, while parrots don't waste time in the business of living, they don't give up easily either. Most parrots are quite long-lived. Certain species, such as the cockatoos, macaws, Amazon parrots and the African gray, can live upwards of seventy years!

Brilliant colors, a fascinating anatomy and remarkable longevity are not the attributes that most people cite when praising parrots. It is the ability to mimic speech that seems to draw most attention. While you have surely noted that hallmark of the parrot family the hooked beak, you may not ever have observed parrot's thick, club-shaped tongue. In combination with the syrinx, or voice box, it is the tongue that allows the animal to talk. It is not just human speech that can be closely copied, but nearly any other sound the animal chooses. When a parrot whistles, by the way, it is not whistling in the true sense of the word. Since parrots lack even the remotest semblance of lips, they cannot blow air quite the way we do. The sound originates in the syrinx, and the final touches are put on the product by the tongue.

In the wild, parrots incessantly bicker, click, mutter and screech at each other through the treetops. The exact subject of parrot conversation is, of course, unknown, but mimicry is almost certainly part of it. Growling like a leopard or screeching like a hawk would surely get the message across to other birds, and cackling would make great sense if it kept members of the population in touch so that they could protect each other and reproduce.

I know through sad experience just how well the voice of the parrot carries through the trees. Some years ago I was living in the Sun Belt and had a houseful of parrots. They were kept in a large airy room with plenty of sunlight.

My very favorite parrot was a diminutive spectacled Amazon (read about this species in the "recommended" section) named Yeast. I called him this because of a rare yeast infection that had plagued him when I first took him home. Yeast and I had quite a good friendship going. He was a little bugger when it came to strangers and would bite quite hard when the mood took him. With me, however, he was reliably gentle and a great trickster. He actively explored his cage and had a limited but amusing vocabulary. He could manage "I love you!" in a high squeaky voice and would occasionally add "Come here" to his statement. What made me laugh the hardest, though, was when he ridiculed himself by yelling "Yeast the *beast*" in a throaty voice, over and over again.

One black afternoon, Yeast was sitting on a wooden perch which I had affixed to the top of his cage so that he could sit unconfined and survey the world. He was amusing himself with a rubber toy that dangled from the ceiling by a long cord. His cage was located several feet from the sliding glass door that gave exit to the yard and which always remained closed and locked. Suddenly I heard a scratching and looked up to see my dog at the door, pawing to get in. She had wandered off earlier in the day, and I had been worried about her. Forgetting momentarily about Yeast, I slid the door open and the dog scooted in, heading straight for the bird cages. Yeast panicked at the sight of the dog and took wing, making straight for the open door and squeaking by before I could catch him.

Yeast was unsteady in his flight, and it took him a minute to get oriented. I was off in hot pursuit; but the call of the wild was stronger than the call "Yeast come back!" He gained altitude with alarming ease, and I realized that I had forgotten to check the growth of his feathers and give them a trim. His first stop was the nearest tree, where he roosted in plain sight, preening himself and surveying the situation. I commanded, I cajoled and I pleaded, all to no avail. He sat staring at me, unable to figure out how to get to me if he wanted to and not quite sure if he really did. I went inside to look for something, anything, that would help me reach him. When I returned, he was gone.

During the next week, I put ads in all the local papers, describing Yeast and offering a reward for a call leading to his capture. He stayed in the neighborhood, and I got plenty of calls. In fact, the phone wouldn't stop ringing, and at one exasperating point I was sure the whole town was playing a trick on me. I drove here and saw him, I drove there and heard him, but he was always beyond my reach. The worst part was listening to him. Since he centered his flight pattern about my house, I heard him day in and day out. It was always the same. "Yeast the *beast*," I heard. "I'm Yeast the *beast*! I love you. Come here!"

I tried and tried to come there because I loved him too, but his cries grew more and more infrequent until they stopped altogether. I can only hope that Yeast found a happy home somewhere and did not become the victim of a bird of prey.

I never suspected that Yeast could fly so strongly, for I had clipped his wings. Clipping a bird's wing is very much like giving a haircut. A clipped wing has had a few of the larger, "flight" feathers snipped off with a scissors. It causes the bird no pain, things look a bit more trim when you are finished and the feathers grow back. A fully clipped individual is incapable of controlled flight, but a bird in the middle stages of growing feathers back may manage to gain altitude. Unfortunately, I had not kept a sufficiently watchful eye on the regrowth of Yeast's feathers.

I am frequently asked if a parrot understands what he is saying. This is not a question one can easily answer. A brilliant mimic, after all, is not necessarily a brilliant *bird.* True, he may talk well, but in the deepest sense I doubt that he understands any human language. Yet a parrot can learn to make basic associations, saying "Good morning" at sunrise and "Good night" at sunset. He can learn your name and use it appropriately. I suspect that parrots have the ability to generalize as well, knowing what a dog is, for instance, and saying the word upon seeing either a miniature pinscher or a Great Dane.

The control of objects is one way in which an animal can demonstrate intelligence. Man, after all, is often described as the "tool user" in order to emphasize the importance of being able to control the environment. The parrot's intellect too is brought into sharper focus by its ability to manipulate objects. If you have seen a parrot cavort around its cage, using its beak and claws as a monkey uses its fingers and tail, you know that a parrot can do lots more than perch. While not exactly a Ferrari mechanic, a parrot can pull a tiny seed out of a cupful of marbles or open the door to his cage and let himself out. I had a cockatoo who was so persistent in trying to escape that I finally had to padlock his cage. Several times he watched me take the key, which hung on a wire by the door, insert it into the lock, turn it and free him. One day I walked into the room to find him doing exactly that with his beak. He fumbled a bit, to be sure, but in less than a minute he had the door open and was climbing out. What is really astounding about this achievement is the fact that he learned by *watching me do it*!

Sulfur-crested cockatoo

Okay, we have some idea of what a parrot can do, but how does he know to do it? What senses does he have, and how sharp are they? If you look at a bird's skull, the eyes seem pretty small. If you look inside the skull, however, and examine the brain, you can see that the eyes take up the major portion of what's there. Although the eyes are large (in relation to the brain size), the muscles that move them are small. This is the opposite of what you find in our own heads.

We have small eyes, but we can use them easily and move them around a lot without turning our heads. Bird eyes, though capable of seeing incredible color and detail close up and at a great distance, do not have much mobility. It is the bird's neck that allows him to see what he wishes; it can swivel nearly all the way around.

It would be hard to imagine an animal for whom the perception of depth is more important than it is for the bird. Is that high-tension wire near enough for me to land on? Is that eagle far enough from me that I don't have to worry about being eaten? These, as you can imagine, are critical questions. Yet the ability to discern whether something is near or far in relation to something else depends upon being able to look with two eyes at the same thing. *We* can do this because both our eyes point in the same direction. Parrots, however, have eyes on either side of their heads and thus are not looking at things in three dimensions. An adorable parrot habit that you may have witnessed is "head cocking," a twisting of the head when your bird looks at you as though in utter disbelief. When your parrot does this, his brain takes two or three views of you and interprets the information. Pretty soon your pet has an idea of how far away you are and what you really look like. Parrots must take several views while they are flying too, in order to see precisely where they are in relation to what is around them.

I have gone into some detail about the way a parrot sees because the rest of the bird's senses are not nearly as interesting. The sense of smell in a parrot is very limited, as is the sense of taste. Birds have very few taste buds, and those that they do have are located a bit down the throat rather than on the tongue. If a parrot likes the way dinner looks, he doesn't care if it smells like an old sneaker, he will eat it.

Lacking the ability to perceive all the wonderful sounds made by its friends would certainly handicap the socially oriented parrot. In order to repeat "Polly wanna cracker" your pet has to be able to hear it! A parrot's hearing is as good as you might expect, considering the important role of his voice. Compared with our own ears, those of the parrot are a bit less sensitive to low tones and a bit more sensitive to the high notes.

Another special feature of bird biology is feathers. All the other animals we have considered in this book have either smooth skin or scales. A bird's feathers serve a couple of functions; they allow him to fly and they keep him warm. A pet bird spends a lot of his time preening his feathers. This activity bears some resemblance to tuning up the engine in your car and checking to be sure there is air in the tires. Without such attentions, your car will not ride very well. By the same token, a bird's feathers must be in good shape for it to fly properly. When you notice a parrot taking its feathers in its beak and smoothing them through, the bird is simply grooming itself, making sure everything is in "top flight" condition. The action of the beak is important, since the feathers are composed of hundreds of little "branches" much like a pine tree. If these are all awry, the contour of the feather is not at its best for flying. To preen, the bird first dips his beak in an area at the rear of his body called the uropygial, or "preen," gland. This gland secretes oil that protects and conditions the feathers. Next he takes his slightly oily beak and runs his feather through it in the direction in which the little branches grow. This puts the feather in order.

While the specifics of breeding parrots are well beyond the scope of this book, I should say that it can be accomplished in the home, particularly with the smaller species such as lovebirds, budgies and cockatiels. Larger birds, as a rule, require the space and seclusion of a large flight cage or aviary to reproduce comfortably.

Reproduction begins with elaborate overtures, fitting for so social a group. If courtship is successful, the pair may even bond for life. The preliminaries accomplished, sperm is transfered from the male's cloaca to the female's. Fertilization is internal. The female subsequently lays her clutch and broods it. In captivity, a nest box is required.

In this section I have touched on some of the highlights of parrot biology. Of course, there are many other fascinating aspects to these birds, and you could spend years watching and learning from them. The best way to do this is to have one for a pet. To see if a parrot is feasible for you, read on.

HOUSING THE PARROT

You will be happy to know that housing a parrot is a very straightforward, simple enterprise. There are no special filters and setups such as you need for lizards and turtles. Foliage and humidity are not factors as they are for amphibians and you don't need to worry about monitoring the quality of its water as you do for fish. All a parrot

needs is a clean cage in a draft-free spot in your home, near the center
of activity.

The Cage

Before I delve too deeply into the specifics of the parrot cage, let
me restate one cardinal animal-keeping rule: When decorating your
pet's home, *if it complicates things, forget it!* I have made this comment
elsewhere in regard to other beasts, but it is all the more germane
when we chat about parrots, since these are among the messiest and
most active of all exotic pets. They throw seeds around, rub their
fruit-encrusted beaks all over their perch and (how shall I put it
delicately?) do not have what you would call "dainty" toilet habits.
You will thus be doing frequent cleaning, and especially when you
have scores of birds in every corner of the house, this can be an
onerous task unless your cage setup is a simple one.

The first question we should consider, then, is what the cage
should be made of. Cages are available in brass, stainless steel,
wrought iron and even metal covered with vinyl. Wrought-iron
cages are inexpensive for their size, but are often made in Mexico,
where they are painted with lead-containing paints. Such cages must
be sand-blasted and repainted with lead-free paint—a hassle at best.
Brass cages tend to chip and flake. The chips could be harmful to the
bird if he should chew the bars, and they become quite unsightly
after a time. Vinyl- or plastic-coated cages are easily cleaned and they
are attractive, but tend to be very high-priced. The most practical
material is stainless steel, as it cleans up easily and has no toxic
properties.

A cage is not only your bird's home, it is his castle. Behind castle
walls, the bird is at peace and secure. Providing the right-size home
is a bit tricky. A small cage will be secure, but too confining; a large
cage will allow plenty of space for exercise but not provide a nook
or cranny to retreat into. Parrots are easily stressed, and the remedy
for stress is a safe haven into which the bird can scurry. Many a
well-meaning owner will buy a giant cage for his pet, only to find that
the bird remains skittish and will not calm down. Since parrot cages
come in different styles and shapes, a ready rule of thumb is, as usual,
a bit difficult to produce. To complicate matters further, some parrots
are more active than others. A noble macaw (a dwarf species you can
read about below) will sit on a perch immobile for hours. A lory or

conure (smaller, more active types) will run and hop and jump about the cage as if they had just had a pot of coffee. I can, however, offer some guidelines. At the minimum, your pet should be able to stand on the center of a perch that is placed in the middle of the cage and pivot every which way with his wings spread. His wings should fall just short of touching the bars of the cage. A maximum is trickier to determine, but at any rate your bird should not appear "lost" in the cage, incessantly wandering from side to side, unable to get comfortable.

I mentioned that cages come in a variety of styles. While you have a lot to choose from, some shapes and styles are better than others. The first thing to look for in a well-designed cage is a tray that slides out at the bottom. The type of bottom that comes off completely has some advantages, but all in all, a slide-out tray is more convenient. Choose a cage whose slide-out bottom is square or rectangular. A round cage may be pretty, but you may be folding up newspaper to cover the bottom, and circular newspapers are hard to find.

The second desirable feature in a cage is a big door. At the outset, you see, your pet may be reluctant to leave his castle. A tiny door that forces you to squash your pet into a feathered pancake will not make coaxing him out into the real world any easier. An enormous door, on the other hand, makes it easy for the bird to enter and exit at will and makes it less of a struggle for you during the taming period. (See the next section to learn about taming and training your bird.) The door should be hinged at the bottom or the side. Top-hinged doors are risky business, since they can open when you don't want them to and end up hurting your parrot or your hand. Some cages have removable tops in addition to doors, or simply lift off from the tray at bottom to double as a standing perch. While the idea is good, the examples that I have seen are round and as such are difficult to affix things to and floor with newspaper.

The last feature to look for in a cage is a wire grid on the bottom, above the tray. While some experts feel that a parrot should be able to walk on the floor and thereby spread his toes, I feel that with the proper perches a parrot's feet get all the exercise they need. The grid is a real mess saver, moreover, as it keeps the bird out of its own discarded food and droppings. One of my best talkers absolutely cannot be kept in a cage without a grid. I had her in a gridless setup when I first acquired her. When she became jealous or upset (parrots can get *very* possessive!) she tried to get my attention by playing an enraged bull. First she would climb to the bottom of the cage and begin to shuffle amid castaway seed shells and feces. Next she would bow her head and wait. If no attention was forthcoming, she would paw the ground violently, spraying detritus everywhere, even outside the cage. Now, mercifully, her efforts are thwarted by a simple piece of metal.

I have mentioned the cage bottom (beneath the grid) repeatedly, so we may as well address the choices available to you. Basically you have the same choice you had for flooring a snake cage. You can use dried corn bits or you can use newspaper. Corncob bits look natural and set off the coloring of most birds in an attractive way. This flooring also clumps about waste so that it can be easily picked out. Corn bits absorb odor well too, but birds don't smell much, so this is a minor advantage. I have gone away for several days and come back to a roomful of birds and little or no smell at all. Perhaps the odor was masked by the cat box.

Newspaper has the advantage of being disposable and cheap. If you are compulsive about cleaning your pet's cage, a chore that should be performed *at least* every third day, you may opt for the daily newspaper change: Pull it out, crumple it up, throw it away and replace it.

Once you have selected and floored a well-designed cage of the appropriate size, you must set it up with a few accoutrements that are needed for your pet's well-being. Perches are right at the top of the list. Most cages come with one perch already installed, but you need more. You don't wear the same pair of shoes, day in and day out, every day of the week, so don't expect your bird to be happy with the same foot position either. A bird's feet will become cramped if it is forced to stay on one perch all the time. You should have at least two perches, and they should be of different diameters.

Position the perches at different heights and facing different directions so that your bird will have a choice of where to sit. Remember to position the perches in front of the food and water cups so that your bird won't have to eat hanging upside down and clutching the bars of his cage. In *front* of food and water cups is different from *above* these containers. Perches positioned directly over cups lead to a situation that I think you can imagine for yourself. Perches for the *top* of your bird's cage are also available. These secure with washers and wing nuts to the cage bars up top and will help the cage double as a T stand (a perch with two cups and a tray underneath sitting on a stand several feet high) in a pinch.

Let's talk about cups some more. Your bird needs at least two cups, preferably three, affixed to the sides of the cage. One cup should be half-filled with cool tap water, the other with mixed seeds (I will go into detail about seeds and other foods below). The third cup should be reserved for supplements to the diet and treats. The food and water cups should be as large as is feasible within the confines of the cage you have selected. The "treat" cup can be smaller. Like cages, cups are made of a variety of materials. Stainless steel is acceptable, but it tends to pit after a time. Porcelain is not practical, as it is difficult to clean and splinters immediately should you or the bird drop it. (That might sound a bit odd, but some large parrots do occasionally attack their seed cups when seized by a passing fancy, and from time to time a macaw, Amazon or cockatoo may actually wrestle such a cup loose and hurl it to the floor!) Heavy plastic or nylon cups are best. They are easy to clean, are inexpensive, last forever and stay whole if dropped.

Your pet may like to stick his beak deep into his seed cup and rummage around vigorously. As it often appears that such birds are looking for something of value, I call this personality type a "prospector." Such activity may not make your pet rich, but it will surely make a mess. Because of its scatter-resistant qualities, a *deep* seed cup is better than a wide one.

Many birds like to prospect in their water cups as well. I have a sun conure (see the "recommended" section) who loves his water dish. When I first acquired him, I made the mistake of giving him a giant water cup. The little guy would attempt to jam his entire body into the water, gurgling and splashing like an infant. All parrots can use a weekly bath to keep their feathers in good condition, but some seem to *really* enjoy it. If your pet is such a creature, you may wish to give him a smaller water dish, as frequent baths are better had from a plant mister or with you in the shower in the morning (just be sure the water is not scalding hot and you give the bird a chance to dry off before exposing him to chilly air). Aquatic activities in the cage seem to wreak havoc with everything from flooring to the carpet around your pet. If your pet is a prospector and you don't wish to deprive him of the pleasure, move the cage to the kitchen, where the floor is easily mopped and swept!

The Playpen and Toys

Parrots are natural clowns. It's hard to say sometimes whether they mean to be this way or whether normal parrot behavior is just humorous to humans. In either case, just like dogs, monkeys and humans, parrots love attention and require play to develop normal personalities. In fact, parrots are so smart they bore easily, and a bored bird is an unhappy bird. Unhappy birds make unhappy owners! You must therefore devote a little time each day to playing with your pet or watching him play on his own.

The best and easiest way to arrange play time for your bird is to employ an actual playpen. There are commercially manufactured pens, available in your pet shop, which are well designed. These are usually wooden, square affairs with swings, ladders, perches and seed cups affixed to a steady base. You can just as easily construct your own if you are at all handy, using dowels for perches and ladders and buying the cups. Alternatively, you can purchase a T stand and then add store-bought items such as swings and ladders to create a real parrot gym of your own design. As long as you are within eye- or earshot, the bird can use it as a sort of second cage. Naturally, since a playpen leaves a bird unconfined and unprotected, your bird can't be there all the time. A cage is still needed to keep your pet from wandering off and eating detergent from underneath the kitchen sink, becoming the neighborhood cat's fanciest dinner yet or simply falling into the commode when you are not around.

Both the playpen and the cage should be *littered* with toys, but these should be added one at a time so your bird is not overwhelmed. I am a big believer in toys. Without you to play with the bird has to amuse himself, and toys are the only way he can do it.

The importance of playthings is best illustrated by one cockatoo's experience many years ago. This bird had steadfastly mutilated himself by pulling out his own feathers with his beak. This masochism had reached the point where the bird's personality was deteriorating and he appeared as naked as a rubber chicken used for pranks. The owners were distraught and brought the parrot to me in hopes that I could help. I quizzed them about diet, time spent with the bird and every other variable I could imagine. They admitted that though they loved the bird very much, they really did not pay as much attention to him as they would like, as they both worked long hours.

Moluccan cockatoo

They had no other pets, and the bird was alone all day and much of the evening. We tried salves, treats and love, but to no avail. Finally I went to their home to look at the bird in his environment. He was housed in an ample, well-designed cage, utterly devoid of toys and with only one perch. I told them that I thought I knew what was going on and instructed them to leave a radio playing in the house while they were gone. Next I told them to go to the pet shop and purchase no fewer than *ten* toys of different types, no two the same. These were to be introduced one at a time over a ten-day period. The couple followed my advice, and within a couple of weeks the bird was a horse of a different color. His temper had improved, and he had ceased mutilating himself. After several months he was resplendent in his normal glorious white plumage, his only bald spot where it was supposed to be, on the top of his head.

Your pet shop may carry an abundance of parrot toys. Ideally, you will find toys made of leather, wood, twine and rubber. If this is not the case, you will have to fashion some toys on your own. Never fear. Precisely because parrots have such active and inquiring minds, *parrot toys are everywhere!* All you have to watch out for is painted objects that could prove toxic and plastic and metal with sharp edges that could cut your bird.

Leather and wood are great parrot-toy materials. Sure they will be chewed up briskly, but so what?—in a sense, you are giving your parrot his toy just so that he can chew it up with a vengeance. That's how many parrots get their jollies. Branches and twigs with bark intact can be great parrot toys—just check to be sure the wood hasn't been sprayed with an insecticide that could hurt your pet. There is perhaps no greater pleasure for a parrot than slowly stripping the bark from a twig with the tip of his beak.

Odd shapes and holes seem to fascinate parrots. Bits of different-sized wood can be fine parrot toys. Try wooden forks and spoons sold for salads and soup stirring. The unfinished type is best, since it presents no risk of paint or varnish toxicity. You can add a little vegetable oil to a wooden toy. This is great for your pet's feathers —and tasty too!

Most parrots love to look at themselves, and mirrors are great parrot toys. Use a shiny piece of metal with blunt edges, though, rather than glass. If a parrot attacks his own image and breaks the glass you might have trouble on your hands. Suspending such a toy from the top of the cage with a length of leather or twine will allow your bird to swing from it as well, and swinging is a great parrot pastime.

My parrots not only enjoy chewing and swinging *from* their toys, they also relish whacking the cage bars *with* them. It is probably the noise they enjoy. Making noise with toys is half the fun. Often providing lots of toys is a good way to get your bird to begin to vocalize (more on talking below). One of my yellow-naped Amazons loves to descend to the kitchen counter where I eat my breakfast. After partaking of my eggs and toast, he waddles over to the side of the plate and picks up a fork or spoon, whichever is closest. With eating utensil in beak, he attempts to climb back into his cage, a few inches away from the counter. This presents a problem, since he needs his beak to reach the bars and the beak is occupied with holding the fork or spoon. Leaning *way* over, he barely hooks the edge of the cage with the available portion of his beak. So hooked, he takes a leap and tries to grab the bottom of the cage with his feet. Dropping what he is carrying is inevitable. The only question is whether he makes it through the cage door before it happens. Sometimes he does and other times he doesn't. Once he's inside with the cage, the fun begins. Sidling over to the bars, he begins an arrhythmic smacking of the cage with the fork or spoon. Smash with the handle, bam with the round end, twang between the bars. Knock, knock on the rail, and so on until he breaches the limits of my sanity and I take the utensil away.

Speaking of making noise with a toy, most parrots love a bell. If the noise bothers you, it can always be reserved for your absence. Use a clip and affix it to the bars as you scoot out of the house. Open bells are great, but the closed, spherical type is a no-no because your bird can get his toes or beak caught in the cracks. This is a good reminder to examine your bird's toy carefully before you give it to him, trying to figure out if there is any *conceivable* way he could hurt himself with it. If there is, throw it out.

The very important job of giving your pet good toys is not only entertaining, but a challenge to your creativity. So long as it is safe, just about anything can amuse your pet and help him to be relaxed, attentive and interesting.

FEEDING YOUR PARROT

I cannot imagine where the expression "You eat like a bird" comes from! Although a bird does peck at his food, his body is a high-revving little engine that must frequently consume vast quantities of fuel in order to keep going. An Amazon parrot, for instance, will consume more than a cup of food per day. When you think about the size of the bird compared with the size of a cup of seed, you realize just how much food this is for the little tyke!

Through the various feeding sections of this book, you may have noticed that variety has been a critical theme. Often I advise feeding a wide variety of foods to an exotic creature because we are not sure exactly what the creature may eat in the wild. By offering lots of different items, we maximize the probability that we are giving an animal what he needs. Parrots need variety too, but for a slightly different reason. These birds are in many cases "opportunistic feeders," eating whatever may come their way if it is appealing enough. Parrots enjoy seeds, fruits, vegetables and occasionally even gourmet delights such as meat and unprocessed cheese. Let's have a look at how we can construct a good diet for your hook-billed pet.

Parrots are ace seed crackers. Their powerful bills equip them wonderfully well to hull even the toughest shells. A large parrot can deal with walnuts, hazelnuts and even Brazil nuts as easily as you or I can conquer a seedless grape. Seed should provide the bulk of your pet's diet and be available all the time.

There are two ways that you can purchase bird seed. The first way is to purchase the individual seeds from your local pet shop or feed store. While a bit more trouble, this is the less costly method and allows you to balance the mix according to what you know about your particular bird's diet. The second option is to buy a prepared "parrot mix." Such a premixed ration saves you the trouble of doing the work yourself, but often is either generally a poor selection of seeds or is inappropriate for your particular kind of bird. In my experience, the mixes that are put together commercially for *small* parrots such as lovebirds, cockatiels, parakeets and Senegals (see below) are adequate. The mixes that I have seen for *large* parrots such as cockatoos and Amazons are less satisfactory. The reason for this is that such mixes are predominantly made up of sunflower seed. While a tasty and nutritious treat for hookbills, sunflower in large quantities is mildly addictive. Eating too much sunflower tends to cause a bird to lose his taste for other foods. I had one bird who fell so in love with sunflower seeds that she made only a token pass at nearly every other food I gave her. When I finally switched her over to a sunflower-free mix (safflower is a good substitute and seems not to have the same addictive properties), she nearly starved herself before accepting the new menu. Since some birds can be very stubborn, such diet changes are best effected by gradually adjusting the ratio of old diet and new (the same principle as the blender tactics that I suggest in the turtle and lizard chapters) until you have your bird eating the diet of your choosing.

When putting together your own mix, you should add in as many kinds of seeds as possible in order to determine your pet's likes and dislikes. Rape (in the mustard family), millet (available on a twig and called a "millet spray"), oats, and canary seeds are great for smaller birds. While larger birds may eat these small seeds, it seems that safflower, pumpkin and, in small quantities, sunflower are preferred.

Give your pet a jumble of different seeds at the outset. When you throw out the shells and provide fresh seeds, check to see which seeds have been eaten. Look at the hulls carefully, because some birds excise kernel from shell as expertly and undetectably as a brain surgeon.

When you buy seed, examine it closely to be sure it is fresh. Seeds are, after all, living organisms, and are less nutritious dead than alive. Fresh seed has a heavy, almost puffy feel to it and will sprout readily if left on a moist towel. (Birds love freshly sprouted seed, by the way, and sprouting is a great way to introduce your pet to a seed he may disdain.) Dead or aging seed is shrunken and less hefty. Watch for cobweblike material in the seed. So called "webby" seed is infested by a moth that breeds in the seed, producing a stringy substance. While moths are certainly not bad for birds, they are bad for your house, as they will rapidly spread from your pet's quarters to yours, dotting walls and ceilings in short order.

Once you have procured your seed, the next priority is to keep it fresh. I use a large plastic garbage can lined with a plastic garbage bag for extra freshness. I seal the seeds in with a tightly fitting lid. Seeds do need to breathe, however, and whenever I feed my birds I stir the seed up from the bottom to improve the circulation of air and leave the lid off the can for a few minutes.

Because most hookbills are noted seed eaters, many people ignore the importance of vegetables and fruits in their diet. Yet no parrot can thrive on seeds and nothing else. Fruits and greens should make up between 10 and 20 percent of his diet. (Don't overdo a good thing, though, or your pet will suffer from diarrhea.) Since parrots are creative feeders, you should be a creative keeper! Try all kinds of things! The different varieties of hot peppers, for example, are traditional parrot favorites and are quite rich in vitamins. Zucchini and other squashes as well as fresh sweet corn, raw potato, carrots, onions, garlic cloves, celery, cabbage and other vegetables are good foods. Melon, especially papaya, is relished as well, as are oranges, apples, plums, pears, grapes, bananas and sometimes even lemons. There is no saying precisely what your pet may prefer. Parrots are such individualists that a half-dozen of the same type of bird are likely to have six different preferences when it comes to fruits and veggies. Your parrot may devour everything on the list above, or may eat only apricots and turnips!

If you feel the urge, as I sometimes do, to share your lunch or dinner with your bird, feel free to do so. All that you need avoid is processed and prepared foods high in preservatives. You want me to spell it out? Well, then, feed your pet all the natural cereal, chicken and egg you wish, but avoid beef jerky, salted pretzels, potato chips and escargots. Your dinner should not be a substitute for your pet's but rather function as a special occasion, a time to spend with your bird that you might ordinarily spend without him.

While it is fine to share appropriate foods with your parrot, there are certain other items that should not be shared. Alcohol, for instance, can kill a bird. While it might seem obvious, let me state it for the record: *Don't get your bird drunk!* Wine or booze is absorbed far more quickly by a bird than by a person, with potentially dire results. If you want to give your parrot a special treat, try some sunflower seeds, a dog biscuit, raw peanuts or a dab of peanut butter.

Because we cannot know the precise nutritional requirements of every type of bird, I have recommended time and again giving as varied a diet as possible. To cover our bases still further, I suggest providing a vitamin-and-mineral supplement as well. There are several such supplements now on the market, and most of them do the job. "Blair's Super Preen," however, is the best preparation I have found. It is manufactured by RHB Laboratories, Inc., of Santa Ana, California, and is available at many pet shops. This compound comes in pellets and powder. I prefer the powder, for though it has the nasty habit of going up your nose, it is easy to administer by simply sprinkling it over the seed.

If you are unable to go to the trouble of preparing a balanced seed mix for your bird, there is an alternative. A quality pellet food from a well-known company can, if used in conjunction with fruits and vegetables, provide well for your feathered friend. Some such pellet diets are fortified with vitamins and minerals already, and are carefully designed to provide adequate levels of protein, roughage and carbohydrates. There is also the advantage of easy preparation and storage (no moths!) and no seed hulls to clean up from the floor around the cage. The Lafeber Company of 7278 Milwaukee Avenue, Niles, Illinois 60648, makes a variety of good pelleted foods and treats.

TAMING, TRAINING AND TALKING

Taming

When you get to the "recommended" section, you will discover
that I discuss and suggest purchasing a "hand-fed" baby bird whenever possible. Such birds have been raised from early stages by
people. They "imprint" on their captor, taking the person who feeds
them for a mother! These animals require little in the way of formal
taming, as they are already used to being handled and fed by humans.

For one reason or another, however, not everyone ends up with
such a tractable and instantly delightful pet. Expense (hand-fed babies can cost up to twice what a wild-caught adult of the same species
will command), availability (these birds are not available everywhere
and not at all times of year), a romance with a particular bird or even
just a hankering for a challenge may lead some prospective parrot
owners in the direction of an older, wild-caught bird. A bird who has
just been snatched out of the wild with a net and gloved hands is not
terribly interested in being your best buddy. He may have had the
tree he lived in cut down from underneath him at night, or even have
seen his young molested in order to command his attention. You are
going to have to work hard to replace his wariness and fear with trust
and devotion; but it can be done. The same principles that I outline
below can be used at first on a relatively tame, even hand-fed, animal
who just needs some time to get used to you.

There is no such thing as a best, surefire method for taming a bird.
Nearly everyone who has owned and worked with parrots for a
while has the idea that his or her method is best. There are, however,
some basic principles and guidelines to use as a starting point. If you
get to thinking in the right way about what you are doing, the details
are less important. It helps to have some innate sensitivity toward
animals, but knack or no knack, enough patience will result in a tame
bird.

The very first step, of course, is to conquer your fear of your pet's
beak. I can hear the hemming and hawing already, but you may as
well admit it: I *know* you are at least a little afraid of that formidable

seed cracker at the front of your new friend! If you have a macaw or cockatoo, you have good reason to be wary, and if you are working with a *wild* adult, you unfortunately must either use a stick (gently, so as not to bring back bad memories of his capture), wear a pair of strong leather gloves or both. Smaller, younger parrots may use their beaks to grab on and steady themselves, but are unlikely to do much more. The bottom line is that you must be prepared to get pinched a few times when you start to work with a parrot. Most often this occurs when the bird is using its beak like a third hand or foot, grasping or balancing itself. It is certainly not a pleasure, but a parrot pinch is nothing you cannot tolerate. Parrots bite only out of fear. If you do get nipped, just remember how easy it is for you to overpower your pet, and remind yourself that he knows it!

All right, you have selected your new bird and are about to take him home and begin the taming process. You are eager to get the little guy out of the noisy pet shop and into the quiet of your place. Your enthusiasm is wonderful, but remember one thing: *The taming process begins the minute you have selected your bird!* When your bird's routine has been broken, he is confused. Everything is new. This is the time to begin building his dependence upon you. Dependence is an important ingredient in a relationship with a wild creature. The very first step in creating and enhancing that dependence is to clip your bird's wings.

Wing clipping is a misnomer that tends to bring awful notions to mind. Unlike wing pinioning (a permanent, surgical procedure, performed by a veterinarian, rendering the bird permanently unable to fly), clipping resembles nothing so much as a haircut. The procedure is simply to select three or four of the longest feathers on one wing and snip them off near the base. This utterly painless and temporary technique (the feathers grow back in less than a year) accomplishes the goal of unbalancing the bird's flight. When he tries to fly he spirals uncontrollably and soon learns not to try for the window or open door. (Remember the tragedy of my pet Yeast and don't succumb to temptation and let your bird fly around the house.) Because the bird does not enjoy being restrained during clipping, and because there is some potential for injury in inexperienced hands, it is best to let the seller or a veterinarian clip your bird for you at least twice a year.

Okay, your bird is clipped and has made it home. If you have a T stand or playpen, place your parrot on it. If not, put your bird on the top of his cage (on a perch up there if you have affixed one of the type that secures with wing nuts) and close the door so the bird cannot get inside. What you are trying to do here is *lock the bird out.* Once it regains the familiar security of a cage, you are going to have to battle to get it out again! Now step back and watch the bird for a while. Try to use this time to accustom yourself to your bird's behavior. Watch the way he ruffles and cleans his feathers and watch the way he moves. Listen to his noises and try to sense whether they are sounds of pleasure or displeasure. This initial day or two is one of the most important periods in your relationship with your animal. The whole key to taming success lies in your ability to understand the signals your bird is sending you. Notice which times of the day or night he is most active and which times he is quiescent. Some birds are noticeably more amicable when they first arise; others tend to be crabby in the morning and receptive at night. The best time to approach and start really working with your bird is in a calm and receptive period. Don't use food as an enticement in the beginning. If you do, you set a poor example for subsequent training. Your bird should want to do things for *you,* not for a seed.

Sooner or later (you may have to go out, and it is best to leave an unattended bird caged), you will have to put your bird back into his cage. When it comes to taking the new bird out again, you may run into a little difficulty. I had a yellow-naped Amazon who was a classic case of Parrot-Jekyll and Parrot-Hyde. When he was on or in his cage, no one could go near him. If you approached he would act sweet and timid, even bowing his head to offer it for scratching. As soon as you were within striking distance, however, he would jab out at you like a tricky boxer. I cured him of this nasty habit by leaving him out of his cage for a few weeks. With no wire to surround him and make him feel secure, his attitude began to improve. After a few uptight days he began to accept motion around the house with more aplomb and could eventually be approached without fear of attack. Keeping a bird a bit off balance in new surroundings may seem a bit unkind, but actually it is the simplest and easiest way to start things off on a good foot.

So far, so good. The bird is out, standing on a perch, in a playpen or atop his cage. You have mustered your courage and are unintimidated by the hooked bill. You are thinking that the next logical step is to get the bird onto your finger. Take my advice and skip this.

Instead, go right to getting the bird on a wrist or forearm. Fingers are bite-sized morsels, wrists are a bit more difficult to engage.

Some experts recommend using a stick or glove as an intermediate stage. Let the bird bite the glove rather than your hand, they say. Let him chew the stick! Unless you are taming a truly large bird (big cockatoo or macaw) that is capable of really hurting you, I don't agree with this advice. First, many birds come to you with a great fear of sticks and gloves. I had a blue-headed pionus that I acquired as a young bird. He was a feisty devil who struck out with his beak in my direction every time I approached him. Not wishing to have my blood let, I tried a stick. It was a disaster. Every time I got the stick in his general vicinity, he shrieked, spread his wings, flapped, rolled his eyes and made me fear for his heart. The mere contact of a stick was enough to send him into paroxysms of terror. Finally, I put away the stick and tried a gloved hand. No difference. The minute he felt the touch of the glove, he had a fit. At length it dawned on me that this was a panic reaction more than just normal avian reserve. I took off the glove, summoned all my courage, gritted my teeth and proffered my bare forearm. He stepped smartly on, and there is nothing more to tell. I can just presume that someone wearing gloves captured him in the jungle and then manhandled him using a stick. Take the bare-wrist approach and push up under the ribs and against the chest a bit to ease your bird off his perch.

If your bird keeps flying off your wrist, he will only spiral to the ground. Don't do this over the kitchen linoleum. Take him into a carpeted area, or at least put a towel down on the floor. You will avoid injury from repeated hard landings with a little padding underfoot. Keep persuading him onto your wrist each time he flies off. Depending upon the temperament of the bird, you may be in for several days of sit and chase, sit and chase. After a while, however, every parrot knows it is time to hang up the laundry. Once he is sitting quietly on your arm, half the battle is won. The next step is to teach him to step from one wrist (now you can try a finger) to the other by repeatedly pushing up under his ribs until he steps on.

Once you have gotten this far, you will want to persuade your pet to let you touch him. Favorite scratching spots are under the wings and on top of the head. Touching your bird is important in establishing the right rapport. Sometimes, though, a bird is really dead set against it. This is not the case with young or hatchling birds nearly so much as with much older, wild-caught birds. Years ago I had an experience with a mature red lory. This bird, also known as the Moluccan lory *(Eos bornea)* for the islands from which it hails, is one of the most gorgeous creatures known to aviculture. The Moluccan is a nectar feeder, irascible, loud and messy. Its bright red beauty, however, makes it worth it if you have a large aviary.

I purchased Lucy at a bird fair in the Midwest. I brought her home and tried to tame her, but to no avail. She bit, screamed and clawed her way rapidly out of my heart, resisting all my attempts at familiarity. She was one of the rare birds that actually seemed to enjoy biting for biting's sake. Once she secured a hold, she simply would not let go, gouging flesh and blood with relish. At length I decided that what I had was a real battle of will on my hands. It was time for drastic measures. I took the bird in hand and stepped into a dark closet. For three hours Lucy and I sat in total darkness. At first she bit me mercilessly. Thank goodness I couldn't see the blood and no one else could hear my language. Then slowly but surely she settled down. By the end of the joust she was sitting pretty on my hand and was enjoying it as I ruffled the feathers on her head with the bloody stumps that were my fingers. I have described this awful case simply to show that nearly any bird *can* be tamed. If you follow my advice and acquire a young, hand-fed animal, the whole process will take place painlessly in a couple of days.

Training

Once you have your bird tamed, you may feel up to teaching it some tricks. So long as what you do is not harmful to the animal, tricks can only increase your enjoyment of your bird and the amount of time you spend together. The first step in teaching any kind of trick is to take note of a natural behavior and use it as the basis for a trick. You may notice, for instance, that your bird pushes his food around with his beak before he eats it. If so, your bird already does a trick. It is up to you to make it more elaborate. If you get a wooden parrot wagon (a typical commercial parrot toy available at your local pet shop) or a Matchbox sports car, you should be able to transfer the pushing habit onto the toy by loading it down with a seed or two. After a time, the bird should begin pushing when no seed is present.

Many birds learn to bow their heads in anticipation of a scratch when their owners approach. This is another example of a natural behavior easily capitalized upon. Try giving the command "Bow, Polly" every time you approach with your hand and the animal bows. After a sufficient number of repetitions (how many varies with the bird), your pet should bow his head as soon as you utter the phrase, even if you are across the room. Playing with his natural tendencies and coordinating them with your verbal commands, you can find a virtually limitless repertoire within your bird's natural behavior. You may find it necessary to reward your bird with a seed at odd intervals just to pique his interest. Sometimes an animal as intelligent as a parrot gets a bit bored doing the same thing over and over again.

Talking

Talking birds can be a pain. Sure, once in a while they say the right thing at the right time and make you laugh. The rest of the time they upset the neighbors with untoward remarks and offend your guests with ethnic slurs. Still in all, people love a bird that talks, and Greta, my African grey parrot with her two-hundred-word vocabulary, is definitely my favorite bird.

Unless you buy a bird that is already talking, there is, of course, no guarantee that yours will. Yet there are a number of ways to maximize your chances of getting a talker. The first step is to choose a bird who makes a lot of noise. Noisy, active birds are more likely to be impressionable to the sounds around them. This is just what you want. He may try to imitate your dog, your refrigerator, your belches or your washing machine, but at least it's a start. Next, try to secure one of a species that has a good reputation for talking, such as a blue-fronted Amazon or African grey parrot. (Remember that you pay a premium for noted talkers. If you are not concerned with having a talking bird, don't pay extra for one.) Third, try to get a young bird. For some reason, younger birds seem to learn more readily and do not have as many of the fears and complexes that make for a quiet and reticent animal.

The best approach to training a bird to talk is the same approach I recommend for training a bird to do tricks. Find something the bird already *almost* says and capitalize on it. Before you even start, your parrot already has a great repertoire of noises. Don't try to make him say "Einstein was misguided concerning relativity" when all he can utter thus far is "Bwaaaap." Instead, seize upon it when he says

"Screpumbok, Candafay?" and work on shaping that into "I can talk, can you fly?" or whatever.

Yeast, my little spectacled Amazon who flew away, came to me with "Breep-da-*breep*" (accent on the first and last syllables) already in his vocabulary. I took this and gently molded it into "Yeast the *beast*!" With the little fellow on my shoulder (a bad place for a newly acquired bird unless you desire multiple pierced ears), I walked around the house repeating "Yeast the *beast*" in time with his own rhythm over and over again. I ended up with both a parrot that said "Yeast the *beast*" and painfully inflamed vocal cords.

Once you have isolated something that your bird sounds as if he might be trying to say (be creative, now!), you really want to get to work on it. Pick the active periods when your bird is already yakking in Amazonese to repeat the phrase. The only way a bird will learn to say something is through hearing you repeat it over and over again. Incidentally, birds seem to be more interested in a woman's voice than a man's. Perhaps because a female voice is higher and thus closer to the range in which a bird's normal vocalizations take place, women who I know have more success with the same birds than do men.

Those of you who feel that a talking parrot is of the utmost import but have more valuable things to do with your time than repeat sweet nothings in your parrot's ear have two options. One is to simply buy a bird that seems a promising mimic and let nature take its course, waiting to see what, if anything, your bird picks up. The second option is to purchase an "endless-loop" cassette like the ones used in phone-answering machines. Available at most electronic-appliance shops, these special tapes have no beginning and no end. They simply repeat a twenty-or-thirty-second message over and over again. Record the desired phrase once on this tape and then play it near your bird when you are not home. Absolutely never put this machine on when you are in the house! Listening to "Herman want to clean Mummy's teeth?" over and over again is simply more than the human nervous system can stand.

As it is with taming and training your bird, patience is a virtue when it comes to teaching a bird to talk. I know of some young parrots that talked quite distinctly after a few days in a new home. Other older, less tame birds of my acquaintance started talking spontaneously when they had been pets for four or five *years* and their owner had long since been resigned to their silence. It is a good sign if your bird starts talking soon, and a poor one if he doesn't, but the die is certainly not cast. Keep at it, especially at those phrases that seem natural for your bird. Use the cassette not as a replacement for your personal involvement with the parrot, but rather as an addendum to one-on-one training.

In the end, if you have tried for several months and have gotten nowhere, give up. Remember, talking isn't everything; in fact, it is a rather mixed blessing. It may be that your bird is not receptive to your voice. It may also be that he is not at a stage in his growth and development when talking is a priority. It is also entirely possible that he will not be a talker. Drop the training, but don't give up the bird. I had a sulphur-crested cockatoo once that looked at me as if I were crazy when I tried to teach him to talk. I had, you see, this particular phrase that I thought would be amusing for him to repeat. I tried repeating "Open this cage, Arthur!" over and over again, in high and low tones and with the added services of an endless-loop cassette. I would approach him, greet him with "Hi, Toby" and start repeating the request for release. All this was to absolutely no avail. He simply wasn't interested in either saying it or gaining freedom from his cage. Months went by with no result, and I finally followed my own advice and gave up. Several weeks later, I was giving him his breakfast when he cocked his head and looked me right in the eye.

"Hi, Toby!" he said with a bit of a squawk.

ACQUIRING A PARROT

I have already admitted that parrots are my favorite of all exotic pets. How, then, have I waded through the myriad and vast panoply of parrot pets to come up with just a few to suggest? How have I decided between so many beautiful birds, many of which I have kept as little friends? Well, it has not been easy. I have certainly left out a lot of great potential pets. Not only that, but my choices may not jibe exactly with what you hear or read elsewhere; after all, this is a very personal business. I have taken the same factors into account when assembling this list as I have in assembling the other lists in this book, namely: availability, price, temperament and variety. Parrots, in general, are the most costly of exotic pets, so be forewarned that you may be looking at an outlay of several hundred to several thousand dollars. For those of you whose commitment is less strong, there *are* a few choices herein that will not send you to the poorhouse.

Shopping for a Bird

When you start to shop for a parrot, you will find a vast and devoted number of parrot enthusiasts. Some are devoted to the animals themselves and some to the money to be made selling, training and unfortunately even smuggling them. Prices for the same species of bird will fluctuate wildly from place to place and from time to time. Some of the factors that influence the price of the bird of your fancy include how popular the bird is, its reputation as a talker and its age and condition. Popularity ebbs and flows and should not be a major factor in choosing a bird. You may not, after all, be looking for the same qualities in your pet as everyone else is. Not everybody likes paisley colors, for instance, nor a bird with a lot of spunk (read a less brightly colored, more aggressive bird). A bird's health is, of course, important, but it too can change. What should be very important to all new buyers, however, is age.

A new and booming industry has sprung up around the exotic-bird market. It features and supports individuals and establishments who are highly committed to breeding and raising baby parrots. While some babies are still brought in from the wild (not a practice to be encouraged, as the mortality among young and parents alike is high), many are now born here in this country. This is wonderful news, as it takes the pressure off wild populations, some of which are in dire straits. The end result of all this effort is the hand-fed baby bird. Taken from the nest at an early age and fed by spoon, such birds have "imprinted" on people, mistaking them for parents, and have thus lost all fear and inhibition in their interaction with humans. A hand-fed baby bird will trust you, the pet owner, far more completely than a wild-caught bird.

Such a well-attended bird is a pet at its fullest potential, and as such commands a high price. It is worth every cent. In fact, it is more important that your bird be young and hand-fed than that it be one of the more illustrious parrot species. If you have, say, $400 to spend, you can get either a $400 adult bird, or a hand-fed $250 baby bird for which someone who did the raising is asking $400. The latter is by far the better choice! Don't get caught up in a race to acquire rare and valuable birds just for the sake of keeping up with the Joneses. What species (or race) of bird you have is far less important than how young it is and what kind of attention it has received.

The first step in parrot shopping is to go to a bird show or a large pet shop where you can actually see a lot of birds and get an idea of the parrots' prices and personalities. Bird shows are advertised in the paper and local pet shops. If you live in an area where this kind of thing doesn't exist and your pet shop has a limited selection, you might try a nearby zoo. Some zoos have truly excellent bird collections.

After you have a clue as to what type of bird you want, start looking in the newspaper for classified ads and also check some of the pet publications. *Bird World* is one publication that regularly runs large numbers of private-party and dealer ads for thousands of different birds. If you cannot secure a copy from your pet dealer, write *Bird World* at P.O. Box 70, North Hollywood, California 91603. Another popular publication is *Bird Talk.* Most pet shops carry it, but if you cannot find it, the address is: *Bird Talk,* P.O. Box 6040, Mission Viejo, California 92690. Leafing through these magazines will give you an idea of the American commitment to aviculture and will also start to inform you about the birds themselves and appropriate prices.

Very often the best source for a bird is your next-door neighbor who, unbeknown to you, is breeding cockatoos in a flight cage behind his garage! Your local newspaper's pet section might surprise you!

The Healthy Bird

Below you will find some guidelines. They are for your use when examining a bird you wish to buy. You should by all means take your bird to a veterinarian at once and have its blood and stool checked, as well as a more professional physical performed. Be sure that you have a return or exchange option with the seller, allowing you to bring back a sick bird within an agreed-upon period (a week should be long enough). *Get this in writing!*

1. A healthy bird has clear, bright eyes, with no goop around the lids.

2. Feathers, including tail, should lie fairly smooth and not be

puffy. A slightly disheveled appearance, however, may simply signify the need for a bath. A tattered tail is permissible if the bird is in a small cage.

3. The nostrils and beak should be clear of mucus.

4. The vent (where feces exit the body) should be clean. Feces themselves should be semisoft, not runny.

5. A missing toe or nail can be acceptable if it doesn't bother you, but should entitle you to a discount.

6. Unless the bird is clipped, it should be able to flap and fly. Examine the wings and check for obvious broken bones.

7. The bird should be spunky and full of life. Let no one convince you that a moribund bird is "just moody," or "pining for the fjords." If someone tells you that, tell him you are not "in the mood" to buy his bird.

8. The bird should not be hostile. He doesn't have to be tame, but he shouldn't try to rip your lips off either.

9. The bird should be fairly young. Six months is a good age, but three months either way won't hurt. When trying to assess the age of a bird, remember that crusty, scaly legs usually mean an older animal and smooth legs signify youth. Once a bird has reached adulthood, changes in its skin and plumage happen exceedingly slowly (after all, some parrots may live one hundred years!), and it is virtually impossible to "age" him until he reaches the twilight of his years.

PARROTS I RECOMMEND

Now you know where to go about finding a young bird and how to determine if it is in reasonable health. Below you will find my list. The prices are necessarily approximate. I have ranked talking ability on a scale of 1 to 10, with 10 being the best-talking bird. My comments apply only to the general case. Birds are individuals, so don't come after me with a shotgun if your number 10 ranked bird won't talk!

There are nineteen birds on this list, ranging from the tiny love-bird to the giant green-winged macaw. The list starts with some of the smaller birds and works its way up to the larger and more expensive varieties. Remember that you will find only *parrots* on this

Fischer's lovebird

list, not other commonly kept birds such as finches and mynah birds which have less to offer as pets. To include these birds I would need a whole second volume!

1. Fischer's lovebird *(Agapornis fischeri)*

Lovebirds are among the tiniest of parrots, but their chipper personalities and bright colors are enough to charm anyone. I remember cruising Lake Naivasha in East Africa, watching thousands of these birds flit from one nest to another. In this locale, the birds live in the hollows of bare, leafless stumps growing in the middle of the lake. At one time these carcasses were trees, but they have long since been drowned by swollen, rising waters. Fischer's lovebird is quite striking in appearance, with a white ring about its eye and a bright red beak. The overall color of the bird is green, with blue highlights here and there.

That these creatures are called "lovebirds" is one of the great mysteries of parrot taxonomy. They are in fact aggressive little birds who will take on even the most fearsome of adversaries. In pairs they may *look* cute, but they often squabble, and in groups are quite unsociable toward people. These little birds can become the most clownish, active and intelligent of pets, but they absolutely *must* be acquired at a very young age. Taming a fully grown lovebird to the point where it is a reliable and affectionate pet is like trying to squeeze water from a stone. Find someone in your area who breeds them and get yourself a fledgling, or better yet, if you are experienced, a bird that still needs to be fed by hand. (Your veterinarian or local zoo can give you a good formula for spoon feeding. But be aware that this is a tricky proposition and not the best idea for a beginner.) These birds breed readily in captivity, though not as readily as some of the other lovebirds, and more people breed them than you might imagine.

My first Fischer's was a little fellow named Isaac whom I happened upon at a pet shop. I spoon-fed him for some weeks until he was cracking seed on his own. He was an adorable companion, spending much of his time in the breast pocket of my shirt or picking leftovers from the kitchen counter. He also provided companionship for some of my larger birds when I was not at home. I never feared for his life in the presence of big parrots. "Afraid" was simply not in his vocabulary. Nor was anything else, by the way, as lovebirds are not known for their talking ability.

SIZE: 6 inches
TALKING ABILITY: 1
PRICE: $30–$45

2. Peruvian grey-cheeked parakeet *(Brotogeris pyrrhopterus)*

Not as beautiful but surely more reliable and easier to train than any lovebird, the grey-cheek has been called the ultimate small-bird pet. At any age it is amenable to immediate training and can learn to speak passably well. This bird can make a great friend for anyone, even those who are a bit reluctant to own a bird. I have never met an owner of a grey-cheeked parakeet who did not adore it. Birds of this species, by the way, are available on a seasonal basis, generally in early spring.

SIZE: 6 inches
TALKING ABILITY: 3
PRICE: $100–$135

Senegal parrot

3. Senegal parrot *(Poicephalus senegalus)*

Although it is generally agreed that a hand-fed baby lovebird makes a cute pet and that a grey-cheeked parakeet is a delight, my next choice is a generally underappreciated bird in this country. Long a popular pet in Europe, the Senegal parrot is bulkier and a bit larger than the grey-cheeked and much more interestingly marked. The head is gray, with wicked-looking orange eyes, and the chest is orange or yellow. The rest of the bird is basic green. The appearance is more elegant and fine than it is striking. The eyes, by the way, are a good measure of the bird's age. When the animal is immature, the eyes are gray.

Senegals are a bit tough to tame when they are fully adult and are capable of quite a nasty bite for a bird this size. Try to find yourself a gray-eyed youngster and taming will be easy. In temperament these birds are more mellow than the lovebirds, though not so sweet as the grey-cheeked. Senegals can learn to talk well and possess a certain swaggering character that is a bit difficult to describe but makes them immediately attractive and endlessly entertaining.

SIZE: 9 inches
TALKING ABILITY: 4
PRICE: $40–$60

4. Black-headed caique *(Pionites melanocephala melanocephala)*

The black-headed caique (kah-*ee*-kay, generally mispronounced "cake" in the pet trade) hails from South America. While only a reasonable talker, this bird can be a lovely and responsive pet. He is active, highly intelligent and wonderfully marked: his front yellow and orange, his body green and his head and beak black with some blue in the eye ring.

Like the Senegal, the caique has a chunky look (his tail is quite short) and a distinctive personality. He is stubborn, and only a young individual (look for smooth, not scaly, feet) is easily trained. There is something in his aggressive independence and aloofness, however, that is admirable, and with time, thanks to his great intelligence, he can become an exceptional pet. Of all the birds on this list, this is probably the least easy to find.

SIZE: 10 inches
TALKING ABILITY: 5
PRICE: $350–$400

5. Blue-headed pionus *(Pionus menstruus)*

The pionus is a parrot whose common name is the same as its genus name in Latin. There are several different pionus species, displaying different color schemes. These include the white-capped parrot *Pionus senilis* and Maximilian's parrot *Pionus maximiliani.* The blue-headed is probably the best-known pionus in this country. Slightly larger than the caique and a bit easier to come by as well, he has a reputation as a laid-back, imperturbable bird. Also known as the "red-vented" parrot, he wears an overall livery of green, with the head a lovely chalky blue (more pronounced in the male). The vent, of course, is red.

I own a blue-headed pionus named Julian who spends every moment I let him sitting atop his cage. He rarely seems to feel insecure enough to need the bars around him. When first acquired, he was calm, but would bite if you came too close. His biting was not the uptight, panicky type of biting you see in many freshly caught adult birds (Julian was several years old when I got him) but rather a calm and deliberate action of self-defense. He has never talked, and I don't expect that he will. Despite mediocre credentials in the talking department, the pionus is a great choice if there is a lot going on in your household. It takes a lot to shake up this wise little fellow.

SIZE: 11 inches
TALKING ABILITY: 3
PRICE: $175–$225

6. Spectacled Amazon *(Amazona albifrons albifrons)*

For slightly less money than you may spend on a pionus, you can get yourself one of the fabled Amazons. The smallest and least costly of the group is the spectacled or red-white-and-blue Amazon. The names refer to the rainbow of feathers on the top of the head and around the eyes, the balance of the body being green. Spectacled Amazons come from Mexico and Central America. Because they are loud and have a screechy voice, they don't have a great reputation. Again, however, I feel compelled to buck the trend and recommend them highly, for all of my experiences with these birds have been great! Being very vocal, they learn to talk readily and are willing to perform anytime. My own spectacled Amazon, Yeast, was an actively hilarious bird. Yeast spoke often, loudly and clearly, though his voice was certainly high-pitched. I took him with me on trips now and again, as he was well balanced and adaptable. On one occasion I left him in a hotel room in Los Angeles while I went out to get a newspaper. When I returned I witnessed what must rank as the funniest parrot misadventure I can recall. Turning the corner in the hall, I paused as I saw a maid with a service cart in front of my door.

"Hello?" said the maid after knocking on the door.

"Hello!" came the reply from inside.

Parrots: yellow-naped Amazon,
blue-fronted Amazon,
spectacled Amazon

"Can I make up the room now?" asked the maid.

"Come here!" came the voice from inside the room.

At this the maid took her key ring, found the correct key and inserted it into the lock.

"I love you," said a coy voice from inside the room. The maid froze with the door open a crack. "I love you!" repeated the voice. "Come here!"

At this the maid quickly slammed the door, removed the key from the lock and pushed her cart down the hall as fast as it would go.

I suspect that spectacled Amazons are underrated simply because they are common and inexpensive. Retailers would naturally rather you spent five times the price on some rare creature. I can promise you that you won't be getting five times the bird.

SIZE: 11 inches
TALKING ABILITY: 6
PRICE: $150–$200

7. Lilac-crowned Amazon *(Amazona finschi)*

This bird is a bit larger than the spectacled Amazon. The feathers have a dark tinge to the edges, especially on the breast, which gives them a scalloped effect found also on the African grey. The overall color is green, the eye is orange and the beak is horn color. There is a purple cast to the head.

This is a likable, slightly timid bird well suited to a gentle rather than an exuberant owner. Also known as Finsch's Amazon, this beautiful animal is easy to come by, makes a good talker and is moderately priced.

SIZE: 12 inches
TALKING ABILITY: 7
PRICE: $200

8. Blue-fronted Amazon *(Amazona aestiva aestiva)*

This great South American pet is duly appreciated in Europe, but seems to be underrated here. In fact, this may be the least expensive ticket to a beautiful, really talented talker. In my opinion it is second only to the African grey when it comes to the spoken word.

The body is green, the bill dark and the head yellow with blue, hence its name. The burnt-orange eye is large in relation to the head, giving this bird a sensitive look. Unlike Finsch's Amazon, however, it is far from timid. Blue-fronts seem to have a lot of energy and are perpetually either talking or moving around.

SIZE: 15 inches
TALKING ABILITY: 9
PRICE: $350–$425

9. Yellow-naped Amazon *(Amazona ocrocephala auropalliata)*

The blue-fronted Amazon may be one of the world's great talkers, but the all-around-best-pet crown of the Amazon kingdom must go to the yellow-naped Amazon. This is a plainly marked bird, whose appearance belies its tremendous intellect and personality. The over-all color is green, with some red and blue on the flight feathers. The name derives from a patch of yellow that develops on the neck and forehead. As the bird ages, this coloring may spread as far down as the shoulders, but some specimens barely develop a patch at all.

This ultimate Amazon is a large, hefty bird that can deliver quite a nip when so inclined. Although active, intelligent and a fantasti-cally gifted talker, this bird does have a tendency to be a bit "beaky." That is to say that it uses its beak a great deal in fun and play as well as in anger.

As a rule, Amazon parrots show their intelligence with displays of affection and by talking. My older "nape," Dudin, however, is also a very acrobatic bird. He loves to hang and swing and roll around. Stephen, my younger nape, is a terrific trickster. He loves to lie on his back on the floor and dart out his feet and beak (gently) at your passing hand. He is not uncomfortable in this most vulnerable posi-tion and will hold it as long as you are willing to play.

Though the yellow-nape is still an expensive bird, its price has dropped considerably in the last few years. This is due no doubt to a great deal of effort on the part of breeders in this country. If you manage to find a hand-fed baby in your area, try to be sure that he has been domestically bred, as opposed to taken from the nest in the wild.

SIZE: 16 inches
TALKING ABILITY: 9
PRICE: $600–$900

10. African grey parrot *(Psittacus erithacus)*

Returning to Africa, the land of lovebirds and Senegal parrots, we encounter a parrot with a much-deserved reputation for excellence. The African grey is what you might call an avian paradox. It is both cheap and expensive, a sweetheart and a louse. It is also my favorite of all parrots.

This bird is ash gray over the body, lightening to pale gray at the head. The tail is bright red, and the feathers show the attractive scalloped effect referred to in the discussion of Finsch's Amazon.

The African grey is the finest talker in the parrot world, bar none. In the land of mimics, it is rivaled only by the mynah bird, a far messier and less intelligent animal. Not only does the grey demon-strate an ability to make associations between words and objects or events, it also has an astounding memory and a *quality* of voice that is matchless in the parrot world. I have related some of the antics of my pet grey, Greta, in the introduction to this chapter. Anecdotes, however, do little to convey how fixated this bird is on me and my actions. Greta picks up nearly every word that I repeat frequently in the house. She clears her throat the way I do, blows her nose the way I do, answers the door and telephone the way I do and replays loud, emotion-packed conversations like a feathered tape recorder. She also has the annoying habit of calling the dog. I would like a nickel for every time I have found the poor dog pawing at the door, trying to get into the house so that she could respond to Greta's call!

My recommendation of the grey requires some qualification. If not acquired at an early age (baby greys have black eyes, young greys have grey eyes and mature greys have straw-colored eyes), African grey parrots can be tough to tame and demonstrate a horrible habit known as the "grey growl." This is the sound the wild animal makes when distressed, and it is obnoxious enough to put anybody off. If you so much as approach the cage, most wild-caught greys will start growling. It may take months of hard work to expunge this grating sound from your bird's vocabulary. For this reason, my general recommendation that you stick with a hand-fed baby bird is even more emphatic in the case of the grey. A hand-fed baby grey is the number one, absolute best, no-contest winner of the pet-parrot game. There is no other bird that will so totally relinquish its soul to you if hand-fed from the nest. Your grey may start talking at only a few months old and would sooner give itself a heart attack than bite you. The bond between you and any hand-fed bird will be strong, but in the case of the grey it is unbreakable. This relationship, how-ever, will probably extend only to you. Other members of your household will likely be treated with tolerance but not affection.

The hand-fed grey is very expensive. There is, however, a way around this. Lurking on the sidelines, ignored by the cognoscenti and spurned by all those who don't know better, is the greatest deal in all of parrotdom. Of all the pieces of advice that I offer in this book, this is the most astonishing and valuable. Here it is, *the big secret:* There is a subspecies of the African grey known as the Timneh parrot (*Psittacus erithacus timneh*). In every way it is identical to the bird I have just discussed, save that it is an inch or so smaller and has a maroon tail with a dustier dark, brownish body. The Timneh is just as good a talker, just as affectionate a pet and just as smart as its oft-termed "Congo" cousin. The price, however, is quite different. A typical price for a Timneh grey is $200, and I have seen Timnehs for as little as 69 greenbacks! Can you imagine a more irresistible deal? The greatest pet bird in the world for less than $70! If there is a catch, it is that these birds are available mostly as adults. Young birds are a bit more difficult to find, but they are available too. Try to find one that has black eyes and you need not worry too much about its being hand-fed. For the price, it is well worth a little extra work.

SIZE: 13 inches
TALKING ABILITY: 10
PRICE: $400–$800

11. Petz's conure *(Aratinga canicularis)*

Another fine deal comes to us from western Mexico. This parrot is a member of the conure group. Conures resemble Amazon parrots and come from roughly the same area. They are, however, generally smaller, cheaper, noisier and less proficient when it comes to the spoken word. This particular conure is a green bird with an orange crescent on his head, which lends the alternative name "half-moon" parrot. To me, the half-moon is an avian imp. It is playful and active and a great companion if acquired young. An older bird tends to turn his vocal talents to screaming rather than talking and is thus a bit more of a headache.

I knew a half-moon that was the treasured pet of a lady who slept in bed with the bird (not recommended, owing to the frequency of "roll-over" deaths). It would even pull the covers over its own body and lie contentedly on its back.

SIZE: 9 inches
TALKING ABILITY: 4
PRICE: $80

12. Sun conure *(Aratinga solstitialis)*

This Central American bird is at the other end of the conure spectrum from the half-moon. It was once considered so rare that it

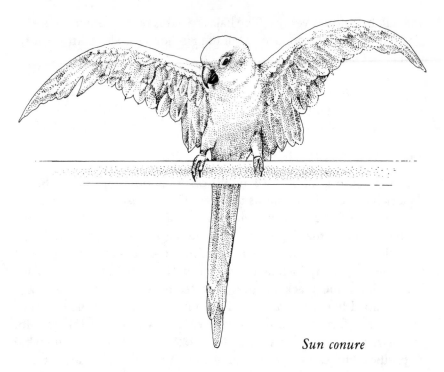

Sun conure

was almost never seen in captivity. Nowadays this spectacular yellow species is being bred regularly by private breeders in this country. When young, it is green with traces of yellow on the breast and wings. As it ages, the yellow spreads until the only green left is streaked through the wings. The beak is black and the eyes are brown. This bird is different from the typical conure, being a bit less noisy and somewhat more poised. Sun conures make fair talkers and fine pets.

SIZE: 13 inches
TALKING ABILITY: 6
PRICE: $350–$475

13. Janday conure *(Aratinga jandaya)*

Brazil gives us this magnificent conure, who is squawkier than the sun conure. Don't let this put you off (unless you live in a studio apartment), as the bird can learn to talk and is so marvelously colored that he seems worth even earplugs! His belly is red, as are his beak and tail; his chest is yellow. The balance of his body is emerald green. The Janday is to the conures what the Fischer's is to lovebirds: a little jewel.

SIZE: 13 inches
TALKING ABILITY: 5
PRICE: $175–$200

14. Noble macaw *(Ara nobilis nobilis)*

Leaving the conures, we move on to another group of South American birds, the fabulous macaws. The largest of these birds are the largest of the parrots, while the smaller ones look a lot like conures. One of the tiniest of the macaws is the noble macaw. When I say tiny, I mean small enough to fit into the pocket of the giant of the group, the forty-inch hyacinth macaw. This green bird has a black beak, with some black on the wing feathers too. The head has a bluish cast. I like little macaws. They give you much of the elegance and charm of the big birds without requiring a huge bank account and a walk-in closet for a cage. The noble macaw has an agreeable disposition and can talk reasonably well. You will often see birds of this species huddled together in groups in a dealer's cage. They appear timid and withdrawn as they cling to the bars and to each other. Once you get one alone, however, he will show an eagerness to have you as company that shines through even his strongest fears.

SIZE: 14 inches
TALKING ABILITY: 6
PRICE: $200–$225

15. Green-winged macaw *(Ara chloroptera)*

Macaws are screamers. I have to say this right at the outset. If I don't, many of you will go running out to buy as soon as you have laid eyes on one and then you will claim I didn't warn you. These are not birds for those who like to sleep long after sunrise! You can get some peace if you cover the cage, but remember that many large parrots do like to vocalize, most often at sunrise and sunset, and the green-winged is no exception.

Less well-proportioned than some other macaws, the green-winged has an enormous beak that makes for a top-heavy appear-

Green winged macaw

ance. While the beak may look outsized, it also lends a charm that one finds in something less than perfect. (It can also snap a broom handle in half, so watch your fingers with an untamed bird.) Except for a few green feathers on the wings and a white patch at the face, the entire bird luxuriates in deep burgundy feathers. Unlike the ill-tempered scarlet macaw, which it closely resembles, it has no yellow on the wings—and no yearning for your blood. The green-winged macaw is a well-tempered bird, highly intelligent and a good talker. If you can afford one (he is one of the more affordable of the giant macaws) and have adequate space, this imposing bird will do you proud.

SIZE: 36 inches
TALKING ABILITY: 8
PRICE: $700–$1,500

16. Blue-and-gold macaw *(Ara ararauna)*

Far more popular than the green-winged is the blue-and-gold or blue-and-yellow macaw. Named for his blue head, neck and wings and yellow chest, this bird has a reputation as the smartest and most playful of all macaws. He will learn to talk in a low, resonant voice that befits his majestic appearance.

I bought my blue-and-gold as a baby who still required hand feeding (not recommended until you have had considerable experience). He is a lovely pet with a curious but typically macawlike habit:

he blushes when angry or upset. Whenever he gets mad at me, or at another bird, the blood rushes to the white area around his eyes and turns it distinctly red!

SIZE: 32 inches
TALKING ABILITY: 8
PRICE: $500–$700

17. Goffin's cockatoo *(Cacatua goffini)*

The last parrot group that we will consider is the cockatoos. These Australasian birds have personalities quite distinct from those of the other parrots we have considered thus far. Cockatoos often talk, but do not enunciate as clearly as some Amazons or the African gray. Rather, they demonstrate their intelligence by using their bodies and beaks. Give these athletes of the parrot world a cage a bit larger than you might furnish for birds of other sorts, as they especially love to climb and swing. As a rule cockatoos are quite jealous and become very closely attached to one owner.

Goffin's cockatoo is one of the smallest and hails from the Indonesian islands. Like all cockatoos he sheds a fine white powder, much like talcum, which keeps his feathers in shape. (If you are sensitive to dust or down, a cockatoo may not be your best choice.) He is all white, with a small crest on top of his head that can be erected when he is excited or alarmed. There are some faintly red feathers near the eyes. Goffins are among the easiest of the cockatoos to tame and train, learning to talk quite well. They are also the least expensive members of this remarkable group.

SIZE: 13 inches
TALKING ABILITY: 7
PRICE: $200–$250

18. Moluccan cockatoo *(Cacatua moluccensis)*

The twenty-inch Moluccan cockatoo comes from the Moluccan islands. It is a very stout-bodied bird, with a coloring suggesting white clothes that have been washed with red ones. This bird has a scream that rivals the largest macaw's and, if bought as a wild adult, is a very trying bird to tame. If bought young, however, and best of all, hand-fed, it is a sweet and tremendously affectionate creature. Its considerable bulk makes it an impressive sight, particularly when it is chewing through a toy, its favorite activity.

SIZE: 20 inches
TALKING ABILITY: 6
PRICE: $600–$750

19. Sulphur-crested Cockatoo *(Cacatua galerita)*

The sulphur-crested cockatoo is an Australian species represented by several different races. We see them on the market as the lesser, greater, medium and Triton sulphur-cresteds. The pet potential and personalities are largely the same, but they differ a little in size and feathering. All are majestic white birds with enormous wingspans and yellow crest feathers atop the head. The male sulphur-crest has dark, almost black eyes, while the female's tend toward burgundy.

I have had two males over the course of the last five years, and both have been master escape artists. Toby, whom I mentioned earlier, enjoyed traipsing over the cages of my other birds and was lucky enough to survive with toes intact. Eventually I had to *padlock* his cage!

You may recognize this parrot from the television series *Baretta.* The star's pet bird, Fred, is a greater sulphur-crested. Australia protects its parrots by law, so any that you see being legally sold here must have been bred in this country. As an unfortunate result, this most personable, intelligent and talkative cockatoo is terribly expensive. I have included it anyway, as it is a popular and rewarding pet and for many parrot lovers, a pet to aspire to.

SIZE: 20 inches
TALKING ABILITY: 7
PRICE: $1,200–$2,500

ON COLLECTIONS

Now that you have a specific idea of some birds that might be right for you, I must issue a word of caution. Don't get more than one, at least to start out with. Pet parrots are highly intelligent individuals with special characteristics and needs. Some are quite demanding, and taming one and truly gaining its trust can be a long process. It pays off in spades, but any parrot is work. Two birds are more, not less, trouble. I would be embarrassed to admit how many hours a day I spend cleaning parrot cages. If after a period of time you feel that you are ready for more than one bird, be aware that some birds simply do not get along. In this case you may have some problems to contend with.

If you do elect to start a small bird collection, the most responsible and rewarding move you can make is to get your bird a mate in hopes of breeding the pair. Most birds are not readily distinguishable by sex. A special surgical technique may be required to determine whether your bird is male or female. There is also a new method for determining the sex by analyzing a fecal specimen. This is preferable because it can cause your bird no harm. Your veterinarian can advise you further.

Sometimes when birds breed, they lose interest in their human companions. If you have a wonderful relationship with your bird and you are thinking of expanding, you should keep this in mind. By this time you should have a clear picture of just how enchanting such a relationship can be. Be sure you think about what you are getting from your bird and what more you want before you get in too deep. Remember, a parrot is a lifelong companion!

AMPHIBIANS

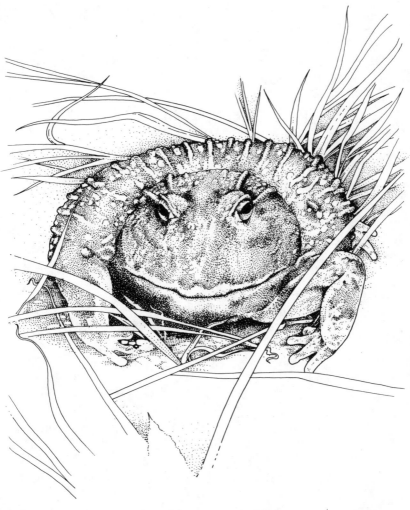

African burrowing bullfrog

On the grand scale, if it were not for amphibians we would all be minnows. Without amphibians, Mozart's *Jupiter Symphony* would be a chorus of gurgles and Frank Lloyd Wright's most brilliant creations would have been conceived in duckweed and lilies. Amphibians were the vertebrates who stood on the doorstep of evolutionary greatness and opened the door. Before we could graduate from the fish stage and drag ourselves out of the primordial oceans, there had to be salamanders and frogs. Organs and such needed time to arrange themselves properly.

Because amphibians are secretive and small, and because they are tied to the water, our debt to them passes largely unnoticed. Generally thought of as scaly, slimy, slippery and unlovable, they are actually among the least destructive, offensive and dangerous of all animal groups. There are no venomous amphibians, none destructive to man's foodstuffs or livestock and, except in the most innocuous—indeed, pathetic—way, none that compete with us for dominion over this planet. Their ravenous appetite for those crop-eating, man-biting insects actually makes amphibians more of a boon than a plague. What's more, they make terrific pets.

So who are these misunderstood creatures?

They are, of course, frogs and toads, salamanders and newts. There are also such exotica as sirens and caecilians, delicate and unusual beasts interesting mainly to zoologists who study amphibians and reptiles.

Everyone knows frogs and toads, but how many know the difference? Well, let's clear all that up right now. All toads are frogs, but not all frogs are toads. "Frog" is the name for any tail-less amphibian. Some frogs have smooth, damp skin and live near the water, while toads tend to have dry, tough skin and live in more arid areas than many other frogs. They spend less time in water, but are still tied to it for breeding purposes. Salamanders are amphibians *with* tails— elongated, lizardlike creatures, immediately distinguishable from a lizard or any other reptile by their moist, smooth, scale-free skin. Your first encounter with a salamander may have been on a rainy night's walk in the woods. Like all amphibians, salamanders are secretive creatures that spend much of their life under logs and stones or wedged into cracks and crevices. A warm, wet, spring night is the perfect time to find a multitude of these creatures.

That retiring disposition, combined perhaps with the fact that amphibians dry out very quickly when taken from their natural environment, makes them less readily available than other forms to the pet trade. Yet when they can be acquired they are well worth the effort, as these creatures can be more magnificently colored than the gaudiest bird and more poised and inscrutable than the most regal of serpents.

Is there a person among us who has not marveled at the changing of a tadpole into a frog? Anyone who has seen the tail resorb, the eyelids develop and the snout take shape simply must wonder how it all works. Amphibian biology is more special and intricate than that

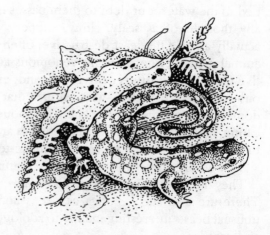

Spotted salamander

of perhaps any other vertebrate group, for as their name suggests, most amphibians live two distinct lives: as totally aquatic larva and as land-dwelling adult. You have probably found amphibian biology astonishing without even knowing its more exotic aspects, such as the young salamander that does all his developing inside his mother's body, sustained by the bodies of his less-well-developed brothers and sisters. And did you know that frogs use their eyeballs to swallow?

In addition to being fascinating creatures, amphibians are inexpensive to buy and maintain and require only the most modest of setups. If you wish to keep things as simple and straightforward as possible, a bare plastic sweater box with a half-inch of water at the bottom will suffice. Conversely, your pets will also thrive in any elaborate reproduction of their natural environment you care to construct. If you want to turn a corner of your living room into a tropical rain forest complete with pool, waterfall and live equatorial plants, amphibians will populate it with pleasure and dazzle you with their calls and colors. In such an environment they may even breed for you. Amphibians really are easy to get along with.

AMPHIBIAN BIOLOGY

Animals with backbones have not always dominated the terrestrial landscape of this planet. Such advanced life forms had actually made their start in the primordial oceans, beginning the colonization of the land with gasping forays. Even though amphibians and their eggs dehydrate easily and are thus still tied to the water, they represent the vital pioneers of dry-land dominion. It is the fact that they made the important first step that makes amphibians critical in our own evolutionary history, and it is the duality of their lifestyle—the fact that they are "living bridges" between land and sea—that makes amphibians as a group very complex.

You can, after all, talk about the existence of a parrot easily enough; it flies, talks and picks things up. Likewise you can easily consider a fish, which swims all the time, or a rattlesnake, which lives in the desert and eats rodents and birds. The amphibian, however, with his elaborate natural history, defies ready generalizations.

Before we get into the topics of reproduction and metamorphosis (changing from larva to adult), let's talk a bit more about the basic life processes of the average amphibian, beginning with digestion.

This will help you better understand what makes your potential pet tick and how best to meet his needs and wants.

We call the form that the amphibian takes when it first emerges from the egg the larva. Frog larvae, or tadpoles, are generally filter feeders. That is to say they filter water through the mouth and gills and extract plant and animal material. Although frog larvae are only very rarely totally carnivorous, salamander tadpoles do eat living insect prey by sucking it into the mouth. As both frogs and salamanders mature, they become totally carnivorous. To help catch insect prey, many salamanders and frogs use tongues controlled by an elegant arrangement of muscle and cartilage. Some salamanders can shoot out their tongues to a distance half as great as the length of their body and do so with unerring accuracy. At the end of the tongue is a bulbous, mucus-coated glob to which an unlucky bug adheres, then to be withdrawn into the mouth. Frogs use a similar mechanism and catch prey by flipping the tongue out. The frog tongue, by the way, is attached at the front and flips out from the back forward—precisely opposite to the way we use our tongue. Once in the mouth, food is exposed to cone-shaped teeth and then proceeds down the short esophagus into the stomach and thence the intestine. There is some differentiation between the small and large intestine, but frogs seem to show this more than salamanders.

The amphibian digestive system ends in a cloaca, the same combined reproductive and excretory organ that we see in reptiles and birds. The cloaca features an outpocketing that forms the urinary bladder.

Other than the agile tongue, there is nothing terribly unusual about the digestive system of the frog or salamander. When it comes to *being* digested, however, the situation changes. While there are no seriously venomous amphibians, there are plenty of poisonous ones. Nearly every amphibian is somewhat poisonous, and some are extremely so. The distinction between *poisonous* and *venomous* is an important one. Venomous animals feature chemicals that can be used in either defense or offense. A venomous animal is capable of delivering his venom into an attacker or prey, usually by a bite or a sting. Poisonous animals, on the other hand, are harmless unless you try to eat them, in which case you are either sorry, sick or dead. A mushroom is poisonous, but not venomous. A rattlesnake is venomous, but makes pretty good eating. Amphibians have glands on their skin and sometimes behind their heads that make them pretty poor fare.

When it comes to breathing, we also find amphibians a bit unorthodox. They must, after all, cope with a dramatic change of lifestyle in mid-course. How do they manage an exchange of gases when they are at first aquatic and then terrestrial? The answer is simply that they adapt the respiratory system to suit the stage of life. Larvae employ gills to extract oxygen from the water, and terrestrial-phase adults breathe with lungs. There are exceptions, too. Some salamanders, termed neotenic (neoteny is a fancy word for the retention of juvenile characteristics into adulthood), stay babies forever (even though they can reproduce) and never make it out of the water. They breathe with gills from birth to their dying day. They are not inextricably bound to the water, though. Should the pond or stream in which they live become stagnant and less well oxygenated, for instance, their gills will expand in size to increase in efficiency. And if the pond dries up completely, they develop lungs, complete the metamorphosis to the adult form, and shuffle off into the mud!

After oxygenated blood has been exposed to the gills or lungs, it is pumped throughout the body by a three-chambered heart, featuring two chambers for the return and one for the expulsion of blood. Kidneys and a liver keep the whole system clean.

You now have under your hat an outline of what goes on inside the amphibian, but what about his interface with the outside world? What does the amphibian perceive with its primitive brain? Well, for one thing, an amphibian's eyes serve their owner pretty well, but are geared more toward detecting movement than toward perceiving definite shapes the way we do. Frogs, as I mentioned earlier, use their eyeballs to help them swallow! The eye is mobile in the socket and can move out and in—bulge and unbulge, you might say. When a frog takes a big bite of something, it depresses its eyeballs, which protrude into the palate from above. The big bumps suddenly appear at the top of the throat and help force the food down like little thumbs. That's not the only remarkable aspect of the anuran (frog) eye. With the eye relaxed, the frog is focused on objects close to him in the environment. That is to say, the frog must work to focus on things at a distance. This makes a lot of sense for the frog, since the things that matter most happen only inches away. A descending shoe is an example; so is an outstretched hand or a fleeing locust. These are concerns of the moment, right close by. People, on the other hand, see distant objects when the eye is relaxed, and must employ the muscles of the eyeball to bring the nearby into focus. This is why you tend to stare off into space when you are tired. You are doing no more than giving the muscles of your eyeball a rest.

When we take an overview of the attributes and capabilities of any particular animal group, we see that Nature, while majestic, is very frugal with her favors. An animal rarely has what it does not need. If frogs are able to see things that are very close and instantly to perceive the slightest movement, it is because they must be able to do so in order to survive. By the same token, when we consider hearing, we see that frog hearing is acute at some frequencies and not at others. The reason frogs hear certain tones particularly well is that sounds, especially the mating calls of the males, are important to the perpetuation of the species. It is, after all, the calls we all hear on balmy spring evenings that serve to bring frogs together and make baby frogs. These calls, and their frequency, duration and intervals, are specific to each kind of frog, and each species hears particularly well in the range of the calls of his own species. The call of the male is designated to attract only females of his own species. Females, in turn, have hearing specially formulated to detect their own Romeos' wailing. To all the other croakers and grunters on a pond, the female turns a literally deaf ear. Without these calls, and the ability to hear them, frogs would not know where their mates were hiding and might well try to copulate with a patch of rotting moss.

At a given pond or bog, salamanders and frogs of several different types may be at work perpetuating their genes. You might imagine that with all those amphibians out there squirming around in an orgiastic frenzy, a bit of confusion could develop in paradise. Species-specific calls do a lot to ensure that the correct partners hook up, but other safeguards are at work as well. One of these is quite amusing: When frogs meet at the appointed place and time, often a marsh or pond early in spring, the males and females enter what is known as "amplexus." In less esoteric terms—they hug each other. It is actually the male that does the hugging; the female just smiles. Because of the large numbers of frogs involved, mistakes do happen, occasionally resulting in a male grabbing another male. Instead of the willing response of the female, the overly amorous gripping male is greeted by a characteristic, sharp grunt called the "release call." This is quite a distinctive sound and apparently gets the point across. I know of one frog expert who likes to determine the sex of a frog by imitating amplexus with his thumb and forefinger. If the frog he picks up is female, she remains quiet, but if it is a male in his hands, the response can be quite vociferous!

In addition to calls, amphibians have elaborate courtship rituals— a prescribed series of movements that male uses to identify female and vice versa. These rituals are especially elaborate in salamanders, who are essentially voiceless. Salamanders are perhaps more old-fashioned and romantic than frogs, dancing well into the night before engaging in the nitty-gritty. Usually it is the male who does the wooing. He may begin by fanning the female's face with water moved by his front legs. Often he waves the scent from so-called "hedonic" glands at the female with his tail, thereby arousing her. He may rub the products of these sex glands onto her to achieve the same effect.

Reproduction may be seasonally staggered so that not too many different species are actually breeding in the same spot at the same time. Some frog species, for instance breed explosively once a year, with an entire population in on the action. Other varieties may trickle into and out of the breeding site over a period of some months. There are, in addition, "opportunistic" amphibian breeders. *Scaphiopus,* the spadefoot toad, is an example. The animals of this burrowing species live in dry areas and wait patiently throughout the year for the rains to come. As soon as it is really wet out, they pop up from their burrows and dance the rumba.

Perhaps because amphibians are still busy trying to decide just what kind of animals they are, their methods of fertilization are quite diverse. There are, in fact, so many different ways for amphibian sperm to meet amphibian egg and develop into a larva that we can take only a cursory view of this vast subject. The general pattern in frogs is for the female to lay eggs and the male to deposit sperm upon them. Fertilization is thus external—taking place outside the mother's body. Internal fertilization is very rare among frogs, but a great deal more common among salamanders. Some salamanders also fertilize externally.

In frogs and salamanders both, the size of the clutch varies with the size of the mother's body. Large females have lots of babies; small females have fewer. In addition, as you might expect, if there are a lot of eggs, each egg is small, whereas fewer eggs means larger eggs. The size of the egg he sprang from, however, seems a poor predictor of how large an individual of a given species will grow.

Perhaps the most interesting thing about amphibian reproduction is the degree of parental care evidenced by many species. Reptiles, generally considered to be higher on the evolutionary ladder than amphibians, do little if anything to care for their young (crocodilians, monitor lizards and a python or two are the exceptions). Yet amphibian mothers often guard their nests and even brood their clutch in dramatic ways. In one species, the male even does the work. The daddy midwife toad, *Alytes obstetricans,* wraps his string of fertilized eggs around his waist and goes about his business taking the eggs with him. Other frog mothers hold their eggs in pouches. Yet another species takes the burden even further and carries the developing embryos right in the vocal sac of the throat. This approach is taken to the ultimate degree by frogs of the genus *Rheobatrachus,* who swallow the eggs and retain them in the stomach, where they go through the tadpole stage and are finally regurgitated to appear as small frogs in the adult form.

Most amphibians, of course, don't go through a tadpole stage in their mother's stomach. The usual pattern is for eggs to turn into larvae in a pond or stream. Frogs-to-be and future salamanders then swim around happily waiting to change into adults. The larval, or tadpole, stage usually lasts for anywhere from eight days to three years, after which an adult emerges from the process. All frog tadpoles change into frogs, but as pointed out above, some species of salamander are neotenic and find it advantageous to remain larvae.

You can see from our discussion of amphibian biology that while there is a great deal of variation, there are surely patterns. Amphibians are primitive animals that display some fascinating predilections and behaviors. There is not a student or fan of natural history among us who does not have plenty to learn from these creatures. As much as any of the more "advanced" pets I advocate in this book, amphibians display the principles and infinite newness of all living creatures nurtured and observed in the home.

Now that you have a bit of background in the world of the frog and salamander, let's leave the lofty stuff and get down to the brass tacks of keeping pet amphibians alive and happy.

A HOME FOR YOUR AMPHIBIAN

I noted earlier that maintaining amphibians can be as simple as sticking them in a clean plastic box (amphibians have no use for heaters, filters or decorations) or as complex as turning your living room into a tropical jungle. In this respect the amphibian cage offers something for everyone. There is no evidence that the amphibian knows the difference, but I would certainly recommend you make a stab at putting together a vivarium, if only because it enhances *your* enjoyment of and involvement with your pet. Let's have a look first at the simple cage and then at the amphibian vivarium.

The Simple Cage

When I say simple, I mean simple. Ideal containers for this purpose are five- to ten-gallon all-glass aquariums or plastic sweater boxes. The glass container is more attractive and less prone to scratches than the plastic, but is also heavier and more difficult to move and seal. Like reptiles, amphibians are fine escape artists and need to be well contained with a tight lid. Amphibians do need air, however, and you must make a few air holes (say, three on the top and one at each end) in a sweater box to allow proper airflow. Punching a hole in clear, hard plastic can be exasperating, as plastic tends to crack easily when its integrity is insulted. I like to heat a Phillips-head screwdriver to cherry red on the stove and then poke a clean, smooth hole in the plastic with the hot metal. If you use this method, be careful not to inhale the fumes that rise from the melting plastic, as these can be toxic.

Choose a container that is big enough so that your frogs or salamanders (should you decide on more than one) are not on top of one another and yet is small enough for you to lift easily. Two small frogs should be fine in a five-gallon aquarium. If you have very large or toxic animals (more on this below), try a ten-gallon tank. Avoid crowding your pets, as this encourages the emergence and spread of disease and makes keeping the cage clean all the more difficult.

Amphibians foul the half-inch to inch of water you give them rapidly, especially if they are large and you feed them often. You must therefore dump out the water and replace it every two or three days. Have some smaller plastic boxes with tight lids and a couple of holes punched in them available so that you have someplace to put your pets while you clean. Soft plastic freezer boxes fill the bill perfectly.

While amphibians are not as sensitive to water hardness and pH level as fish are, they are terribly susceptible to chemical poisoning by cleaning agents. Scrub the tank thoroughly using only table salt, and then rinse it painstakingly until all traces of salt are gone. *Use no soaps of any kind on an amphibian cage, as these are invariably toxic to your pets!*

Naturally, you cannot filter a half-inch of water in a sweater box. Even if you could set up a system to filter your pet's water, however, this would be inadvisable because of the substances amphibians exude that a filter cannot catch. Many species of amphibians, as we have previously discussed, sport glands under the skin and behind the head that produce toxic skin secretions designed to keep away predatory birds, snakes and dogs. To put it plainly, they taste terrible. When left in the same closed environment (a small plastic box, for instance) for long periods of time, these secretions build up until they are at a level harmful to the animal itself! Can you imagine being so toxic that you cannot live with yourself?

Many years ago I was thrilled to acquire my first pair of "arrow-poison" frogs from South America. (There are, technically speaking, a few different species that fit this description, mostly in the genera *Dendrobates* and *Phyllobates.*) These are small, terrestrial frogs that are so brightly colored in either gold, blue, green or red that they don't appear real. Unlike most amphibians, they have a reputation as difficult captives. These creatures get their name from a poison produced beneath the skin known as "batrachotoxin." It is one of the most potent animal toxins known. Before it was "discovered" by science, the poison was a well-known entity to the South American Indians. These natives still capture the frogs and gently toast them, skewered by a twig or two, over an open flame. The poison drips into a collecting vat held beneath the animal. Each frog yields only a minuscule quantity of poison, so many animals must be toasted to fill a vial with the stuff. The Indians dip their blowgun darts into the liquid and use the powerful nerve poison to drop small mammal quarry when they go hunting.

My newly acquired frogs lasted only three days in a five-gallon tank with an inch of water. I could not figure out why these costly and apparently healthy frogs had resigned so ungraciously from my care. I autopsied them and found no signs of disease or injury. I cleaned out the tank thoroughly and put it away, not feeling like killing any more arrow-poison frogs. It was not until years later, when I was better informed, that I was able to keep these animals successfully by not crowding them and by cleaning their cages and changing their water often. It seems that their poison, strong enough to sting human skin and drop a monkey in its tracks, is also strong enough to perfuse the water at the bottom of a tank and kill the frogs themselves. My frogs probably succumbed to their own juices!

The Amphibian Vivarium

In choosing an aquarium or box for a simple cage, you are limited by how much weight you can carry, since frequent cleaning is a must. When it comes to the vivarium, however, you will be constructing a dry-land tank, humid but without water, that will more or less run itself. You should pick a cool, convenient spot in your house where the lighting is dim and the activity level is low. There should be a fair amount of space, for where the vivarium is built, the vivarium will stay! Even a small tank, after you are done with soil and stones and such, will be a fearsome load should you have to move it.

I have seen specialized vivaria successfully executed by experts in ten- and twenty-gallon aquaria. For our purposes, however, a small cage is a poor idea because it leaves you no room for error. Small cages are too easy to overwater, overheat, overlight and overcrowd to be advisable for the beginning hobbyist. The minimum size for the first amphibian vivarium is thirty gallons. Remember that you will probably end up adding more creatures to your tank than you start with, and it is always far better to have more room than you need than not to have enough. Vivaria are at their best when they duplicate a natural community, permitting some interaction between your pets to take place. I will discuss mixing animals later.

Important, too, is the shape of the tank you choose. Lizards, snakes and fish do best in long, low aquaria whose bottom surface area is maximized. Not so amphibians, many of whom are able to utilize vertical space for climbing. Plants, an integral component of any vivarium, require vertical space too, particularly the types I will recommend below. Choose a high- as opposed to a long-style tank. In the fish trade such tanks are often referred to as "show" models.

To achieve proper drainage, the bottom of the tank should be covered with about an inch and a half of pebble gravel. Over this, put down some activated charcoal, which will serve to freshen the substrate. On top of the charcoal, lay down an inch or two of vermiculite, the mica-like absorbent material sometimes scattered through potting soil. This is available from a garden shop or florist. On top of this put about an inch of good-quality soil, and lastly lay down a layer of peat moss or sphagnum.

Once you have chosen and floored a tank, the fun really starts. If you are a frustrated interior designer, you are in for the time of your life. There is virtually no limit to the number of attractive plant species available to you, and there are scores of interesting mosses, rocks and woods for the choosing. Just be sure to select materials and plants that are compatible with a highly humid environment.

Speaking of a highly humid environment, your vivarium must be misted daily with a plant mister. The humidity should be high enough that you see water condensed on the glass. A shallow pie pan full of water stuck in a corner of the vivarium will help keep the vivarium humid, offer some recreational dipping space and enhance the chances of amphibian progeny appearing in your home.

I want to avoid issuing too many "do's" and "don'ts" when it comes to the vivarium. Your setup should be a very personal thing, an expression of your own creativity and your regard for your animals. Use the following suggestions as jumping-off points. Try to think like a secretive amphibian when you construct the tank. Remember to include lots of space for climbing and lots of out-of-the-way spots where your pet can sleep, hide or just plain vegetate. It is challenging and fun to create secret niches for amphibians, especially salamanders, to discover and utilize. You might, for instance, construct a small hiding cave out of quartz, petrified wood or some other material that appeals to you. Include twigs and branches for climbing, particularly if your miniature forest is to include acrobatic tree frogs. Supply some split or rolled cork bark for a ready-made hiding tube.

Plants should be left in their pots rather than put directly into the ground, since salamanders and some of the burrowing frogs just love to get down into the soil and root around. Any plant that you fancy should be okay, so long as it can deal with vivarium conditions. Philodendrons make terrific vivarium plants, as they are hardy and inexpensive and have broad leaves that support the climbing activities of many species. Bromeliads are also great vivarium plants. These are urn-shaped organisms, with a cup in the middle formed by concentric leaves that collects water when you mist. Frogs love to sit in this kind of moist pocket and survey the world around them, looking like clammy little Buddhas.

All About Lids

Many amphibians are expert climbers and escape artists. Affix a secure glass or plastic cover to the vivarium to keep animals and humidity in, making sure to drill or punch out a few air holes. A screen top will permit too much evaporation. The top must line up perfectly, as any imperfection in fit will result in vanished pets. Tree frogs are the worst culprits. Using their sticky, wide digital (finger) pads, they can adhere to virtually any surface, including glass, and routinely feel the need to test their mettle on every available spot in the house. Your tree frog sees wonderful opportunities for fun and games as he stares through the aquarium glass. Give him just one little crack and he will be sticking to everything in sight: refrigerator doors, desk legs, windowpanes, bookcases and toilets.

You read me right. Toilets. As a boy growing up in an apartment with my parents, I had a large terrarium for some exotic and wonderful tree frogs. This tank had a cranky lid that, to the everlasting joy of these creatures, would pop open at the most inopportune times. One day when I came home from school with a sack of crickets to feed my frogs, I noticed that a large yellow frog was missing. I searched high and low for the little bugger, but to no avail. Knowing how quickly amphibians perish without moisture, I gave him up for dead after several days.

That same winter, my parents decided to replace the fixtures in the bathroom and called the plumber to come and install a new sink and toilet. I was at school and my father was in another room shaving when the plumber appeared in the mirror. My father turned, wrapped only in his bath towel, to see the man standing there with the toilet tank in his arms and a strange expression on his face.

"There is," he exclaimed, "a large yellow frog on the wall."

Knowing my strange proclivities full well, my father didn't bat an eye. Following the plumber into the room, however, he saw nothing whatsoever on the wall. Still cradling the toilet tank, the plumber searched frantically high and low, but without result. My father suggested to the poor devil that he not drink so heavily at that hour of the morning.

I never did find the frog, but I would like to think that he lurks behind some toilet still, waiting for another opportunity to make some stranger believe in the supernatural!

Lighting and Temperature

Amphibians like dim, cool areas with lots of humidity. Room temperature is actually the upper limit for your vivarium or simple cage, the low 60s being the temperature at which many amphibians are happiest. High temperatures are much more likely to harm your pets than low ones, so avoid sunlit locations and spots near heat-producing objects. Right above the kitchen stove, for instance, is a lousy spot for frogs and salamanders.

Incandescent light bulbs, aside from being hard on the eyes, are also a big source of heat. One 40-watt bulb can raise the temperature in your vivarium to the uncomfortable range for your pets, and a 75-watt spotlight may kill them. Total darkness, on the other hand, limits severely the types of plants you can use if you have a vivarium and in any case makes amphibian-watching tough. The answer is to use a cool, full-wave fluorescent light bulb of the type discussed in the turtle and lizard chapters. Vita-Lite by Luxor and Chromalux by General Electric are the brands I recommend. Put the lamps on a timer and let them shine, say, six hours a day.

FEEDING YOUR AMPHIBIAN

Like feeding fish, feeding amphibians is an easy, pleasurable task. For fish there are a multitude of commercial preparations, and for amphibians there are a multitude of bugs. Any type of insect or similar bug, save a huge beetle or highly venomous spider, is fair food for an amphibian. What you will probably have to do with your salamander or frog is to try different bugs, ones that are available either to your collecting net or at the local bait or pet shop, until you find what works out best.

When you are selecting food to offer your pets, remember my remarks about the amphibian eye. Although not terribly acute, the eyes of frogs and salamanders respond well to motion. An insect that lies without moving may be passed up, while a bug that energetically hops, skips and crawls will be promptly detected and devoured. Amphibians benefit from vitamins, too. Put some powdered multivitamin (Vionate is a good brand) in a plastic bag. Blow up the bag, drop in the bugs and shake. This will coat the food items with vitamins and your pet will receive a dose.

Pet shops often carry mealworms *(Tenebrio)* and whiteworms *(Enchytraeus),* and both of these make good food, especially for salamanders. Bear in mind, though, that the crunchy outer skeleton of a mealworm is made of a chitinous material that tends to accumulate in the amphibian's belly, leading ultimately to intestinal blockage and death. Go ahead and feed your pet mealworms, but don't make them the major part of its diet.

Aquatic amphibians, especially small ones, will relish the smaller worms such as *Tubifex* sold in pet shops as fish food. These are best presented as a writhing mass on a flat dish. Larger worms are savored as well, and if you have a backyard, go out and dig up some earthworms. If you don't find the idea too objectionable, many frogs and salamanders enjoy slugs, too. Find these inside drainage pipes and grids. Very tiny amphibians will sometimes take fruit flies *(Drosophila),* but these and houseflies are not the greatest foods because they can easily escape and become a problem in your house.

The old standby for feeding amphibians and other small insectivores in the home is the cricket. They make such great pet food that most of my own collection is fed crickets much of the time. Crickets of the genus *Gryllus* are available at nearly every pet shop, even in the winter months, since they are farmed in tremendous numbers to supply the trade. If you buy them in bulk and keep them yourself, they are often cheaper, and you're sure of their availability. Keep crickets in a separate small, well-sealed container with holes punched in the top. Empty egg crates or crumpled-up paper towels make good hiding places for captive crickets. Feed them some cereal, and provide water by soaking a piece of sponge and putting it in with the bugs. Occasionally crickets will breed, but getting them to drop eggs is a bit tricky. A small piece of window screen laid over some moss seems to encourage the female to deposit. If you have a fair-sized vivarium with a number of amphibians, keeping and breeding crickets will save you time and money. Listening to them chirp in the evening is pleasant, too.

Like reptiles, amphibians can go for long periods without eating. This doesn't mean that you should simply forget about your pets for months on end, but rather that their forgiving metabolism will allow you some lapses, such as vacation time and long weekends. Large, well-fed amphibians kept cool and moist can go for ten days without eating. (Make sure, though, that there is *some* supervision. Water in the simple cage must be changed every few days, and vivariums must be misted at least every other day lest your pets dry out. If the latter is not possible, leave a dish of standing water in the tank until your return.) I enjoy watching amphibians eat. Frogs are particularly entertaining. They seem embarrassed by the act, stuffing the food into their mouths with their feet, as if they didn't want anyone to see. Feed your pets twice a week and you should have no problems. Give them as much as they will devour in one sitting.

Mealtime is a fine opportunity to get to know and understand your animals. Very often an amphibian that doesn't seem to recognize that you exist will quickly respond to you when you come bearing insect gifts. Most amphibians eat their meals in one piece, so don't be surprised if an agile tongue comes out and snatches an entire cricket from your grasp. Move slowly as you approach your pet and then let the movement of the insect prompt the salamander or frog to take the food from your fingers. I have a pair of White's tree frogs (*Hyla caerulea*) from Australia that sit with catlike aplomb and wait for me to offer a tidbit. As I approach their mouths, they betray nothing until suddenly the tongue flicks out and the bug is gone. A fire salamander that lives in my back room spends most of his life under a clump of sphagnum moss. He relishes worms of all types, and I have even enticed him to a bit of lean beef now and then. A way of getting an amphibian pet to eat meat is to set the lean cut in motion by clumping it about a piece of thread and then swinging it in front of the animal to simulate insect activity.

For most amphibians meat is a treat, not a part of the staple diet. Really large frogs, however, such as Blomberg's toad (*Bufo blombergi*), and any of the bull or horned frogs (discussed later) *require* the quality of protein found in red meat and are best fed baby rats and mice of appropriate size. Simply drop a live infant rodent into the tank, just as you would a bug. Keep an eye on the proceedings to make sure all goes as planned and remove the mouse or ratling after a few minutes if the amphibian lacks appetite.

Avoid using adult mice or half-grown rats unless feeding the absolute largest of frogs—say, a foot-long African burrowing bullfrog (*Pyxicephalus adspersus*). There is more about this rat-eating giant in the next section. You will also find information about where to find your amphibian pet, which one to choose and how to know if it is healthy.

ACQUIRING AN AMPHIBIAN

If the notion of an amphibian pet appeals to you, the best thing to do after reading this section is to go to your local zoo, aquarium or pet shop, in that order, and see what such creatures really look like. What excites you on paper may not so move you in the flesh. The converse, however, is more likely. If you are curious but still view these forms as "way out" and slimy, seeing them will help settle your mind. I can, for instance, extol the virtues of the blue arrow-poison frog below. I can tell of its unreal, electric blue and its terrific vibrancy and contrast. I cannot, however, render the full effect of so startling a beast in words. You just have to see it. After you have investigated some amphibians and decided on what you want, the first thing to do is set up a home for your future pet. *Prepare the cage THEN purchase the beast.* This is a rule I cannot state too often.

Other than the nearby woodpile, there are two principal sources for pet amphibians. One is the local pet shop, the other the large mail-order house. The former is your best bet, since you can see the animal firsthand and have some recourse if it dies on you during the trip home. Also, there are people in the pet shop who can give advice that goes beyond the scope of this book. Pet shops, though, tend to be more expensive than mail-order houses, even after shipping costs are considered. Mail-order businesses depend for their livelihood on repeat orders and are thus somewhat bound to provide merchandise of quality. You can learn of a mail-order dealer or two by getting in touch with your local reptile and amphibian club or with a nearby zoo or museum. Any local veterinarian who deals with exotic animals should also be able to help. When you contact a "herp" club, by the way, ask if any active trading of animals is going on. Explain your situation and see if the club can provide you with local sources for any animals you'd like to acquire.

Sex and Age

The sex of the animal you buy is unimportant unless you wish to breed your pet. It is not even always obvious, moreover, to which sex your prospective pet belongs. Of course, I always encourage breeding, but not all types of amphibians will oblige under captive conditions. Try to get help from a knowledgeable salesperson should you wish a sexual pair of amphibians.

The age of an amphibian once it has reached adulthood is likewise tricky to ascertain. Most of the species that I mention here are long-lived. Even if you acquire a mature adult, it will probably live for several years given the proper care. To some extent you can figure out how old an amphibian is by its size. Like reptiles, amphibians just keep growing, slowly but steadily, throughout their lives. Assuming that both animals have always had enough to eat, a larger individual of the same sex will be older than a smaller one.

Handling the Amphibian

There is one major inside tip concerning the handling of salamanders and frogs, and that is: *Don't!* These creatures depend upon the moist mucus layer of their skin to protect them from disease and injury. By handling them you remove this layer and imperil their well-being. If you have to move them, either use a net or wet your hands thoroughly, touching them for the briefest possible interval. Not only can handling harm your *pet,* but because of their skin secretions, it can harm you! *Remember always to wash carefully after handling any frog or salamander;* and for Pete's sake, never rub your nose while involved in amphibian work! You may not get nose warts, but you will be itching, burning and sneezing for a week. Amphibians may be stored in small plastic food-storage boxes while their cage is being cleaned.

The Amphibian Physical Exam

To be as sure as you reasonably can be that the pet you've chosen from a shop is in good shape, inspect it in an unhurried manner employing the following guidelines:

1. Does the animal look banged up? There should be no cuts, scrapes or bruises. These are prime sites for secondary infections.

2. Does the skin bear any fuzzy or bumpy red or white lesions? These are signs of fungal or bacterial disease and can be difficult to cure.

3. Are both eyes present, intact and clear? Amphibians have amazing regenerative powers, but don't count on your pet's regrowing an eye.

4. Does the animal look well fed? One very common cause of a lousy-looking frog or salamander is dehydration. Lots of pet shops allow their amphibians to dry out, mainly because they don't know any better. If there are no marks on the creature but it looks like a withered prune, ask if you can put it in a bowl of water. Do so and watch for a few minutes. If dehydration is the problem, the animal should begin to fill out in a matter of minutes as its skin absorbs life-giving water.

5. Is the animal missing any limbs? That might be okay! Salamanders are great at regrowing lost limbs and tails. If you discover a slightly disfigured salamander that is otherwise in acceptable condition, you might want to try to get a discount on it from the pet seller. Give it time and you will have the pleasure of watching it regenerate the affected part until it is as good as new!

On Mixing Animals

The simple cage should be reserved for a single animal or perhaps a pair of the same species. Vivaria, on the other hand, can be greatly enhanced when they support several animals of different types. Overcrowding is a bad idea, as it causes stress and disease and ruins the "hands-off" quality that a vivarium should have. I rail against overcrowding in the lizard chapter. The problem is that it is difficult to give a rule of thumb, as amphibians come in all different shapes, sizes and ages. A cardinal rule that I have given elsewhere and will repeat here is that if you cannot lose all the animals in your vivarium (that is, come in and see absolutely nobody home now and then), either you have too many pets in one tank or the tank is too small.

Large predatory frogs such as the burrowing bullfrog cannot safely be mixed with other animals, nor can very large aggressive salamanders such as the Pacific giant. Highly toxic species such as the arrow-poison frogs must also be kept alone or in small groups of their own kind, lest they inadvertently poison their tankmates. Amphibians of widely disparate sizes should always be kept apart, as nearly any amphibian will attack what it can swallow given half a chance and enough time.

AMPHIBIANS I RECOMMEND

Below you will find a list of ten frogs and eight salamanders that I think make especially good exotic pets. I have tried to come up with a representative list, taking into account availability, price, hardiness, attractiveness and any special features that bear on selecting the candidates. Picking ten frogs from the approximately 2,500 world-wide was especially difficult, but the 310 salamanders of the world presented a more manageable bunch. Their world headquarters is North America, so I have confined my eight choices to native species. Prices, unless otherwise noted, pertain to average adult amphibians. Salamanders are measured from snout to tip of tail, frogs from snout to where the tail would begin if there were one.

1. Spotted salamander *(Ambystoma maculatum)*

This is a common creature of the woods, ponds and swamps of the East Coast and Southland. It is a large, powerful salamander, jet black with yellow spots. Spring rains bring such beasts out *en masse* to breed and lay eggs. The eggs may number 250 per female, and they incubate for about a month and a half before yielding half-inch larvae. The aquatic tadpoles need about three months to grow another three inches, whereupon they are ready to metamorphose into the real thing. By the next year they are four-inch salamanders. These hardy and fearless little creatures are diggers and pushers, so remember to leave any vivarium plants you may use in their pots.

CAGE: simple or vivarium
FOOD: crickets, worms, slugs, beetles, flies, meat strips and baby
  mice
SIZE: to 8 inches
PRICE: $7 in pet shops, but easily found within their natural
  range with the spring rains

2. Tiger salamander *(Ambystoma tigrinum)*

A member of the same genus, this creature is very similar to the
spotted salamander, though it is not so brightly colored. There are
eight races of this amphibian spread across the states, the Eastern
form being the largest. This is a black salamander, featuring yellowish-
brown blotches. The breeding patterns are similar to those of its
spotted cousin, this animal having a slightly shorter incubation period and a longer larval stage. Larvae transform into adults at about
five inches. Though they greatly resemble *A. maculatum*, tiger salamanders are much more impressive, thanks to their sheer size.

CAGE: simple or vivarium
FOOD: insects of all types, meat strips and baby mice
SIZE: to 13 inches
PRICE: $8

3. Pacific giant salamander *(Dicamptodon ensatus)*

This mottled purple bruiser lives very well in a forest vivarium as
long as it is kept *very* damp. This is one of the bulkiest salamanders
in the world and hails from the Pacific Northwest, where it frequents
logs, bark and rocks. Pacific giants like to climb, so be sure your tank
is well secured. When this species is first caught it emits a rattled
clicking, rare in the otherwise silent world of the salamander.

CAGE: simple or vivarium
FOOD: various insects, particularly worms, when young, baby
  rodents when adult
SIZE: to 12 inches
PRICE: $18

4. Common newt *(Notophthalamus viridescens)*

You know that most amphibians go through two stages after emerging from the egg. First they are larvae, and then adults. Well, our next recommended salamander features a new twist to the sequence. It goes through a third phase! The larvae emerge from the egg, eat, grow and transform into a rough-skinned, fire engine–red terrestrial phase known as an "eft." They truck clumsily across the forest floor in the our Eastern states, and I caught scores of them as a boy.

After one to three years they transform again, returning to the water to live out their lives as the red-spotted olive-and-yellow aquatic, air-breathing adult newt.

> CAGE: vivarium for the eft stage, simple for the newt
> FOOD: small insects of all kinds
> SIZE: to 5 inches (rarely)
> PRICE: $3; the newt stage is much the most commonly available

5. Eastern red salamander *(Pseudotriton ruber)*

This animal is similar in color to the eft stage of the common newt. As it get older, however, its color darkens to the point where an older individual will appear a purplish brown. This salamander likes very cool damp spots. If your house is warmer in summer than 70 degrees, you might consider refrigerating this beast in a plastic container with damp moss and air holes.

> CAGE: vivarium with plenty of good dim hiding spots
> FOOD: small insects of all kinds
> SIZE: to 7 inches
> PRICE: $9

6. Slimy salamander *(Plethodon glutinosus)*

This is another East Coast salamander that likes a cool, moist environment such as you might find under rocks and in the leaf litter of the forest floor. The slimy salamander is a shiny black creature with white flecks. Actually he doesn't feel slimy at all, but rather *sticky* from the copious mucus produced by his skin. Slimy salamanders are less shy than the previous species and you have a good chance of

seeing them out and about, wriggling in the home you have created
for them.

CAGE: simple cage or vivarium
FOOD: small insects of all kinds
SIZE: to 7.5 inches
PRICE: $6

Slimey salamander; dusky salamander

7. Northern dusky salamander *(Desmognathus fuscus)*

This is a variably patterned plain brown animal with spots and stripes. There are several varieties of this salamander from different locales. All breed in spring. Eggs are laid in summer, and the female curls about them and provides protection (never mess with an angry mother dusky!) until they hatch. The larvae transform at about eight months of age. These animals require cool, moist surroundings like most of our salamanders.

CAGE: simple cage or vivarium
FOOD: small insects of all kinds
SIZE: to 4.5 inches
PRICE: $5

8. Rough-skinned newt *(Taricha granulosa)*

We have to travel to the West Coast to find these spunky salamanders. They feature a potent toxin in the skin that is a fine deterrent to would-be predators. They can't hurt you, though, unless you feel like having a newt sandwich. When approached and threatened, these fellows close their eyes, sway their backs and bring the head and tail up into the shape of a U, much as a scorpion does. The limbs are extended forward and the toes are flexed. This energetic arching brings the bright yellow belly into view—a warning signal, perhaps, to a predator who has lost the memory of the last time it went for a bite.

Rough-skinned newts spend a great deal of time underground, emerging with early-spring rain to move about through grasslands and lay eggs. The young metamorphose in August and are sexually mature at about four years old. They do not go through an eft stage.

CAGE: simple cage
FOOD: small insects of all kinds
SIZE: to 7 inches (rarely)
PRICE: $3

9. African burrowing bullfrog *(Pyxicephalus adsperus)*

In order to enjoy salamanders properly, particularly in the vivarium setting, you must be somewhat vigilant. That is, you must search for your pets, since they are wont to descend into the substrate, never to be seen until you look. While frogs too lead still lives, at least they are more visible. Tree frogs frequently stick to the glass of vivaria, whereas aquatic species often hang motionless in the water. Semiaquatic frogs remain motionless a great deal of the time too, huddling in mud, sand or gravel. The pale green African burrowing bullfrog, also known as the groove-crowned bullfrog, is a sedentary semiaquatic type, but it can also be active, predatory and aggressive when hungry.

This is one of the largest frogs in the world, with an appetite to match its prodigious maw. When young it will daily devour bugs at an alarming rate. As it grows it will tackle mice and ultimately small rats. I acquired my first burrowing bullfrog many years ago and kept it in a bare two-and-a-half-gallon tank with an inch of water. I tossed in crickets whenever I had a few to spare. Its feeding proceeded in this rather haphazard fashion until I noticed that it could no longer turn around in the aquarium and that it seemed less than content with its insect fare. I took it out gingerly, as when it is hungry this voracious animal will occasionally go for a finger, and put it on the floor. I offered a mouse by the tail, and *poof,* the mouse was gone. I offered another and it met a similar fate. The frog's pale underbelly swelled, but it still had the active, inquiring look of the hunter. Shortly thereafter I transferred the frog to a ten-gallon aquarium. The hungry looks it gave other animals in surrounding cages made me uneasy.

The next day I came home to find my animal room in utter disarray. Tanks had been knocked over and cracked, water was everywhere on the floor, crocodilians were sliding through the mess hissing and my tortoises were loose and lumbering around. Parrots were screaming, and snakes were holed up in corners. Many of my prized animal books were sopping and ruined. The door to the closet was open, and my eighteen-foot Burmese python was casually surveying the wreckage. Nearby, a large wooden cage lay tipped on its side and empty, a trail of blood leading up to it. Sensing disaster, I began to look for the monitor lizard that should have been in the wooden cage and found him on top of the ten-gallon tank that had once held my African bullfrog. I suspect that my giant python had pushed the closet door open and roamed around the room, upsetting some cages. When he tipped over the monitor's cage the lizard got loose, causing more damage and eating my frog. I had no other casualties, but I had loved that frog and have never been able to bring myself to buy another. The moral is, pay careful attention to securing your amphibian and reptile pets, as a pet on the loose can be a heartbreak waiting to happen.

> CAGE: simple, and unlike cages for other amphibians, warmed to 80 degrees F., but no more. Use a low-wattage bulb at first, increasing the heat slowly by changing to a bigger bulb so as not to risk roasting your pet. This animal is much too large and powerful for a vivarium. Because of its predatory habits, do not house it with other animals.
>
> FOOD: insects of any sort when young, small rodents when large
>
> SIZE: to 8 inches
>
> PRICE: $30

10. Bell's horned frog *(Ceratophrys ornata)*

The South American horned frogs are another group of bizarre, predatory frogs with sharp teeth and a willingness to use them. They are also some of the most spectacular forest-dwelling giants available to the frog fancier. The back of this spectacular frog is green, red and black, providing a variegated camouflage that serves it quite well in nature.

> CAGE: alone in a simple cage or vivarium
>
> FOOD: insects of all kinds when young, pink mice and larger mice when adult
>
> SIZE: to 7 inches
>
> PRICE: $35

11. Blomberg's toad *(Bufo blombergi)*

In every "recommended" section I try to include one "way out" animal. This is usually an expensive, rare and hard-to-find creature that is included to titillate the reader as much as to present a real option. The recently discovered Blomberg's toad is such an animal.

It hails from southwestern Colombia and is the largest true (meaning it belongs to the genus *Bufo*) toad in the world. It is tan above and chocolate brown on the sides. The belly is brown. This animal is less moisture-loving than the preceding two. I have never seen a juvenile of this species, but the adults are peaceable, dignified, noble animals. Like all toads, Blomberg's features poison glands on the back of the head, so be sure to handle yours as little as possible and rinse after frog work.

CAGE: extremely large vivarium or bare cage; this is a mobile animal

FOOD: rodents of approximately one-third the size of the frog or smaller

SIZE: to 9 inches

PRICE: difficult to assess and varies considerably; probably in the vicinity of $100

Bell's horned frog

12. Colorado river toad *(Bufo alvarius)*

A great deal smaller and surely less exotic than the preceding species, this is nonetheless an impressive toad. It is olive above and cream-colored below and is remarkably smooth-skinned (for a toad). This frog comes from mountain canyons, especially near springs and reservoirs. Like all toads, it has poison glands on the back of the head that produce a noxious substance. In this particular animal the poison is potent enough to kill a dog. It won't affect you unless you decide to have your pet for dinner. This frog is active chiefly at night, so don't keep it in your bedroom unless you wish to be awakened from your dreams by a cacophony of grunts and splashes. Just to show you how serious the Colorado river toad is about making it into the next millennium, when it breeds, it doesn't kid around. Females have been known to lay eight thousand eggs at a sitting!

CAGE: simple
FOOD: insects of all kinds, pink mice
SIZE: to 6 inches
PRICE: $20

Colorado river toad

13. European green toad *(Bufo viridis)*

Another true toad, this animal might just be the ideal amphibian pet. It lives well in a vivarium and is not overly destructive to whatever creative planting you have done there. Its bright green-and-brown pattern makes it very attractive, and it will eat almost anything. It is active, responsive and happy at room temperature, but is so hardy that in nature it survives fifteen-thousand-foot elevations and frigid temperatures. It is distributed all over the European continent and on into Asia and is quite common and popular with European hobbyists.

> CAGE: simple or vivarium
> FOOD: any kind of harmless (no black widow spiders or huge biting beetles) insect and pink mice
> SIZE: to 4 inches
> PRICE: $10

14. European tree frog *(Hyla arborea)*

While charming and entertaining, tree frogs are as a rule more delicate, more difficult to keep healthy and shorter-lived than any of the semiaquatic predatory frogs or the toads. This species, however, seems to have a really solid grip on life. It is a chunky green animal, which can change hue all the way to brown when threatened or disturbed. I have kept scores of European tree frogs in a large, tall vivarium with a variety of leafy plants. They love to be misted with a plant sprayer and to be kept a bit warmer than some other frogs. Years ago I purchased a pair of these frogs and put them in a tank. They turned brown because they were angry and upset at being rudely scooped up and transported to a new abode, so I left them alone, hoping they would return to their attractive green. The next day I sneaked up to the tank to have a look and found no sign of them anywhere. These are small frogs, and I figured that they had simply hidden someplace. I looked long and hard, but to no avail. There were no obvious holes or cracks through which they might have made good an escape. In desperation I began a systematic search, turning over leaves and rocks, but found nothing. At long last I gave up, sure that they were drying and dying somewhere in my home. The next day I went through the procedure again, only to find the two frogs clinging inconspicuously to an inside corner of the glass. They had been there all along, pressed small and tight, the color of their bellies matching the white of the aquarium glue; all but impossible to see.

The ability to change color as I have described is characteristic of many tree frogs and gives the animal added protection in the form of camouflage from predators. If I couldn't find the two frogs in a vivarium when I knew they were there, you can see that their tactics are effective.

> CAGE: tall vivarium heavily misted and kept in the warmest part of the room
> FOOD: small crickets and other comparably sized insects; worms not relished
> SIZE: to 1.5 inches
> PRICE: $12

15. Barking tree frog *(Hyla gratiosa)*

Frogs of the genus *Hyla* are characterized by the same grasping suction pads on the fingers that allowed the previous species to cling to the aquarium glass and escape detection. The present handsome species is a master trapeze artist, employing its grasping sticky toes to help it leap about from leaf to twig. This frog can change from green to brown to gray and has light spots on the back that look a bit like tiny staring eyes. It gets its name from its call, which is hoarse and sounds vaguely barklike.

> CAGE: tall, heavily misted vivarium
> FOOD: crickets and other insects
> SIZE: to 3 inches
> PRICE: $15

16. Asian painted frog *(Kaloula pulchra)*

I confess, this might just be my favorite frog. It is a subtly marked species, featuring brown, cream and black, and it likes to burrow. I had one that burrowed so effectively, in fact, that I lost him for over a year! It wasn't until I tore the tank completely apart to prepare it for new occupants that I discovered a half-dried-out but still healthy painted frog way down under the dirt in the back of the vivarium.

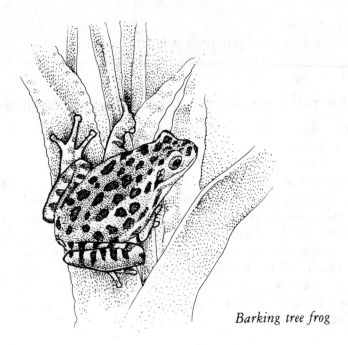

Barking tree frog

This is a mellow little guy with a very accepting personality. Its name, I am sorry to say, makes absolutely no sense.

CAGE: simple or vivarium, kept in the warmest part of the room
FOOD: insects of all kinds
SIZE: to 3.5 inches
PRICE: $10

17. Fire-bellied toad *(Bombina orientalis)*

Completely opposite in every way to the painted frog, the fire-bellied toad is flamboyant, raucous and active. It is not a true toad at all, appreciating far more aquatic environs. The fire-bellied toad is green and black above, red and black below. The colors are not subtle and muted like those we find in so many other frogs, but bright, bold and shiny. The red in the belly is due largely to a tongue-twisting pigment, canthaxanthin, found in its insect diet. This creature, like many amphibians, has toxic skin secretions, so be sure to wash your hands after any neccessary handling.

CAGE: simple
FOOD: as wide a variety of insects as possible
SIZE: to 2.5 inches
PRICE: $8

18. Blue poison-arrow frog *(Dendrobates tinctorius)*

If the colors of the fire-bellied toad are bold and shiny, those of
the poison-arrow frog are positively atomic. Although it is tremendous what man can do with synthetics these days, I have never seen
a manmade material—nor a neon sign, for that matter—that can
match this frog's intense color. Earlier in the section I spoke of the
high toxicity of the poison secreted by the skin glands of this frog
and its use in Indian blowgun darts. You cannot handle this creature
at all, for you can actually burn yourself. It is unlikely that the skin
on your hand will be affected, but woe to him who rubs his eyes after
contacting one of these frogs! Maintained with care and caution,
however, these fabulous little jewels are the crown of the amphibian
kingdom.

CAGE: simple cage with water changes every other day or a
vivarium covered with moss, the moss changed weekly. No
more than two frogs to a five-gallon aquarium. A hiding place
such as a piece of cork bark is required.
FOOD: a wide variety of suitably small insects; baby crickets
make a good staple
SIZE: to 1.5 inches
PRICE: $30

FISHES

Fishes: blue discus, golden ram

It could be that there are as many different fishes as there are stars in the night sky; close, anyway. This is largely because fishes have so much space to expand into. Oceans, lakes, rivers and streams, remember, represent three-dimensional space in greater abundance than we can comprehend. With all this room come many different environments, some as vast as the open ocean and others as tiny as the bosom of a lily pad.

Earlier chapters had us walking the perimeter of a garden of earthly delights and making a careful selection here and there. When it comes to fish, however, we are wading neck-deep in options. As a result, this chapter is even more selective than the rest. It is designed to serve as a basic guide through the mass of equipment, paraphernalia and species that comprise the fish aquarist's tools and his subjects. I do not try to be comprehensive—the scope of the subject makes that impossible—but rather attempt to give you a glimpse of the principles that underlie an enormously popular hobby.

When we looked at snakes, we dealt with a small group and I managed a representative sampling. The same was true of turtles, salamanders, frogs, parrots and to some extend, lizards. When it comes to fishes, though, the best I can do is pick some individuals that I think make good pets. Reluctantly, I am omitting saltwater animals (they are among the most fascinating and spectacular of all aquatic forms) because the marine aquarium is an expensive proposition that, while rewarding for the advanced hobbyist, is a nightmare for the average pet owner.

Can a fish be a pet? You bet. As a vertebrate animal, the fish has the right equipment to be able to behave in fascinating ways and even to learn some basic things. Your fish can learn to know his feeding time, to nibble from your fingers and to distinguish you from a stranger.

If you are confined to the house, a fish, like many of the animals described in this book, is an ideal pet. It rarely makes a mess you have to clean up, it won't whine to go outside every two hours and it won't squawk and wake you with the sunrise. If you feel an aversion to slimy creepy-crawlies, a fish won't offend you. If you forget to feed it once or twice, a fish will forgive you. You won't sneeze from its dander, or have to vacuum its hairs off the furniture. If your budget is limited, buying and feeding fish surely won't tax it. Feeding a fish costs only a few dollars per year.

Fish have more to offer than relief from anticipation of the drill while you sit and wait in the dentist's office. In certain ways a fish offers you a better opportunity to learn about animal behavior than any other exotic creature. There are several reason for this: First, a fish is a relatively simple vertebrate whose behavior patterns are repeated over and over and are thus easy to discern. Second, the animal is contained within an aquarium, which is a showcase of sorts. It is unlikely that the fish is off rooting in your lawn or tearing apart the back of the sofa. Whatever your fish does, it occurs right in front of you and is hard to miss if you spend any time at all watching. Third, it is inexpensive to get more than one fish, and a small aquarium community, like a vivarium community, will result in fascinating interactions.

Should you decide to set up an aquarium for a number of fish, you should strongly consider sticking to one species, or at least type, of fish (tropical catfish, for example). Time and again I have alluded to the desirability of breeding exotic animals, but have been forced by the limitations of space to skirt the specifics. Again, I cannot describe how best to get all fishes to breed, but in most instances fish are less picky than other creatures concerning the when and where of love play. Breeding an exotic species is thus a reality within the grasp of the amateur fish keeper and can also be quite lucrative! Consider that breeding fish can be your way of paying back Nature for the strain to which you subject her with pollution, overpopulation and habitat destruction. When you breed a fish at home, that is one breed less that has to be taken from the wild to satisfy the hobby.

FISH BIOLOGY

Because this is such an enormous and fascinating topic, this section should really be called "highlights of fish biology." Despite the vast variety of the fishes swimming through the waters of our world, one thing unites them: They all are bound by the constraints of an aquatic existence. In some ways living in the water makes things easier on a body and in other ways it imposes hardships. The skeleton of a fish, for instance, isn't necessary to support its body; water holds the body up instead. On the other hand, water is hundreds of times more dense than air, so moving through a rough sea is a lot tougher than muscling your way through even the nastiest wind. In order to cope with the drag of the water and to take maximum advantage of the support it lends, most fishes have, during the long course of evolution, developed a characteristic streamlined shape and a slimy secretion that covers their scales and helps them slip through the water.

Despite these common governing factors, there have evolved three distinctly different types of fishes: the jawless fishes, the fishes with skeletons of cartilage and the bony fishes. The fish that interest us as pets are of the latter type.

Fishes are vertebrates, and as such are similar to us. When a fish swallows his food, it goes first down his esophagus and then into his stomach, just as do chiliburgers and escargot when you and I indulge. A look at a fish's esophagus can reveal a lot about his eating habits. Some fishes are filter feeders, meaning that they strain water through the mouth, catching food in what amounts to a big toothbrush. The esophagus of these animals is small, because microscopic food doesn't put much strain on the throat. One can equate filter feeders to people who never take a bite of solid food, surviving instead on liquid nourishment. Carnivorous fishes, like sharks, on the other hand, have an esophagus that is distensible, acting like a tube of Silly Putty, stretching every which way to accommodate such diverse items as a tuna's fin, a human foot or a spare tire.

Some fishes lack stomachs, but all have intestines. A long, coiled intestine tells you that the fish is a plant eater. Plants are more difficult for fish to digest, so they need more gut to do it. Carnivorous fish have a fairly straight intestine. Fish also have livers, pancreases, spleens, kidneys and busy little hearts. A fish's heart is pumping blood not to lungs for oxygen but to gills. In case you weren't sure, fish breathe oxygen just as we do, but they have to get it out of the water first. Gills allow them to do so.

Imagine for a moment that you are floating in a swimming pool. Just for the sake of fun and frolic, you take a breath and dive under the water. You sit on the bottom, but find that you can't stay put. Waving your hands helps, but this tires you out and soon you shoot to the surface. So what if you cannot stay submerged at a particular depth without waving your hands around? No big deal to you, maybe; but despite the effectiveness of propulsion by fin and tail, fish can't afford to waste time and energy trying to stay at one depth. (Floating at a specific depth, by the way, is termed being "neutrally buoyant.") It is crucial in the life of a fish that he be able to hover at any depth without working really hard to do it. I think you can see why. Suppose the hungry bass, cruising the lake, sees a tasty minnow about ten feet below him. He points himself down, mouth agape, pulse racing, stomach juicing, only to find he can't quite get down there. Instead he keeps floating back up to where he started. Just as he is beginning to get upset, the bass spies a nice, plump tadpole pulsing along lazily on the surface. With a deep grin (to himself; fish lips can't do that) he starts for the top, only to find himself sinking back to his original depth. Before he dies from lack of food, friend bass is going to go quietly nuts from frustration.

Fortunately for the fish of the world, they are able to rise and fall at their whim and to stay at the desired depth without really working at it. They do this, in essence, by being born with a balloon inside. This is called the gas gland or "swim bladder" and is the part of the fish that sometimes comes out of his mouth if you reel him in from depth really quickly. As the fish rises and falls in the water, the gas gland swells and shrinks to adjust its buoyancy. Picture strapping a lead weight to your waist. You go for a swim in the lake, but not being the suicidal type, you take a life vest with you. The vest is empty when you start. You sink like a stone until you are so deep you are scared. Quickly you open a gas cartridge into the vest and it buoys you up.

What is hi-tech to you is utterly natural for the fish. The fish transfers the gases that are dissolved in its body to the bladder. The bladder swells, and up goes the fish. When the fish wishes to go down, it sucks the air out of the balloon and plummets like a marble in grape juice.

The actual mechanism whereby a fish is able to rapidly fill its gas gland and empty it at will is complex. The best way to explain it, for our purposes here, is to say that it works by diffusion. If you take a dried-out old sponge and immerse it in warm water, the result will be a full and spongeful bloom. Water enters the sponge by diffusion. Diffusion depends upon concentration of things. There is a greater concentration of water outside the sponge than inside, so the sponge fills with water. If the sponge has been treated with some water-soluble chemical (red food dye, for instance), this will diffuse out into the water when the sponge is immersed and turn the water red.

Now that we see how our imaginary bass can catch the minnow or the tadpole if he is hungry, we wonder how he knows the prey is there. Fish have a primitive brain, yet they manage to do fishly things under a variety of circumstances. The brain of the fish, by the by, is primitive only compared with the turtle's or our own. Compared with a sea sponge or a cockroach, a fish is a mental giant! Feeding this paragon of aquatic intellect is a set of senses with which we can certainly identify. Let's talk about fish eyes for a moment or two. As you might imagine, there are all different kinds of fish eyes. Fishes that live in total darkness, for instance, have eyes that don't function well if at all. Fishes that live right at the surface of the ocean amid the crashing surface of a bright tropical reef have eyes that yield all the necessary detail. Color vision is in most cases of no consequence, since water filters out light very quickly as one descends into the depths. Fishes that have to inspect something very closely before they eat it have eyes set right up near the front of their heads so that they can employ binocular vision. Other fishes, those in constant fear of being chomped, for example, have eyes set widely apart to give them the maximum possible field of view. Water, moreover, does some strange things to vision, as you know if you have ever tried to read the Sunday paper underwater. The fish eye is specialized so that it bends light appropriately for the subaquatic environment. If your goldfish jumps out of his bowl onto the kitchen table, however, he cannot even read the funnies!

What about fish ears? The ear in most vertebrates consists of inner, middle and outer portions. Fish have only the inner ear, but when the ear is combined with the gas gland, the fish can hear pretty darn well. Some fishes use extensions of the swim bladder to help pick up vibrations in the water. Fishes with such connections are able to hear higher frequencies than fishes that lack this feature. Sound carries distinctly and quite far underwater, but since water provides more resistance than air, it takes more energy to make a sound underwater than up here on land. If you had a good pair of fish ears, you would probably be able to detect a cacophony of grunts, whistles, clicks and grinds. The range of fish hearing is almost as great as the range of our own. When you tap the glass on your aquarium, be assured that your pet undoubtedly gets the message.

I had a pet oscar once that I had trained to come to the surface and wait for food when I tapped the glass. Oscars are large carnivorous South American fish, members of a group called "cichlids." (More about cichlids below.) One day the metal thermometer that hung on the side of my oscar's tank failed to give a reading. As a temporary measure, I borrowed a floating tubular glass thermometer that had been bouncing around in one of my marine aquariums and placed it in my oscar's home. The movement of the water from the powerful filter had the glass tube tapping erratically against one side of the tank. Soon I heard this peculiar gulping sound. Wandering over to the tank, I found my pet frantically leaping at the surface, mouth agape, expecting food. The poor fellow had mistaken the rhythmic tapping of the device for my finger ringing the dinner bell.

Fish have taste receptors, so they'll know if you try to feed them a bunch of jalapeño peppers ground up to look like fish food. Oddly, though, the fish's taste buds are not all located in his mouth. In fact, though concentrated mostly in the head, his taste buds are scattered all over his body.

So our pet fish can see his prey, maybe hear it and certainly taste it if he gets in close. There is another important fish sense, however, that is a bit harder to grasp since we don't share it. This is the so-called lateral-line system. It is, in effect, a collection of inner ears running down the side of the fish's body. The result is a highly sensitive system that cues the fish in to whatever movements are going on in the water around him. This is the most sensitive organ most fish have to help them detect predators and prey, to perceive objects in the water and to determine which way the current is flowing.

By now you should have a fair idea of how your pet fish "sees" the world and how he deals with living in the aquatic environment.

Since you have some general sense of what is inside a fish as well, let's talk about how fish reproduce. First off, you caviar lovers out there know that most fishes lay eggs. The fact is that fishes lay so many eggs that if all the fish eggs in the world survived and grew up to be adults, there would be no room for redwood trees, moonlit beaches or human beings. Instead, we would be up to our noses in fish. As it happens, predators eat fish eggs and fry (baby fish), disease destroys fish eggs and fry, and consequently lots of fish eggs never even get to *be* fry.

There are numerous different ways of fertilizing and incubating eggs, each one offering certain advantages and disadvantages to the mother and offspring. If the mother lays her eggs and leaves them, without a care in the world, for instance, she runs the risk of having them eaten when she is not around. She will still, of course, be able to lay another day. If, on the other hand, she carries them with her, she has a better chance of protecting them; but her fate is their fate. If she becomes appetizer for a shark, so do her young.

Species of fishes that lay large numbers of eggs generally have a higher mortality in the clutch. Species that lay fewer eggs seem to take better care to ensure their offspring's survival. A good example of this is "mouth brooding," a technique practiced by many common aquarium fishes (such as some African cichlids) in which fry are protected in the mouth until they are old enough to fare for themselves, the mother fasting all the while so as not to ingest her babies.

Some fish engage in orgiastic luaus, males and females congregating together and releasing sperm and eggs in great impersonal clouds, letting water bring them together and hoping for the best. Still other fishes (tuna, for example), pair up to make babies. The female will release the eggs and the male will release the sperm that binds with the eggs. Fertilization is thus external. Internal fertilization occurs in some fishes, and is a bit more intimate, the male actually inseminating the female with what amounts to a penis. Sharks hold on to their mates with special structures called "claspers" from which there is seemingly no escape until the act is completed. If fertilization is internal and the mother holds the young until they come to term, she may even develop a primitive type of placenta to nourish the little ones as they grow up.

I have highlighted some of the interesting aspects of fish biology in the hopes of piquing your curiosity. Are you ready for the nitty-gritty of how to care for your pet fish? Read on!

THE HOME AQUARIUM

Aquaria have come a long way since I first set up a home for some fish twenty years ago. It used to be that tanks were slate-bellied monsters held together by stainless steel and glue. Nowadays tanks come in all different shapes and sizes and are made entirely of glass or acrylic. Nontoxic adhesives hold these containers together. Even though you have a lot more choice now than you used to and tanks are relatively inexpensive, the same rules for choosing what is best for your pet still apply. Remember that we are concerned with constructing the best possible environment for your exotic pet, not with designing attractive living-room furniture. My emphasis in this chapter is, as always, on the animal itself. If we manage to come up with an aquarium that is pleasing to the eye too, well, that's a bonus.

Choosing a Tank

When you pick a tank, start out with a medium-sized one—say, twenty gallons. Ironically, a smaller tank is more difficult to manage, as everything happens so quickly. The "buffer" of size is missing. If something goes wrong with the water, the whole tank is bad before you know it and you lose your fish. Too large a tank, on the other hand, is probably a waste of money when you are just starting out and also takes up lots of room. A medium-sized tank gives you enough protection against untoward events (dropping the pepper shaker into the tank or knocking the dish soap tankward) and at the same time will not put stress on your space and wallet.

The shape of the tank is important as well. I said in the last section that fish breathe oxygen after first extracting it from the water. The shape of the tank you choose will have a lot of bearing on the amount of oxygen in the water. If you think about it, you will realize that the oxygen in the water has a sort of free exchange going with the oxygen in the air. The water and air are touching, and molecules are traveling back and forth. A very deep tank has only a little bit of water in contact with the air. The rest of the water remains stagnant. As the fish breathes and takes the oxygen out, the tank becomes a bit stuffy, like a room with closed windows. To help keep your fish in what amounts to "the fresh air," choose a tank that is shallow, wide and long. Below we will see how to further oxygenate the water with pumping equipment.

Flooring and Decorating the Tank

What you put on the bottom of your tank can make the difference between a successful, low-maintenance aquarium that stays clean for a long period of time and an unbalanced, fouled tank that requires frequent attention. Remember that the dirt, waste and excess food present in the aquarium always ends up in the substrate. Certain friendly bacteria live down there, helping to break down the waste. The success of this process, however, depends upon the material you use. River rocks and shale are pretty, and pebbles can add variety, but for ease of maintenance nothing beats regular old aquarium gravel. Even the *size* of gravel you use is important. If the gravel is too large, pieces of detritus get caught and overwhelm the ability of the bacteria colony to degade them, fouling the tank. If the gravel is too small, there is insufficient free flow of water and air through the substrate, suffocating the helpful bugs. The best size for gravel is "medium-grade" natural gravel (the number and name vary with the supplier); any color is fine. Black seems to show many fishes off to their best advantage, but the ultimate choice of color will depend upon your taste and the decor of the surroundings.

The next consideration in setting up the tank is decoration. Live plants in an aquarium certainly improve the appearance of a tank and can enhance the environment for certain fishes. The downside, unfortunately, is that such plants are difficult to manage, foul the tank rapidly and in general are more trouble to us as *pet owners* (rather than aquarists) than they are worth. For years I have used plastic plants with great success. Some of these are quite realistic-looking, and none decay in the water. Also, plastic plants do not entice your fish to rip into them, thus turning them into flotsam.

At many points in this book, I can be caught emphasizing the "bare-cage" approach to pet keeping. This is in line with my philosophy of spending as much time as possible enjoying your pet and as little as possible cleaning up after him. To this end I suggest that rocks, plants and plastic decorations (except where otherwise noted) be kept to a minimum. When given too many places to hide, fish tend to do so, which means you rarely if ever see them. A few hiding spots are a good idea, but don't overdo it. I remember a sixty-gallon aquarium of mine in which swam some twenty small African cichlid fish. Each species was represented by a pair, so as to encourage breeding whenever possible. When it came time to break down the tank for cleaning, I took out my net and began to scoop out all forty fish. In the process I found that one of my male fish, a bright blue beauty, was missing. Since I kept a very careful watch and tally of all my pet fish, I was sure that he had been there the day before, and I began to fear the worst. I searched the tank without success. He was not to be found. At last I had no choice but to assume that my poor little friend had been eaten by another fish. I siphoned off all water and removed the rocks and plastic plants in order to make the tank easier to move. Taking out the last remaining rock, I found the little fellow gasping for air in the gravel, where apparently he had been hiding until it was nearly too late. He revived when I placed him in an aerated bucket with the other fish. I have learned through experience that an overly elaborate, overdecorated aquarium is a good way to have your fish disappear.

Keeping Your Fish Warm

Not every fish tank needs to be heated. If you are in the Sun Belt, you may be able to get away without a heater, particularly if you are keeping a cold-water species. In the majority of situations, however, tropical species do require supplemental heating. The fishes that we will discuss in this book require temperatures in the 68-to-86 degrees F. range. It is up to you to keep track of the temperature with an aquarium thermometer. I prefer the old-fashioned stainless steel thermometers that hang on the inside edge of the tank. The new strip thermometers that are pasted on the outside are also reliable and certainly attractive, but I personally find them a bit hard to read.

Keeping the water warm is a simple proposition. Nearly any type of commercially available aquarium heater will do. Such units have built-in thermostats that allow them to turn themselves on and off, maintaining the temperature that you preset. The vast majority of such heaters are built within a glass tube. Inside is a wire heating element set in a ceramic holder as well as a thermostat and switch. Most heaters clip onto the outside of the aquarium. In order for them to work properly the water must be filled to an indicated level on the tube. There is also another type of heater that is fully submersible. This latter type is more costly, but is of a more advanced design that allows the heater to be placed out of sight behind a rock or other decoration. A submerged heater should not be placed underneath the gravel, by the way, as this does not allow for proper dissipation of heat.

Aquarium heaters come in different wattages, ready to heat any tank from the smallest to the biggest. You don't want too strong a heater, as a thermostat malfunction could kill your pet before you even notice. (Remember the "buffer" concept: choosing the largest tank feasible and the weakest heater that will do the job will make any accidental cooking take long enough for you to detect it.) Too little wattage, on the other hand, will not be adequate to the task of keeping your scaly friends warm. If you have a ten-gallon tank, a 50-watt heater will do. A twenty-gallon tank will require 75 watts and a fifty-five-gallon tank (a common large-size aquarium) will require about 150 watts of heating power. Most modern aquarium heaters are both sensitive and reliable. Once you've set yours up, simply keeping a regular eye on the thermometer is all that is required. Two heater brands I recommend are Supreme and Ebo-Jaeger.

The Well-Lit Aquarium

While they lack the complex lighting requirements of some reptiles, fish need light eight to ten hours a day (a plug-in timer is helpful), just as we do, to see properly and stay happy. We can't put an aquarium by the window, though, because sunlight is too potent and encourages the rampant growth of algae. Incandescent bulbs are no good either, as they emit a great deal of heat and upset our careful temperature balance by warming the water to excess.

The lighting method of choice is a fluorescent fixture. If provided in your choice of blue or purple, a fluorescent bulb will light the tank in a pleasing cast without encouraging undue algal growth and will not heat up the water. Many aquariums are sold as "packages" containing the tank itself, a glass top and a fluorescent fixture. If you purchase a tank separately, fluorescent fixtures are readily available, and your pet shop can help you with the right size. Don't forget the top, though, if you buy just the lamp, as *all fish tanks must be covered to prevent your fish from leaping out!*

Filtering and Aerating Your Tank

I have suggested that you use long, low tanks as opposed to narrow, deep ones. The reason was to maximize the exchange of oxygen between air and water. Remember that fish must extract oxygen from water in order to breathe. The more oxygen you put in, the happier your fish will be. In addition to choosing the correct aquarium, the easiest way to achieve highly oxygenated water is to pump bubbles in by mechanical means. A large number of suitable air pumps are available at your local pet shop, and your dealer can advise you as to how powerful a model you need. The majority of these pumps (Silent Giant, Whisper and Apollo are some good brands) work on a plastic diaphragm that is pushed out and in to pump air. You connect the pump (always placing it *above* the waterline, so that water won't flow back into the unit should it fail or be unplugged) via plastic tubing to a porous "air stone" sunk into the aquarium, and voila! bubbles. Stones of varying porosity are available, producing small, medium and large bubbles. I prefer medium-sized bubbles as they produce a greater oxygen exchange with the water than large bubbles and move more water (keeping oxygen-rich water circulating) than small ones. Putting more air into the water enables your tank to support more fish as well. (More on the number of fish you should put in a tank below.) Mostly, however, it really improves the quality of life for your pets, and that is the name of the game.

Well-oxygenated water is necessary, but your pet's environment has got to be clean, too. Even the smallest fish in the biggest tank needs *some* kind of filtration. Whether this means cleaning the tank frequently, scooping out dirt with a strainer or sucking it out with a siphon hose, some kind of filtering is going on. Luickily for us fish lovers, technology has brought us a host of powerful and effective devices for purifying your pet's water of even the most microscopic organisms and debris.

There are a couple of strategies for the novice fish keeper who has two or three fish in a medium-sized tank and wants to keep them happy and healthy. The first strategy is to get a device that removes the water from the tank, runs it through a mechanical filter such as a fiber mesh and some absorbing charcoal, and returns it to the tank. (So-called activated charcoal, by the way, functions just like a miniature sieve, filtering out chemicals instead of food and feces.) This combination of a flossy substance for trapping big particles and charcoal for trapping small particles is very efficient. Such outside filters are very potent, turning over as much as six hundred gallons an hour. If you have a twenty-gallon tank being filtered by a unit that pumps, say, three hundred gallons an hour, the water in your pet's tank is being totally cleaned every four minutes. Another high point of this kind of filtration is that aeration is occurring by simple movement of water. The principle is the one that makes you prefer to drink from a swift-running stream rather than from a still pond: the water is simply freshened by flow. Having the charcoal and the floss outside the tank is another plus, since you need not upset the tank itself or its inhabitants when you clean out the filter. Please remember that powerful outside filters create enough suction to draw a small fish up into the intake tubes. Cover the ends of the tubes with the plastic strainers provided with the device to prevent your pet's untimely demise. The size of the filter you require depends upon the size of your tank and the number of fish in it. Most models (Aquaclear and Dynaflow are two filters I recommend) come in a variety of sizes, and your pet shop can help you choose the size you need.

The second tactic I mentioned for keeping fish water clean works on a slightly different principle. Instead of drawing water to a chamber outside the aquarium, purifying it there and returning it fresh, this unit sits right inside the tank! The "undergravel" filter begins by sucking the dirt right down to the bottom of the tank, where it wants to fall anyway. There at the bottom, under the layer of gravel you have provided, lurk our helpful bacteria. The best and most effective units that work on this principle utilize a pump to push the water back up from underneath to spigots at the waterline, thus increasing the downward flow (water must rush in to replace what is being pumped up). These filters are especially good for varieties like rams and discus, which prefer a quiet environment without too much current.

If you have been thinking about the filtering process, you may have realized that a combination of the outside, mechanical filtration with the under-the-gravel, biological filtration represents the ideal case. This much filtration, however, is rarely necessary in the home aquarium unless a tank is very crowded.

Water Hardness and pH

As you might surmise, water is not the same everywhere. Minerals at the shoreline, as well as at the bottom of a body of water, have a great effect on the water's properties. Vegetation that falls into the water, together with pollutants and acid that falls with the rain in certain parts of the world all have a great impact on the intimate world of the fish. All fishes are adapted to particular kinds of water, and while some show a remarkable tolerance for variation, most fishes have certain basic requirements in their water that we must heed if we wish them to thrive. It may be annoying, and sometimes precludes the mixing of certain fishes in the same tank, but there really is no way around it.

The two key measurements of water properties are hardness and pH. The former is an expression of the presence of minerals, chiefly calcium and magnesium, in the water. Hard water leaves a white scum on your pipes and in your tank and is full of minerals that form these deposits. Soft water is relatively devoid of these substances. Since tap water (never use distilled water for fish, as it lacks critical trace ingredients such as copper) in different cities across the country has different hardness, you may have to alter the quality of the water from your faucet to suit the fishes of your choosing. Inexpensive chemicals for this purpose are available cheaply from your local pet shop.

The second measure, pH, is an indication of how much unattached hydrogen there is floating around in the water. Water molecules, as you know, consist of two hydrogen atoms and one oxygen atom bonded together into the stuff we call good old H_2O. These bonds, like most things, are imperfect, and sometimes there are hydrogen atoms running around with no oxygen to bond to. The pH system measures the quantity of these on a scale of 14, with 7 being the neutral amount found in the water that helps make up the blood of most vertebrates. A pH of less than 7 means the water is acid, like vinegar, while a pH higher than 7 means the water is alkaline.

It is not too important that you understand all the chemistry involved in hardness and pH. What is important, though, is that you realize that these two qualities matter a very great deal to your fish and you have to pay attention to them. Again, your local pet shop can furnish you with an inexpensive and simple means of assessing and adjusting both pH and hardness. Once the pH and hardness are appropriate for the fish you plan to put in the tank, I recommend adding a small amount of "water conditioner" before actually, physically introducing the fish. Sold under various brand names, a conditioner adds a protective coat to the water and the fish similar to the natural slime that fish exude. This added "buffer" helps avoid injury during the highly stressful first minutes of life in a new small world.

The Right Number of Fish

Fish make water dirty, and you already know that it is important for the fish that you keep the water clean. Pumps and filters make this a relatively easy job, certainly preferable to hefting the tank onto your shoulders for a trip to the garden hose, but you can still overwhelm these devices by overcrowding your tank.

The acquisitive urge hits most of us sooner or later, especially as we become involved with fish and find out how beautiful and fascinating they really are. I remember that early on in my fish-keeping career, perhaps fifteen years ago, I purchased a four-foot-long, fifty-five-gallon tank and set it up bare, with a powerful outside filter. Next I went to the store and bought two tiny baby oscars less than an inch long apiece. My friends said I was crazy, but I stuck to my very extreme posture, knowing that in principle at least, it was best not to crowd my fish.

Unfortunately, I was too impatient to let these fish grow into the tank. I soon fell prey to the "just one more" syndrome, a deadly and chronic ailment of nearly all fish keepers. I found all kinds of fish that would live happily with the baby oscars. I added a pump and air stone, then some gravel and an undergravel filter. I put in a couple of rocks, and pretty soon I had a full-fledged community tank of forty or fifty fish. I could no longer find my original pair of oscars. One day I woke to find many fish covered with "velvet" and fungus, two typical fish ailments, and I lost many of my fish, including the original two.

What I had done was exceed the "carrying capacity" of the tank. This term describes a known natural principle of any environment that very simply suggests that you can put only so many animals into a confined space. It is hard to predict the magic number, as it depends upon how much and what kind of food the animals eat and how much and what kind of waste they produce. (A rule of thumb might be to give each fish at least three gallons of water.) Also involved are how the animals get along, whether they have big personal territories and are reproducing rapidly, and of course, how big they are. My tank was substantially below "carrying capacity" when I introduced the two baby Oscars, but I quickly exceeded the tank's capacity with the additional fish. In the end, the natural tendency of the community to return to a more stable number permitted disease to sweep through the "population" and reduce the number of fish, since I would not.

The moral of the story is that fish keeping is great, and so is having a number of fish. Before you get swept away by the variety and beauty of the fishes available to you, though, spend some time considering the fish as your pet. Learn something about him by watching. Learn to predict where in the tank you will find him at a given time of day. Learn what foods he prefers and what seem to be the best for him. Enjoy interacting with him by feeding by hand, and if you have a couple of fish, examine their interactions with each other and learn if and how they communicate. You may find that having just a few fish whose behavior you come to recognize and understand is the best way to enjoy these amazing animals. There is no magic quantity, but by limiting the number of fish that you own you are more likely to experience the joy of having *pets* and not a collection!

FEEDING YOUR FISH

In comparison with the other exotic animals treated in this book, fish support an old, vast and well-established industry. Fish really are big business. There are scores of aquarium companies, scores of filter and pump and heater companies and scores of fish-food companies. High-quality, effective prepared fish foods are available in numerous forms, including frozen, freeze-dried, flake and pellet. A lot of research goes into the formulations of the better labels (Hikari is an example), which are often specifically tailored to a given group or type of fish and include the appropriate quantities of vitamins, minerals, roughage and protein. There are very few fishes that will not thrive, grow and even breed on these prepared foods. Your retailer can recommend given brands and varieties with which he has had success.

To further enjoy your fish and his full range of behaviors, you may wish to give him live food once a week or so. Except where it is suggested as the basis of a diet, live food should be viewed as a treat, a way for you to feel that you are doing something special for your buddy, and should not be fed too often. Remember that you are safer with the balanced nutrition of a carefully devised commercial food.

Earthworms are a commonly available and inexpensive food for your pet. Section them with a knife into bite-sized morsels if your pet is small. If you have a large fish, simply toss the worm in and watch it go down. The only preparation necessary is a good rinsing to be sure that mulch and earth do not foul your tank. You can find earthworms by digging in the backyard, or at your local bait shop. In winter, naturally, they are a bit scarce.

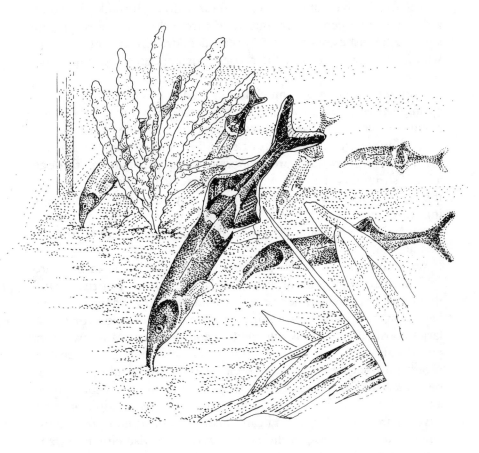

Peter's elephant nose

Tubifex worms and bloodworms (*Tubifex* and *Limnodrilus* species) are another group that fish seem to relish. These worms are small and stringy, though some of the bloodworms can reach several inches in length. If simply dumped into the tank, these worms tend to burrow quickly into the safety of the substrate. This is fine for the likes of catfish and elephant-nosed fishes, as these varieties will penetrate the gravel to reach the worms. Other worm lovers, such as discus fish, are best fed from a worm cup. This is a funnel-shaped device which attaches inside the tank near the top, usually by means of a suction cup. It bears tiny holes from which the worms protrude as they wriggle around. As they stick out, the worms are pecked off by your eager fish. This method of worm feeding rarely allows a worm to escape to the haven of the gravel and rarely fouls the tank. Watching a discus or two gently nibbling worms from the cup is a rewarding sight. Other fishes, such as the African cichlids, will tear at the worms without mercy, revealing their voracious appetites and aggressive personalities.

Another food that is as much fun to feed as it is nutritious is brine shrimp *(Artemia salina).* These little crustaceans (crab relatives) are sometimes known as "sea monkeys" and are available from your pet shop as either energetic adults or eggs. Hatching the eggs is an easy task and represents the more economical approach if you go through a lot of shrimp. Not all fish will go for these little guys, but watching the shrimp themselves cavort around as they are chased is entertaining. It seems that with brine shrimp and tubifex worms the fish get as much of a charge out of the feeding process as they get nutritional benefit.

While it is fun to watch your pet eat live food, you must guard against overfeeding. Some fishes, such as goldfish, will really stuff themselves, whereas other varieties seem to know when they have had enough. Speaking of goldfish, they make great food for other, larger carnivores such as big cichlids and piranhas. Minnows from your local bait shop are equally good and sometimes less expensive.

Several light feedings a day seem to be more healthful for your pets than one or two enormous meals. If this is not practical, most adult fish will do fine on a morning-and-evening schedule, but fry have a hard time of it. If you can't manage to feed more frequently when you have young in the tank, it might be wise either to trade them to your local pet shop for some older fish or to purchase an "automatic" feeder. This is a block of neutral material that comes impregnated with fish food. As the block dissolves, the food is slowly released into the water. You can rely on this device if you plan to be away from home a few days, but don't feed this way too often, as the food contained is not of high caliber.

Speaking of being away, most fishes can easily deal with a day or two of fasting, so long as it doesn't happen too often and the fish are mature and in good condition. Feeding your pets should be an enjoyable activity, a time to interact with your exotic animals and get to know them better. Remember that feeding time is the highlight of your animal's day. When else does your fish pay you as much attention as at dinnertime? You can take advantage of this period of rapt attention by training your pets to come to your tap and wait with gaping maws at the surface. Try to stick to a feeding schedule, feeding at the same time daily. This will ensure that your pets are eagerly awaiting your approach!

CHOOSING YOUR FISH

So you want a fish! But what kind of fish? How do you know if the fish you want is healthy? What are the specific requirements of your chosen pet? This last section provides the specific information that you will need. In it I suggest a variety of species, and you should certainly peruse the chapter before making any decisions. The best procedure to follow once you have selected your pet is the one I suggest throughout the book. First decide which fish you want, then set up its tank, and finally purchase the beast.

Choosing your fish can be a lot of fun. All the world's selection is before you, thanks to a large pet industry. Read the list below, go visit your local museum or aquarium and stop into as many pet shops as possible. Get a look at as many different kinds of fish as you can to get a sense of what types attract you. Chances are good you have preferences you don't even know about yet. I find, for instance, that my tastes run more toward carnivorous fishes than herbivorous ones. In addition, I tend to prefer roundish fishes to long, tube-shaped ones (catfish excepted; I love catfish). There are no value judgments here, of course; all this is just a matter of taste. Simply explore what is around and learn what you like. Once you have settled on a fish or two, read up in this book (or another if I don't cover the fish of your choice) and learn about the animal's requirements.

The sex of the fish you buy is of significance in only two instances: First, there are some fishes in which one sex is the more brightly colored (some African cichlids are a good example), and you may desire the gaudier colors. Second, you may wish to breed your pets. The "hows" of breeding are beyond the scope of this book (most fish just take care of things on their own anyway), but the "whys" should be obvious. It is a satisfying and lucrative situation when your pets reproduce, but telling male from female in order to get a pair may be beyond the ken of either your pet dealer or the available fish guides. A recognized authority at a nearby aquarium or university might be able to help out, but if not, you should purchase at least a trio of the same species to maximize your chances of having a pair. Obviously, if breeding is of primary interest to you, it's advisable to choose a species that can be readily sexed.

The last important aspect of fish choosing is compatability. The first parameter is the actual water the fishes require. Discus fish, for instance, like soft, slightly acid water. African cichlids prefer things hard and alkaline. The second parameter is temperament. While there are never any guarantees that particular fish are going to get along in a particular situation, you can improve the odds a lot by paying attention to a fish's reputation (aggressive or docile) and biology (plant eater or meat eater); but the bottom line will come from the guy who has tried it: namely, your pet dealer.

The Fish Physical

When you have arrived at a decision, run through the following checklist to be sure that the animal you want as your pet is in good health. These guidelines guarantee nothing, of course, as most aquarium fishes live only a few years in captivity and you may be about to buy the Old Man of the Lake. Still, it will keep you out of obvious and immediate trouble.

1. Are all the fins in good shape? Look at both sides of the fish to be sure no fins are missing, and avoid a fish with ragged, tattered fins.

2. Are the fins flowing freely in the current? Fins that are held in tightly against the body (clamped) suggest that something is amiss. (Bear in mind that fish observe a "pecking order." Not all the fish in the tank have equal status. Those that are dominant will display deeper, richer colors and fins that are flawless and held erect like

flags. Take a moment to watch intratank dynamics. Underfish in one tank can be top fish in another, so don't necessarily avoid a fish who is being cowed by larger tankmates.)

3. Are there any signs of fungus or scale disease? Do you see fuzzy yellow or white spots or filaments on the fish? Look at the head and make sure that the scales are not pitted. All of these are warning signs for fish diseases that, while not necessarily fatal, are sometimes difficult to quell and highly communicable.

4. Run the feeding test. Nearly any fish in a pet-shop situation is perpetually hungry. This is not because pet-shop owners are barbarous and stingy, but rather that they are running a business on a tight budget and most fish have big appetites. Ask if you can feed the fish some flake or pellet food. He should shoot straight for it. If he doesn't, try some worms or brine shrimp. Pay for them if you absolutely must. If nothing entices the fish of your heart to chow down, forget him and pick another who will eat for you on the spot. Loss of appetite is often a sign of internal or early-stage disease.

5. How do the eyes look? Are there any bulges or lumps in or near the eyes? What about clarity? Does one eye look cloudier than the other? Eye disease in fish is fairly common and can be difficult to treat. Avoid a fish with suspicious-looking eyes.

All right, you have made your choice and you are ready to take your fish home. The tank has been set up and waiting for your friend for several days. You have used a water purifier to remove chemicals from your tap water and you have squirted a conditioner into the water that will coat the fish and protect his natural slimy coating when he bumps into rocks and glass, investigating the boundaries of his new world. Ask your pet dealer to squirt a bit of conditioner right into the plastic bag with your new pet for added protection, and be sure there is at least a twenty-four-hour guarantee on the animal. A burst of pure oxygen from a compressor will help saturate the water in the bag and make breathing easier for your pet on the trip to your house.

Although the water in the bag provides a buffer both from mechanical insult and from extremes of hot and cold, you should baby your fish on the way home. When you arrive, let the bag float in the tank for a half-hour, thus letting the bag temperature equilibrate with the temperature of the water in the tank. If you were to simply drop the new entry in, he might go into temperature shock. This manifests itself by an inability to orient himself in the water. A fish suffering from temperature shock will float belly up or try to do a headstand in the water. While it looks awful, this is only a temporary condition. Still, it is best to avoid it entirely by floating the bag. While he is floating, the other fish in the tank have an opportunity to come up and examine him, thus giving you an early and safe indicator of potential problems between your fish.

When it is time to release the new fish, take the bag out of the water and cut it open. Pour the water through a net into the sink, allowing the fish to tumble gently into the fishnet. Never touch a fish with your hands, as this will immediately break down the slime layer that surrounds and protects your pet's scales.

Once in the net, the fish should be taken immediately to the tank and may be plopped in without further ado. Never allow any water from a pet-shop aquarium to enter your home tank. The risk of introducing dirt and disease is high. Many advanced hobbyists worry so much about communicable disease in their fish that they actually set up a quarantine tank, a sort of small way station between big home aquarium and the pet shop, in which a new fish will stay for a week. This may sound overly cautious, but it is better than having all your pets wiped out by fungus or bacteria brought in by a solitary newcomer.

FISHES I RECOMMEND

I have already alluded to the myriad of choices awaiting you, the new fish keeper. While this makes things very exciting for you, it makes them very tough for me, as there are so many fishes I enjoy and could well recommend. I have made my choices, as usual, on the basis of availability, hardiness, price and special characteristics. I have done my best to serve up a representative sample of the tens of thousands of the world's fishes. There are three rough categories that I have employed to help break down this bewildering array. The first category is cichlid (pronounced "sick-lid") fishes. These are quite possibly the most popular of all aquarium fishes. They are bony, tropical, warm-water species, highly advanced in their reproductive behavior and also quite territorial, given to displays of aggression and defensive behavior. Their active and sometimes hostile brains makes these possibly the most responsive and lively of all pet fishes.

I have chosen two cichlids from South America and six from Africa. Although there are a number of cichlid fishes that hail from African rivers, most of the celebrated aquarium fishes from the area come out of either Lake Tanganyika or Lake Malawi. These two famous lakes, the seventh and ninth largest in the world, are host to an incredible variety of cichlids that are referred to in the trade simply as "Africans." Both lakes are high in pH and are full of islands, rocky caverns and outcroppings. Each lake has a special fauna. Malawi has more different types of fishes than any other lake in the world, and Tanganyika sports perhaps one hundred and fifty species that occur absolutely nowhere else on earth.

The second category is catfish, to which I am especially partial. These are the noncombative, obdurate citizens of the freshwater environment. They are so tough that nobody messes with them, yet unaggressive and singularly unconcerned with dominance games in the tank, preferring to swim to the beat of their own drummer. Various species of catfish are used as bottom or "cleaner" fish in community aquariums. While they cannot subsist on feces, they will eat any detritus that falls to the bottom, uneaten by the other fish. The housemaid role, incidentally, does the catfish a great injustice. These are beautiful and fascinating fishes in their own right and should not be regarded as merely living vacuum cleaners. Many are nocturnal, and as such can be a special treat for the owner who is also.

The last group in the recommended section is the miscellaneous fishes. These are animals which possess some unique characteristic that makes them either irresistible or fascinating or both. The elephant-nosed fish is an example. You can guess how he gets his name!

For each of the twenty fishes I have chosen, I state the sort of water (preferred pH and water hardness) they need, the type of food that is best and a description of their appearance and temperament. I also give a ballpark figure for the price of each species, though the market fluctuates some and these figures may be a bit low by the time you read this. Realize that baby fish will be at the low end of the price range, while large, healthy adults will sport the stiffest tag. The price you see is for an average, in-between-sized fish.

Remember to consider the water quality, temperature and temperament when considering whether to mix certain fishes. These parameters must match pretty closely or you are in for some problems. Everything on the list should be pretty self-explanatory, so without further delay, here are nineteen exciting creatures for your pleasure:

1. Jewel cichlid *(Hemichromis bimaculatus)*

This is an African cichlid fish and a river dweller. To me it is one of the loveliest of all aquarium fishes. The color, especially in a dominant animal, is a deep and bright red, punctuated by powder blue polka dots. Jewel cichlids are not, unfortunately, as lovely in temperament as they are to behold. They do best by themselves or in pairs, as they are not quite nasty enough to be housed with the African lake cichlids but are too mean to house with anything else. They thrive in well-aerated water, and I have kept a good number of these fish and found them to be extremely hardy. They do well on just about any kind of commercial food that is formulated expressly for cichlids and are most often seen at about an inch and a half to two inches in length. As jewels grow to four or five inches, they will relish smaller fish as dinner. So-called feeder guppies and goldfish make fine fare.

> WATER: not critical
> TEMPERATURE: 78 degrees F.
> TEMPERAMENT: highly aggressive
> FOOD: cichlid diet with occasional live food
> SIZE: to 6 inches
> PRICE: $5

2. Rusty cichlid *(Iodotropheus sprengerae)*

Our next fish is a resident of Lake Malawi. The rusty cichlid is a mouth brooder that guards and raises its young between its teeth, fasting all the while. Like some other Malawi cichlids, it likes a half-teaspoon of noniodized salt (iodine is toxic to fish) per gallon of aquarium water to bring out its marvelous deep brownish-purple color. This is not an easygoing fish, but does make a fine community animal when kept with other "Africans." I think the rusty is one of the finest-looking of all cichlid fishes.

> WATER: hard, with a pH no less than 8
> TEMPERATURE: 78 degrees F.

TEMPERAMENT: highly aggressive
FOOD: cichlid diet with occasional live food
SIZE: to 4 inches
PRICE: $5

3. Malawian eye eater *(Haplichromis compressiceps)*

Unlike the rusty cichlid, this is not a good community animal. Its narrow, compressed head makes it look for all the world like a miniature freshwater barracuda, and it is, in fact, fearsomely aggressive. When the eye eater feeds, it aims its head right at its prey from above, nose pointing straight down to the gravel. The term eye eater is, at least in my experience, a misnomer, since I have never seen it attack the eye of another fish. Make no mistake, however, this unique-looking animal is very aggressive, but that is part of what makes him so interesting. He also spends a good deal of time vertical in the water, like a compulsive headstander.

WATER: hard, with a pH no less than 8
TEMPERATURE: 78 degrees F.
TEMPERAMENT: very aggressive; best housed alone or with slightly less aggressive fish of larger size
FOOD: cichlid diet and live small fish in equal proportions
SIZE: to 10 inches
PRICE: $7

4. Malawian "auratus" *(Melanochromis auratus)*

Equally tough, less expensive and certainly more common than the eye eater, the auratus, while a rough-and-ready fish, is also a bit better suited to community life. Fish of this species grow like weeds if you feed them well and when young are yellowish with broad black head-to-tail striping that become rimmed in blue as the fish matures. If the animal is destined to be a female, the gold on the body will deepen and the black stripe will come to shine. If the fish is going to be a male, the colors will reverse themselves and the body will turn black, the stripe yellow. Give them a few rocks and caverns and these little fish will cavort through them all day long, establishing "home" territories which they will vigorously defend, especially as the time to breed approaches.

WATER: hard, with a pH no less than 8
TEMPERATURE: 78 degrees F.
TEMPERAMENT: aggressive
FOOD: cichlid diet with occasional live food
SIZE: to 8 inches
PRICE: $3

5. Lyre-tailed cichlid *(Lamprologus brichardi)*

Leaving Lake Malawi for Lake Tanganyika, we find a fish that is quite different from the compact, elongated auratus. The lyretail is a mellow, graceful cichlid whose pale coloration is a good indicator of its retiring temperament. The light tan of the body ends in flowing blue fins that are almost fluorescent in a healthy individual. Because they are so gentle, it is best not to keep lyretails with other Africans. In a medium-sized (ten to twenty gallon) tank, a pair will thrive and lose some of their shyness, allowing you to see them constantly. Provide a few plastic plants and some scattered rocks for security, but the elaborate cavework relished by the auratus is unnecessary.

WATER: hard, with a pH no less than 8
TEMPERATURE: 79 degrees F.
TEMPERAMENT: retiring and gentle
FOOD: flake cichlid diet, freeze dried and live foods in equal
   proportions
SIZE: to 4 inches
PRICE: $15

6. Frontosa *(Cyphotilapia frontosa)*

The large hump on its head helps distinguish the male of this species, the last African cichlid on the list. This gorgeous, rare and costly fish is every "African" fancier's dream. The frontosa is a peaceful fish that enjoys rockwork like the auratus and features bright black and blue alternating vertical stripes. I have raised a few of this beautiful species from tiny fry and find that they require regular feedings of live worms or brine shrimp. This fish used to command ten times the price it does now, because it was rarely seen. It turned out that it was not quite so rare as collectors suspected, but rather lived at greater depths. Frontosas are being bred successfully in captivity now, so we are fortunate in having a good number available without putting undue stress on the wild population. If

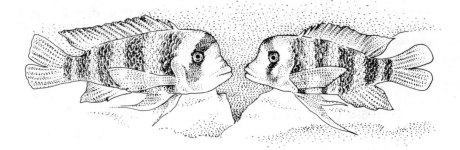

Frontosa

your taste runs to a deep tank, the frontosa will enjoy a bit more depth than other fishes, but is best kept to itself because of its non-combative habits and high value.

WATER: hard, with a pH no less than 8
TEMPERATURE: 79 degrees F.
TEMPERAMENT: shy and gentle
FOOD: live food in quantity, especially worms and brine shrimp; also cichlid flake
SIZE: to 12 inches
PRICE: $20–50

7. Albino channel catfish *(Ictalurus punctatus)*

This first catfish on the list is a native species, and a very striking animal, particularly in albino form approaching its three-foot maximum size. It is unlikely that you can raise this indiscriminate and voracious feeder to that size in your home, but it doesn't hurt to try! You can keep the channel cat in a community tank with other cold-water species when it is young, but as it matures, look out! Any other fish is fair game. I had a young channel cat alone in a twenty-gallon tank and managed to get it to six inches in less than a year by feeding it constantly. Keeping it alone and feeding it so often, I developed a real rapport with the animal and it made a great pet. It would come to the surface immediately when I approached the tank, its red albino eye gleaming in its stark-white body. It is said that the albino form has poor vision, but it surely saw me coming! Should you raise an albino channel cat to a prodigious size and feel that you no longer have room for the animal, your local aquarium may want it. Perhaps you can even talk a local pet shop into using it as a display animal. No one could say that this animal is anything less than wonderfully impressive when grown.

> WATER: hardness not critical, neutral pH (7)
> TEMPERATURE: 62 degrees F.
> TEMPERAMENT: moderate when young, best housed alone when large
> FOOD: any commercial flake, freeze dried or pelleted food
> SIZE: to 3 feet
> PRICE: $2

8. African electric catfish *(Malapterurus electricus)*

Reaching two-thirds the length of our native channel cat, the electric catfish is unlike almost all the other fishes in the world. Employing special organs spread all over his skin, he can generate 350 watts of electricity. What exactly this brown-and-white fish does with all that power is unclear. He may use it to sense his environment, as does the elephant-nosed fish described later, or he may use it as a weapon to stun his prey. Certainly he has a potent defensive weapon at his disposal and should be manipulated with caution. *One should never touch an electric catfish with bare hands,* for while he cannot kill you, he can certainly make you sorry you messed with him! My small electric catfish lives in a ten-gallon aquarium with a strong

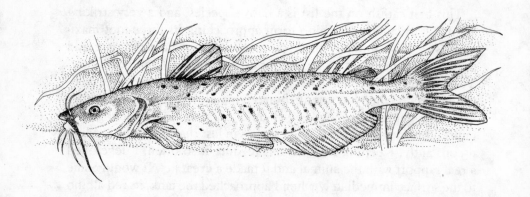

Albino channel catfish

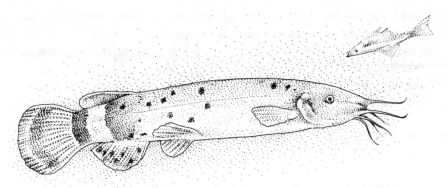

Electric catfish

outside filter clearing the debris left over from the smaller fishes he regularly devours. Needless to say, he lives alone. It seems electric cats don't see terribly well, so a prey item must swim very close by in order to be lunch. It may be a disturbance in his electric field that alerts the catfish to nearby movement.

WATER: medium-soft, neutral pH (7)
TEMPERATURE: 78 degrees F.
TEMPERAMENT: predatory, aggressive, best housed alone
FOOD: small fishes which it eats whole
SIZE: to 30 inches; usually much smaller
PRICE: $50

9. Black-bellied upside-down catfish *(Synodontis nigriventris)*

When you first see this African catfish, you may think him demented. Believe it or not, he actually spends most of his time swimming upside down, his belly to the sky! Perhaps this is a strategy for getting the most possible food out of his environment, for when right-side up he can scour the gravel for worms and when upside down he can eat flake food right off the surface.

This unusual catfish demonstrates a fascinating twist of normal fish biology. The great majority of fishes are darkly colored on the back and more lightly colored on the belly. When a predator views the average fish from underneath, the light belly allows the prey to blend in with the overhead sky and remain unnoticed. Conversely, a predator looking down from above will fail to discern many prey fishes because the dark back melts into the darkness of deep water. In fact, what we see is that this catfish's coloration, like his swimming, is reversed. Thus, when employing his accustomed mode of locomotion, this crazy, clever little fish is perfectly camouflaged.

Despite their mild temper, I prefer to see this species either alone or with other catfish, as frenetic activity seems to send them scooting to safety and makes them hard to see.

WATER: soft, with a pH slightly less than 7
TEMPERATURE: 79 degrees F.
TEMPERAMENT: mild, best housed alone or with other catfish
FOOD: flake or pellet food or live worms
SIZE: to 3 inches
PRICE: $7

10. African polka-dot catfish *(Synodontis angelicus)*

The last catfish on the list is the rarest and costliest fish that I have to recommend. I have included it despite its high price tag because it gives a good idea of the upper limit of the freshwater hobby. This is a striking, nocturnal animal—black with white polka dots, but this description fails to get across the little fellow's majesty.

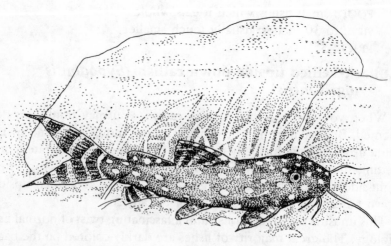

Polkadot catfish

Shy, retiring and nocturnal like most members of his genus, this fish requires rocks to hide under, plastic plants to swim through and a quiet environment. Naturally you should feed him as much live food as possible and take all the precautions discussed to make sure that the water quality is correct. If you decide you want a polka-dot catfish, you will have to special-order it from your fish dealer. Once you have it, hang on to it even if your home breaks up and you lose your job!

WATER: soft, pH of 7
TEMPERATURE: 80 degrees F.
TEMPERAMENT: mild, but because of its great value should be housed alone
FOOD: high-quality flake and pellet food and live worms
SIZE: to 8 inches
PRICE: $150

11. Peter's elephant-nose *(Gnathonemus petersi)*

Those who appreciate the out-of-the-ordinary will definitely appreciate this first of the "miscellaneous" group of fishes on my list. Like the electric catfish, the elephant-nose generates an electric current. Though it is capable of producing only a weak current and cannot shock or hurt the aquarist, it is a heck of a worm hunter. Using organs located on either side of his tail, this creature sets up a pulsating electric field. Interruptions in the field tell the fish that prey, currents or predators are in the area. This system is particularly useful to the elephant-nose because it lives and hunts at night in turbid waters with much stirred-up detritus and silt.

The name elephant-nose comes from the elongated proboscis that this animal uses to uproot worms found by its "radar." The animal is gray with some white markings and appears to have two tails, one behind the other. The bizarre appearance of this fish has made it popular even among people who don't know just how special it really is. For some time now I have had twelve of this species in a sixty-gallon "long"-style aquarium. The tank is thick with plastic plants that obscure the fish a bit and give them a feeling of security. I put several inches of gravel on the bottom of the tank, and during the day I add some bloodworms and tubifex worms to the water. The worms sink quickly to the gravel and bury themselves, largely unnoticed and untouched by the fish. At night the elephant-noses swim accurately through the plants without ever bumping anything or anyone, cruising the bottom, intent on the worm hunt. Suddenly one will orient himself with his tail in the air and ram his nose down into the gravel, wiggling like crazy to drive it deeper. A moment later he will withdraw his "trunk" and there will be a worm hanging from his mouth!

I made the mistake at one point of trying to mix some golden rams (discussed below) with the elephant-noses. The fact that the rams were a good bit smaller than the elephant-noses would, I imagined, not cause a problem, since the elephant-noses were worm eaters, not fish chasers. Was I ever wrong! The elephant-noses went after the rams in true pachyderm tradition. They rammed and butted, snorted and spat, chasing the rams all over the tank until I had no choice but to remove the victims and save the day. Keep your elephant-noses alone or with others of their kind and you should have no problems.

WATER: soft, pH a bit less than 7
TEMPERATURE: 80 degrees F.
TEMPERAMENT: usually not aggressive, but will harass smaller
 fish
FOOD: live worms of various types are best
SIZE: to 10 inches
PRICE: $15

12. Clown loach *(Botia macracantha)*

The clown loach, from Borneo and Sumatra, is another odd-looking creature which unlike most popular fishes is not known to have bred in captivity. It is an orange animal, with black vertical bars down its sides. Clown loaches do well in a community. Like catfish, they are neither passive nor aggressive, disdaining contact with other fish and cleaning detritus from the tank bottom, but unlike most catfish they are not predominantly nocturnal.

WATER: not critical
TEMPERATURE: 70 degrees F.
TEMPERAMENT: noncombative; a good fish for a communal
 tank
FOOD: detritus on tank bottom plus some live food
SIZE: to 13 inches
PRICE: $15 (up to $50 for truly large individuals)

13. Mono *(Mono argenteus)*

The mono comes from coastal waters of the Indian and South Pacific oceans. You may remember that I claimed to exclude marine fishes from consideration because they are so difficult for the novice fish owner to keep alive. They *are* difficult, but this beautiful silver fish with large orange fins and black-striped body is here for a special reason: While at its best in saltwater, the mono does live in estuaries as well, and as such can be kept in a freshwater aquarium with just a teaspoonful of noniodized salt per gallon (remember that iodine is toxic to fish).

I had great success raising a baby alone in a sparsely decorated fifteen-gallon aquarium, and soon had to transfer him to a thirty- and then a forty-gallon tank. Monos do best by themselves or with others of their kind. They are sizable fish, being just as deep from top to bottom as they are long.

> WATER: pH slightly more than 7; a teaspoon of noniodized salt per gallon when you're setting up the tank will help bring out color and improve appetite
> TEMPERATURE: 72 degrees F.
> TEMPERAMENT: retiring
> FOOD: live worms and brine shrimp; flake food
> SIZE: to 9 inches; usually half that
> PRICE: $20

14. West African butterfly fish *(Pantodon buchholzi)*

In appearance the butterfly fish is not nearly so impressive as the mono, but it possesses an enviable talent that makes it just as interesting! Like the marine flying fish, the butterfly fish uses its large pectoral (shoulder) fins to help it skim across the water for short distances. Because of these long fins, which trail in the water, it is best to keep the butterfly fish by itself lest some other fish show an interest in munching on its "wings." In addition, because it can "fly" the fish must be kept in a securely covered tank that has lots of surface area; a "long"-style tank is the right idea. I have found that when feeding, this species rarely descends to depth, preferring instead to wait on the surface until you drop some food into the tank. Flake or pellet will do, but if you want a real treat, catch a fly or beetle, toss it in and watch the fish fly to its meal!

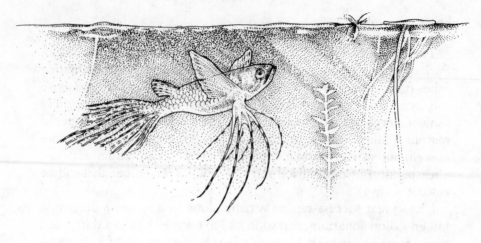

Butterfly fish

WATER: soft, pH a bit less than 7
TEMPERATURE: 77 degrees F.
TEMPERAMENT: moderate, but best kept alone because of its
    delicate fins
FOOD: flake will be eaten, but live insects are best
SIZE: to 4 inches
PRICE: $12

15. Holland's piranha *(Serrasalmus hollandi)*

My choice of the piranha will do little for my reputation as a sane
man, but the fact is that Holland's is one of the smallest and least
dangerous of the piranhas and makes a fine pet in those states where
it is legal to own one. (Some states, including California, New York
and Florida, have laws against all piranhas in fear that they will get
loose and propagate in local lakes and streams. Be sure to check with
your pet store regarding laws in your area.) The South American
genus *Serrasalmus,* to which this species belongs, includes the large
red-bellied and equally large black piranha (pronounced pee-rahn-
yah), well known for their savage attacks on creatures, including
man, that enter waters where large numbers are present. Large piranhas are equipped with amazingly sharp teeth and strong jaws which
allow them to go through flesh like an electric razor on a rampage.

This particular species, with its silver body, yellow belly and red ventral (bottom) fin, is neither so formidably equipped as its larger relatives nor so nasty, though you should always keep fingers, toes and the tip of your nose out of the tank so as not to encourage disaster. Use a large net if you must move your fish—and keep a spare on hand, as piranhas are notorious for biting through nylon mesh.

Interestingly, piranhas are members of the characin or tetra group. This makes them far more closely related to little neon tetras (a common aquarium fish) than to other potential maneaters like great white sharks. Piranhas are good aquarium inhabitants and do well in small groups of equally sized animals. They are neither very territorial nor very aggressive—which belies what they can do should the mood strike them. I remember being deceived by the gentle manners of a baby Holland's piranha that I kept one summer while living on the island of Martha's Vineyard off the coast of Massachusetts. My little one-inch buddy seemed so lonely in his little ten-gallon tank that I decided to get him a friend. My choice was a fire-mouthed cichlid (*Cichlasoma meeki*), an aggressive South American species that is quite territorial and capable of defending itself. I introduced the new fish to the tank, and for several weeks the experiment was a success.

After a time I noticed that the cichlid was making the piranha's life miserable. Slowly but surely, the territory of the firemouth was expanding until he lorded over all but a small corner of the tank. The situation got so bad that I began to feel sorry for the mighty piranha, cowed and beaten into a tiny refuge, barely able to turn around without being bitten on the fin. As the characin came to look more and more ratty, I came to the conclusion that the firemouth would have to go and resolved to return him to the local pet shop the next morning.

The piranha saved me the trip, however, by showing his true colors late that night as I sat at the typewriter working on a magazine article. I heard a splashing sound and turned to see the firemouth leap from the tank and hit the glass cover in a vain attempt to escape the piranha. As the cichlid hit the water, the piranha, in a flurry of motion, neatly severed the firemouth's head from his body and swam a couple of victory laps. Take the hint and don't mix other fish in with piranhas, no matter how tough you think the other fish may be.

Piranhas have one peculiar habit worthy of mention. Periodically they seem to enter some kind of frenzied trance and start smacking the tank with their body and tail. Be sure that you use a submersible heater resting on the bottom of your piranha tank instead of hanging glass against glass down the side. One of my larger piranhas had a fit recently in a tank all by himself and whacked the heater against the side of the aquarium. To my sorrow, I was not home when he did it, and the tank cracked and drained, soiling my living room and costing my fish his life.

Despite the fact that they must have live smaller fish or beef heart for food, piranhas are generally hardy, long-lived aquarium fish. They can give you years of fascination and pleasure if they are accorded the respect they deserve.

WATER: soft; pH a bit less than 7

TEMPERATURE: 75 degrees F.

TEMPERAMENT: the most vicious of fishes; can be kept only alone or with others of its kind

FOOD: live smaller fish, worms, beef heart chopped into small chunks

SIZE: to 5 inches

PRICE: $15 (not available and legal in all states)

16. Oscar *(Astronotus ocellatus)*

You may be thinking, after the story of the piranha and the fire-mouth, that despite the unfortunate outcome of that encounter, tank dynamics sound pretty interesting. Right you are! This is the principal argument for keeping several varieties of fish in one tank. I bring this up now because the South American cichlids, of which the present species is perhaps the most famous example, are especially noted for interacting vigorously with their owner. Like their smaller African cousins, these fish are territorial and aggressive and can be housed together only with the greatest circumspection. Yet the very nastiness and territoriality of these fish is what makes them such riveting aquarium animals.

The oscar comes in several color varieties: basic mottled gray, tiger (black and red) and red. Oscars are perhaps the most responsive pet fish in the world. If you raise one in a large clean tank all by himself, he will thrive on your attention and grow on the food you give him. He will come to know and recognize you and take food right from your fingers. So hardy, voracious and appealing is this species that even advanced hobbyists with very sophisticated setups and goals seem to find time and space for an oscar or two.

WATER: not critical
TEMPERATURE: 75 degrees F.
TEMPERAMENT: will devour smaller fishes
FOOD: all types of live food are best, especially smaller fish; cichlid flakes will suffice
SIZE: to 13 inches
PRICE: $5

17. Red devil *(Cichlasoma labiatum)*

More spectacular than the oscar and certainly more aggressive, the brilliantly colored red devil has such large, protruding lips that even its scientific name *(labiatum)* makes mention of them. This South American cichlid loves to move gravel around and dig, so an under-gravel filter is all but useless for this fish. Instead, use a powerful outside filter to suck up what is left of your red devil's repasts.

I have seen red devils get so mean that they will strike the glass with lips bared and teeth showing if you get too close. Of course, they can't do you any harm, but if you were another fish invading a red devil's territory you sure would think twice. If put into a community of aggressive cichlids of comparable size, the red devil will ultimately come to dominate and then devour his associates.

For a long time I ran a fifty-five-gallon tank that was essentially a fish rogues' gallery. Anytime a fish became intolerably domineering in one of my other tanks, I would (water conditions permitting) put him in the fifty-five. The roster read rather like a *Who's Who* of nasty fish. There was a wary balance among them all, though, as each seemed to know what the others could do. The tank worked out really well—that is, until I put the red devil in. He began by polarizing the inhabitants to one end, making them fight one another viciously for an inch or two of space while he cruised up and down four-fifths of the tank as if he hadn't a care in the world. At last he was the only one left, and he had never actually been in a scrap! He was so terrifying that the other fish would rather fight each other all day than risk his wrath.

WATER: soft; pH of 7
TEMPERATURE: 79 degrees F.
TEMPERAMENT: the worst, worthy of a piranha
FOOD: anything that moves, but will eat cichlid flake too
SIZE: to 16 inches
PRICE: $12

18. Golden ram *(Apistogramma ramirezi)*

This South American cichlid is as different from the oscar and the red devil as chicken pot pie is from tacos and refried beans. The ram is a peaceful, timid fish who appreciates a quiet, dimly lit tank with lots of plastic plants for cover and the company of others of his kind or the discus discussed below. He is a beautifully colored animal, a veritable rainbow. The head is yellow with a red-and-black eye, the chest is purple, the back half blue with darker blue speckles on orange fins, and the entire fish is highlighted in black. To understand the delicate magnificence of this animal you simply must see one.

WATER: soft and slightly aged (has been standing awhile); pH slightly less than 7
TEMPERATURE: *high!* 84 degrees F. is about right
TEMPERAMENT: shy and retiring; needs lots of plastic plants for hiding
FOOD: live tubifex worms and cichlid flake
SIZE: to 2 inches
PRICE: $5

19. Blue discus *(Symphysodon aequifasciata haraldi)*

While perhaps the most quietly and shimmeringly beautiful of all popular aquarium fishes, the discus is, regrettably, as difficult to keep alive as its Latin name is to pronounce. I have included it as a sort of challenge, hoping that some readers will be sufficiently enthused by what they have read here to go out and give a discus a go. The discus is powder blue in color and ovoid in shape, as the name suggests. When he's in top form his color appears to be fathomless, and he moves with the slight twitches of fin of the truly graceful aquatic ballet dancer. Go look at some discus. Perhaps you will feel that their elegance and grace is worth the risk that they may not thrive under your wet thumb. If you do decide to try one, put the tank in a quiet place, pay special attention to the softness of the water, don't mix any other type of fish but rams with the discus—and be sure it isn't your first or only fish.

WATER: soft and slightly aged; pH slightly less than 7
TEMPERATURE: 84 degrees F.
TEMPERAMENT: extremely shy and delicate, easily disturbed; best housed with others of their species or with rams
FOOD: live tubifex worms and bloodworms from a worm feeder, beef heart finely chopped
SIZE: 8 inches
PRICE: $30

Recommended Reading

REPTILES AND AMPHIBIANS

Babcock, Harold L., *Turtles of the Northeastern United States.* New York: Dover Publications, 1971.

Behler, John L., and King, F. Wayne, *The Audubon Society Field Guide to North American Reptiles and Amphibians.* New York: Alfred A. Knopf, 1979.

Belliars, Angus, *The Life of Reptiles,* Volumes I & II. New York: Universe Books, 1970.

Bishop, Sherman C., *Handbook of Salamanders.* Ithaca, N.Y.: Comstock Publishing Associates, 1943.

Breen, John F., *Encyclopedia of Reptiles and Amphibians.* Neptune City, N.J.: T.F.H. Publications, 1974.

Carr, Archie, *Handbook of Turtles.* Ithaca, N.Y.: Cornell University Press, 1952.

Coburn, John Howell, *Beginner's Guide to Snakes.* New York: Paradise Press, 1985.

———, *So Excellent A Fishe.* New York: Anchor Books, 1973.

Cochran, Doris M., *Living Amphibians of the World.* New York: Doubleday & Co., 1961.

——— and Goin, Coleman J., *The New Field Book of Reptiles and Amphibians.* New York: G. P. Putnam's Sons, 1970.

Cogger, Harold G., *Reptiles and Amphibians of Australia,* 3rd ed. Sanibel, Fla.: Ralph Curtis Books, 1983.

Desmond, Adrian J., *The Hot-Blooded Dinosaurs.* New York: The Dial Press/ James Wade, 1976.

Ditmars, Raymond L., *The Reptiles of North America.* New York: Doubleday & Co., 1936.

———, *Snakes of the World.* New York: Macmillan Publishing Co., 1931.

Goin, Coleman J., Goin, Olive B., and Zug, George R., *Introduction to Herpetology.* San Francisco: W. H. Freeman & Co., 1978.

Grzimek, Bernhard, *Grzimek's Animal Life Encyclopedia,* Volume 6. New York: D. Van Nostrand, 1972.

Klauber, Laurence M., *Rattlesnakes,* abridged ed. Berkeley: University of California Press, 1982.

McLoughlin, John C., *Archosauria.* New York: The Viking Press, 1979.

Mattison, Christopher, *The Care of Reptiles & Amphibians in Captivity.* United Kingdom: Blandford Press, 1982.

Minton, Sherman A., Jr., and Minton, Madge Rutherford, *Giant Reptiles.* New York: Charles Scribner's Sons, 1973.

———, *Venomous Reptiles.* New York: Charles Scribner's Sons, 1969.

Parker, H. W., *Snakes: A Natural History,* 2nd ed. Ithaca, N.Y.: Cornell University Press, 1977.

Pope, Clifford H., *The Giant Snakes.* New York: Alfred A. Knopf, 1975.

———, *The Reptile World.* New York: Alfred A. Knopf, 1974.

Porter, Kenneth R., *Herpetology.* Philadelphia: W. B. Saunders Co., 1972.

Pritchard, Peter C. H., *Encyclopedia of Turtles.* Neptune City, N.J.: T.F.H. Publications, 1979.

Reichenbach-Klinke, H., and Elkan, E., *Diseases of Amphibians.* Hong Kong: T.F.H. Publications, 1965.

———, *Diseases of Reptiles.* Hong Kong: T.F.H. Publications, 1965.

Romer, Alfred Sherwood, *Osteology of the Reptiles.* Chicago: University of Chicago Press, 1956.

Rudloe, Jack, *Time of the Turtle.* New York: Penguin Books, 1979.

Schmidt, Karl P., and Inger, Robert F., *Living Reptiles of the World.* New York: Doubleday & Co., 1957.

Stebbins, Robert C., *Amphibians and Reptiles of California.* Berkeley: University of California Press, 1972.

———, *A Field Guide to Western Reptiles and Amphibians.* Boston: Houghton Mifflin Co., 1966.

PARROTS

Bates, Henry J., and Busenbark, Robert L., *Parrots and Related Birds.* Neptune City, N.J.: T.F.H. Publications, 1978.

Freethy, Ron, *How Birds Work: A Guide to Bird Biology*. United Kingdom: Blandford Press, 1982.

Freud, Arthur, *All About the Parrots*. New York: Howell Book House, 1980.

Sutherland, Patricia, *The Pet Bird Handbook*. New York: Arco Publishing, 1981.

Vriends, Matthew M., *Parakeets of the World*. Neptune City, N.J.: T.F.H. Publications, 1979.

Welty, Joel Carl, *The Life of Birds*. Philadelphia: W. B. Saunders Co., 1975.

FISHES

Axelrod, Herbert R., *African Cichlids of Lake Malawi and Tanganyika*. Neptune City, N.J.: T.F.H. Publications, 1974.

Axelrod, H., Emmens, C., Burgess, W., Pronex, N., and Axelrod, G., *Exotic Tropical Fishes, Expanded Edition,* rev. Neptune City, N.J.: T.F.H. Publications, 1980.

Bond, Carl E., *Biology of Fishes*. Philadelphia: Saunders College Publishing, 1979.

Goldstein, Robert J., *Introduction to the Cichlids*. Neptune City, N.J.: T.F.H. Publications, 1971.

McClane, A. J., *Field Guide to Saltwater Fishes of North America*. New York: Holt, Rinehart & Winston, 1965.

Myers, George S., *The Piranha Book*. Neptune City, N.J.: T.F.H. Publications, 1972.

Simon and Schuster's Complete Guide to Freshwater and Marine Aquarium Fishes. New York: Simon and Schuster, 1976.

About the Author

Exotic animals have played a significant role in his life ever since Arthur Rosenfeld found his first painted turtle twenty years ago. Mr. Rosenfeld was born in White Plains, New York, and raised in New York City, where he worked on research, conservation and maintenance of exotic animals. A Yale graduate, Rosenfeld went on to graduate studies in zoology and veterinary medicine at Cornell University and the University of California. Mr. Rosenfeld leads the communication division of a major Texas corporation and resides in Dallas, Texas, with his wife, Arline, and his exotic animals.